# HOLY SATURDAY FAITH

# HOLY SATURDAY FAITH

Rediscovering the Legacy of Jesus

IAN G. WALLIS

*To Lizzie,*
*companion through life,*
*source of joy.*

Published in Great Britain in 2000 by
Society for Promoting Christian Knowledge
Holy Trinity Church
Marylebone Road
London NW1 4DU

The author and publisher acknowledge with thanks permission to use
extracts from *The Old Testament Pseudepigrapha*, Volumes I and II,
edited by James H. Charlesworth, published and copyright 1983 by
Darton, Longman and Todd Ltd, and used by permission
of the publishers.

British Library Cataloguing-in-Publication Data

A catalogue record for this book is available from the
British Library

ISBN 0-281-05025-2

Typeset by Pioneer Associates, Perthshire
Printed in Great Britain by
Biddles Ltd, Guildford and King's Lynn

# Contents

# Introduction

This is a book about faith. More precisely, about the faith of Jesus of Nazareth and how it became the faith of his followers. The title *Holy Saturday Faith* reflects the conviction that the period after Jesus' crucifixion and before belief in his resurrection is of central importance for understanding both the continuation and the growth of the movement he brought into being. Our concern is not principally with who Jesus thought he was or how he was perceived by others, but with his legacy – with what he entrusted to the disciples which enabled them 'to keep faith' after his death. As such, I hope what follows will be of interest not only to those wishing to understand the beginnings of Christianity, but also to those desirous of exploring Jesus' significance for faith today.

Although the case presented in this book is cumulative, readers may wish to pick up the story at different points. To this end, a brief overview may be helpful. Chapter 1 introduces Holy Saturday as a transitional phase for Jesus' disciples characterized by grief over the loss of their beloved leader and reorientation to life without him. Chapter 2 reviews some of the theological resources accessible to the disciples through their Jewish heritage which they drew on in shaping a response to his death. Chapter 3 offers an interpretation of what we know of the disciples' response immediately after the crucifixion in the light of recent studies into grief. Chapter 4, the core of the book, identifies six foundational characteristics of Jesus' practice of faith which he embodies personally and engenders in others, especially his closest followers. Chapter 5 explores how these characteristics give rise to and inform the rich spectrum of expositions of faith rooted in the person of Jesus emerging before or soon after his death. And, finally, Chapter 6 attempts to open up a debate on the contemporary implications of Jesus' habitus of faith by offering a number of reflections and proposals.

I have written this book alongside my responsibilities as a minister of a busy and challenging parish. Although this has brought additional pressures to the task, it does, I hope, reflect a deeply held conviction, namely, that although the tools of critical and rational analysis make an invaluable contribution to our appreciation of Jesus, ultimately his significance can only be discovered through the practice of his faith or, in other words, a wholehearted commitment to human being within God's world. The contents of these pages are, of course, my responsibility, but I wish to express my thanks to the people of Houghton-le-Spring and of St Michael and All Angels Parish Church for allowing me the opportunity to undertake this project and for being willing, knowingly or otherwise, to be a part of it. The Rt Revd Michael Turnbull, Bishop of Durham, and members of his staff encouraged its completion at various stages. My colleagues, Stephen Burns, Joan Haines and Margaret Thrush, have been a source of ceaseless encouragement and undertaken additional responsibilities to enable periods of writing. Similarly, our churchwardens, staff members, Parochial Church Councillors and congregation have offered support, understanding and co-operation.

A glance at the bibliography will demonstrate my indebtedness to scholarly research, and I hope that the findings of this study can feed into a number of key debates about Jesus' and his relation to Christian faith. Keeping abreast of secondary literature has been a struggle, although significantly eased by my being granted access to Durham University Library. In general, I have attempted in the notes to identify those studies which have informed my thinking at different points, rather than narrowly to acknowledge the source of a particular idea or interpretation. I trust that no one's contribution has been misrepresented or diminished, and offer my sincere apologies should this turn out to be the case.

Alex Wright and Simon Kingston, my commissioning editors, have remained enthusiastic about the project throughout. Members of the editorial staff at SPCK have also been most helpful in preparing the text for publication.

Liz, my wife, read the entire manuscript and offered many insightful comments. Her capacity to keep faith with the book and its author throughout a long gestation has been inspirational. I am also grateful for the keen interest and ongoing support of my father.

Feast of St Barnabas, 11 June
'. . . a good man, full of the Holy Spirit and of faith' (Acts 11.24)

# — 1 —

# Setting the Scene:
# Creating Space for Holy Saturday

What happened next? The question of what occurred after the crucifixion can be approached from one of two starting points. We can attempt to reconstruct what became of either Jesus or his disciples and then work out the implications of our findings for the other party. If we start with Jesus, we find ourselves following a well-explored line of inquiry, embracing the evidence relating to the empty tomb, the post-mortem appearances of Jesus and his ascension into the heavens. In principle, all of these are experiential phenomena and open to investigation. We could also include the more speculative issues of Jesus' whereabouts during the period between his death and resurrection, not to mention his continuing heavenly existence and his relation to God. Such an approach would necessarily implicate the disciples as they were the principal witnesses to the continuing history of Jesus of Nazareth. It is reported that they perceived the Lord on a number of occasions and were able to confirm the absence of his body from where it had been laid to rest.[1]

It could be argued that these data represent the sum of what is now available to us were our second point of departure to be adopted, namely, the disciples. For surely their story grows out of what happened to Jesus after the crucifixion. There are, however, grounds for questioning whether this is the full picture. For one thing, there is good reason to believe that the period between Jesus' death and the disciples' conviction he was still with them was considerably longer than the implied three-day scenario of our earliest reference in 1 Corinthians, chapter 15, 'and that he [Jesus] was buried, and that he was raised on the third day in accordance with the scriptures' (v. 4).[2] It seems probable that this reflects a primitive attempt to evaluate Jesus' significance in the light of the story of salvation narrated in the Hebrew Scriptures.[3]

The notion of God acting 'on the third day' to save his people can be found in a number of places. For example, Jonah remains entombed within a large fish for 'three days and three nights' (Jonah

1

1.17 [Heb. 2.1]; cf. Matt. 12.40) before being returned to the land
of the living. Hosea exhorts his listeners to

> '. . . return to the Lord;
> for it is he who has torn, and he will heal us;
> he has struck down, and he will bind us up.
> After two days he will revive us;
> on the third day he will raise us up,
> that we may live before him.' (6.1–2).

We know from later Jewish sources that these verses from Hosea
could be interpreted in terms of the resurrection and, more generally,
we possess ample evidence of belief in life after death being entertained by Jews of the first century CE.[4] 'After three days', then, may
well represent a formulaic expression defining the interim period
following disaster being visited upon God's people and prior to
God's salvific intervention on their behalf. In this case, Jesus, like
Jonah, remains in the grip of death for three days before being
released from captivity and liberated into new life.[5]

Another reason why we should be cautious of explaining the disciples' response to Jesus' death principally in terms of their post-
mortem encounters is the observation that these happenings do not
seem to have been the basis for, nor indeed the substance of, Jesus'
abiding presence within the community of faith which continued
to form around him. In certain respects, this is obvious: while the
resurrection appearances were clearly self-authenticating for those
who experienced them, they were not readily transferable and, in
consequence, could only offer indirect access to Jesus for those who
were not privileged in this way. The portrayal of Thomas in the
Gospel of John, chapter 20, as the one who believes no more than
he can empirically verify, makes this point precisely as readers are
encouraged to discover the 'risen' Jesus not through bodily
encounter but through faith (John 20.24–29; cf. Mark 16.9–13; Luke
24.10–12). As we shall see, Jesus' continuing presence after his death
was principally discerned and communicated through characteristic
resources, practices and perceptions. Central here was the vocation
to share Jesus' faith – to participate in his spirituality, to embrace his
vision of the Kingdom and to engage in his pattern of ministry.[6]

This is a striking observation challenging the oft-repeated dictum
that Jesus' resurrection, together with the outpouring of the Spirit at
Pentecost, was the birth of the church.[7] Clearly, much depends on
what is meant by resurrection, but the point we wish to make is that

the relation between what happened to Jesus after the crucifixion and what happened to his disciples may not be as linear and consequential as is often thought. In fact, we may be closer to the truth when we envisage the causal links in the opposite direction from how they are conventionally understood, with the sense of Jesus' continuing presence emerging from a community constituted by him during his life, envisioned and commissioned by him before his death and sustained in that vision and pattern of ministry afterwards by those who continued to embrace his faith. Within this scenario, belief in Jesus' resurrection is not so much the birth of faith as a radical expression of a faith that finds its definition and fulfilment in him.[8]

But even if we do not wish to go this far, it remains difficult to envisage how the belief that Jesus was raised from the dead could have arisen outside of a community of faith. Such a conviction requires a suspension of unbelief, a willingness to reach beyond the boundaries of everyday experience and the ability to indwell a world informed by God's sovereign power. A world sufficiently familiar to the recipients that it would enable them to interpret and articulate their post-crucifixion sense of Jesus' continuing presence as resurrection. Surely, it is only those who had allowed themselves to be formed by Jesus' vision of the Kingdom and, equally importantly, remained open to its transforming effects who would be in a position to reach this conclusion. Further, without the continuity of testimony spanning the crucifixion, the conviction that it was Jesus *in particular* who had been encountered would lack substance. This is clearly evident from the resurrection narratives where Jesus is not recognized, but his presence discerned through the performance of practices or the engendering of experiences characteristic of him. For instance, Jesus is perceived as bread is broken and meals are shared (Luke 24.30–1, 35; John 21.9–14), as the Scriptures come alive and interpret recent events (Luke 24.17–27, 32, 44–7), and as his ministry of communicating God's Kingdom is continued with good effect (Matt. 28.16–20; Mark 16.15–20; Luke 24.49). And, again, it is as joy, peace, forgiveness or reconciliation overwhelm the disciples that they recognize Jesus (Luke 24.32, 36, 41; John 20.11–16, 19–21, 21.15–17). Significantly, even Paul, who probably never met Jesus, required the witness of the community of faith to interpret his Damascus road experience as a Christophany (cf. Gal. 1.11–24; Acts 9.1–19, 22.1–21).[9]

In the light of all this, it seems our second approach, of inquiring into what took place in the lives of Jesus' disciples after his death, leading to the conviction he was still with them, is not only a legitimate pursuit but also an essential one if we are to appreciate the central position Jesus assumed within the faith of those who knew him and, even more surprisingly, of those who didn't. For, without question, this *phenomenon of transferability*, in which the faith of Jesus – the body of beliefs, practices and perceptions defining his pattern of life – could be communicated to and appropriated by people who possessed no personal experience of him, is one of the profoundest aspects of earliest Christianity.

Our starting point, then, is the death of Jesus or, more specifically, the disciples' response to it. This is what we shall refer to as *Holy Saturday*, the transitional phase delimited by Jesus' crucifixion and his followers' ongoing awareness of his presence with them. Although Jesus' whereabouts and pursuits during this phase attracted much speculation in the early Christian centuries and beyond (see Appendix 2), the circumstances of the disciples are rarely mentioned in as many words. This apparent silence can be variously explained. For instance, if we assume the 'after three days' resurrection scenario communicates not only theological truth about the significance of Jesus, but also temporal truth about what happened forty-eight hours or so after the crucifixion, then manifestly the disciples had little time to do anything. However, if the testimonies and stories celebrating the resurrection are not the origin of Jesus' continuing influence upon his followers but expressions of it, then a chapter in the life of the disciples emerges that is relatively unexamined and highly significant. Here, the practice of the faith of Jesus – participating in his spirituality, embracing his vision of the Kingdom and engaging in his pattern of ministry – becomes the medium capable of giving access to his world and so of enabling him to be encountered afresh.[10]

In future chapters, we shall attempt to give definition and substance to this Holy Saturday process, but before doing so a number of objections need to be anticipated. The first relates to the paucity of evidence for such an extended period between Jesus' death and belief in his resurrection. Surely, there should be more signs of this phase, especially if it was characterized by creativity on the part of the disciples. The vital consideration here is what counts as evidence, for could it not be that certain artefacts of Holy Saturday faith have survived although they are rarely recognized as such? Consider, for example, the development of the gospel genre. For many years, it has been an axiom of biblical scholarship that the entire New Testament canon was written after the resurrection by authors who interpret Jesus and his life from this perspective. The assumption is that the resurrection can be spoken of as a historical happening, at least to the extent that one can talk about documents being composed before or after it. A happening that exerted a transforming, determinative and defining influence upon the disciples and those who became followers through their ministry. And yet a survey of recent literature on the resurrection reveals anything but a consensus as to the nature of this phenomenon. Opinions range from an objective event, in which Jesus' material constitution is transformed into a spiritual body possessing supra-human properties, to a gradual change within the psyches of his followers releasing them from guilt and dejection, and enabling them to minister effectively in his name.[11] This spectrum of views encompasses fundamentally different understandings of resurrection and the timescale over which it occurred, calling into question the assumption that all early Christian authors place a 'resurrection spin' on their witness to Jesus. How can we be so sure when Jesus' resurrection is surrounded by so much uncertainty?

Perhaps a more fruitful approach is to interpret the gospel form as an end-product of Holy Saturday rather than as a response to Easter Sunday. Why did Mark, or whoever created this genre, decide to communicate the enduring significance of Jesus for faith by telling his story – a story with sequence, progression and detail? If it was principally his death and what happened to him afterwards that constituted his importance, there would be little point in relating the substance of what he did and said, and the course his life took. It would have been sufficient to prescribe his contribution in essentially theological terms as is attested in many of the New Testament letters, where Jesus is defined in relation to concepts such as creation, salvation and sanctification (e.g. by Paul). But this is not what we find in the Gospels, especially the Synoptics, where we are encouraged to reflect on the nature and substance of belief in relation to Jesus in person – to appropriate his faith by re-membering or re-collecting the crucial years of his life and by repeating or rehearsing the course of discipleship realized through his ministry.[12] The Gospel of John manages to combine both of these approaches by communicating a mature theological assessment of Jesus within a narrative presentation of his ministry.[13]

It appears that for the Gospel communities, the phenomenon of the resurrection did not mean faith started on Easter morning; rather, the call to discipleship remained rooted in Jesus' summons to follow in the way of the Kingdom. Evidently, the story of Jesus was found to possess a paradigmatic function in defining awareness of and response to God. As a result, second and third generation followers discovered what Jesus means for faith by undertaking a journey similar to that attempted by their predecessors and, ultimately, by Jesus himself.[14] The coining of the gospel form, then, reflects the way in which believers integrated Jesus' story into their own: the journey of faith, which was embodied by Jesus and in which his first disciples were invited to share, must be realized within each community as the significance and identity of Jesus are discovered through responding to his call.[15] This is clearest in Mark's Gospel which concludes, somewhat enigmatically, with an invitation to discover Jesus in Galilee (Mark 16.7).Why Galilee? Because it represents the locus for Jesus' ministry and the context for discipleship, that is, the birthplace of faith and the crucible in which a Jesus-centred response to God finds definition and expression.[16]

A second objection concerns the condition of Jesus' followers after his death. Describing Holy Saturday as a creative period for them may, at first glance, seem unlikely given that the Gospels characterize their response to Jesus' arrest and crucifixion in terms of desertion and betrayal (e.g. Mark 14.43–6, 50, 66–72). Surely, disillusionment following Jesus' inability to deliver the kind of Kingdom they had hoped for (cf. Mark 10.35–7; 11.1–11), together with fear for personal safety owing to their association with him (cf. John 20.19), will have precipitated a swift and discreet retreat to Galilee and return to their former ways of life (cf. John 21.1–14). The implication of all this is that Jesus' death burst the bubble of their aspirations and extinguished their enthusiasm for discipleship, leaving them with broken spirits, dented egos and a sense of having been betrayed and deserted by the one to whom they had entrusted their future.[17]

But is this likely? Two observations require us to think again. First, from what we can gather, Jesus did not assemble a community of followers in order to create a culture of dependency, but to envision and enable a team of co-workers capable of sharing his faith and vocation and, as a consequence, ministering in his name, with or without him.[18] This sense is captured in the saying, 'Follow me, and I will make you fish for people' (Matt. 4.19; Mark 1.17), and is confirmed by the way in which Jesus' apprentices are commissioned to assist him (e.g. Matt.10.1–15; Mark 3.13–19; 6.7–13; Luke 9.1–6; 10.1–12; John 13.1–20), setting about the task with varying degrees of success (Mark 6.13; Luke 9.6; 10.17–20; cf. Mark 9.14–29). In certain respects, this mode of authorization and resourcing is reminiscent of early prophetic traditions, where God's Spirit is transferred from one party to another (e.g. Elijah and Elisha), and may reflect Jesus' own experience.[19]

For example, it seems probable that Jesus, on the occasion of his baptism, was not only identifying with John's call to prepare for the imminent coming of God's salvation and judgement, but also believed himself to have been commissioned by the Baptist and invested with God's Spirit to share in his prophetic ministry (Matt. 3.13–17/Mark 1.9–11/Luke 3.21–2).[20] Further, there are good grounds for thinking Jesus was initially a disciple of John (cf. John 3.22–30; 4.1–3)[21] and we know they both claimed charismatic, rather than institutional, authority for their convictions (cf. Mark 11.27–33). Significantly, Jesus' own ministry may only have flourished after John's arrest and subsequent demise, suggesting a continuum in which he inherits the prophetic mantle or divine imprimatur from his mentor (cf. Mark 6.14–29). In a comparable way, while the disciples, who may well have been baptized by either John or Jesus, serve their apprenticeship under the latter and are commissioned by him, empowerment for ministry occurs after the crucifixion when the Spirit of God, embodied in Jesus, is transferred to them.

A second consideration which militates against the view that the disciples' faith was destroyed by Jesus' demise comes into focus when we reflect on the nature of the relationship they shared. In this respect, Josephus, the principal Jewish historian of the first century (37 CE–c. 100 CE), may well put us on the right track when he records the following comments about the Jesus movement:

At this time there appeared Jesus, a wise man [if indeed one should call him a man]. For he was a doer of startling deeds, a teacher of people who receive the truth with pleasure. And he gained a following both among many Jews and among many of Greek origin. [He was the Messiah.] And when Pilate, because of an accusation made by the leading men among us, condemned him to the cross, *those who had loved him previously did not cease to do so.* [For he appeared to them on the third day, living again, just as the divine prophets had spoken of these and countless other wondrous things about him.] And up until this very day the tribe of Christians, named after him, has not died out. (*Ant.* 18.3.3 §63–4; our emphasis)

In its current form, this testimony is judged to contain Christian insertions, added subsequently to elevate the status of Jesus (i.e. the words enclosed within square brackets).[22] However, the section of interest to us is almost certainly original. Josephus characterizes the disciples' response to Jesus' death in terms of the love they shared during his life ('those who had loved him previously did not cease to do so'). It is significant that a commentator with little sympathy for Christianity would speak in such terms; and his assessment reminds us that, while people sought Jesus for many reasons, those who became his followers were attracted to him as a person. Through what must have been an intensely formative period when Jesus and his closest disciples lived a common life, embraced a common vision and pursued a common vocation, strong affectional bonds must surely have been forged. We gain some insight into this from references in the Gospels which allude to Jesus ministering alongside his followers (Mark 6.6–12; 9.14–29), withdrawing to spend time with them (Mark 3.7; 4.35), sharing intimate experiences and intuitions (Mark 8.27–9; 9.2–13; 14.32–42), celebrating the Kingdom together (Mark 2.18–22) and, at the end, entrusting his vocation to them (Mark 14.12–26).

All this suggests that the fundamental response of the disciples to Jesus' death will have been one of *grief at the loss of someone they had grown to love and respect,* and not primarily one of disillusionment at the demise of their teacher and leader.[23] This point is clearly brought out by the author of the Gospel of Peter, an early Christian work, probably of the first century:[24]

> But I [i.e. Peter] mourned with my companions and, being wounded in heart, we hid ourselves for we were being sought after by them as if we were evil-doers and as persons who wanted to set fire to the temple. Besides all these things we were fasting and sat mourning and weeping night and day until the Sabbath . . . At dawn on the Lord's day Mary Magdalene, a woman disciple of the Lord – for fear of the Jews, since they were inflamed with wrath – had not done at the sepulchre of the Lord what women are accustomed to do for their dead loved ones. She took with her (women) friends and came to the sepulchre where he was laid. And they were afraid lest the Jews should see them and said,

'Even though we could not weep and lament on that day when he was crucified, yet let us now do so at his sepulchre. But who will roll away for us the stone that is across the entrance to the sepulchre, that we may go in and sit beside him and do what is due?' – for the stone was great – 'and we fear lest any one see us. And if we cannot do so let us at least place by the entrance what we have brought as a memorial for him, and let us weep and lament until we go home.' (7; 12)

Nor is this conclusion undermined by their failure on occasion to understand Jesus' message (cf. Mark 4.13; 8.17), to correctly anticipate his response (cf. Mark 10.13–16), to seek their own self-interests (cf. Mark 10.35–45) or readily to accept his death (cf. Mark 8.31—9.1). Without question, the disciples struggled to embrace Jesus' vision of the Kingdom and pattern of ministry, but in spite of all this they continued to follow – no small indication of their personal commitment to him! Even their conduct at the time of the arrest and execution (e.g. Mark 14.50–1) is partially mitigated by the fear and turmoil surrounding these events. Furthermore, rather than simply deserting Jesus in Gethsemane, there is evidence that they offered armed resistance against the Jewish authorities (e.g. Mark 14.47; cf. John 18.10–11).[25] We also need to balance Peter's denial of Jesus (e.g. Mark 14.66–72) in hostile and politically volatile circumstances with his willingness to give public expression to his undying devotion towards him (e.g. Mark 14.26–31; cf. John 13.6–11; 21.15–19).

As we shall see, much of the disciples' conduct after Jesus' death is consistent with expressions of mourning and loss. For instance, the need to meet together for mutual support and comfort, to remember Jesus and to celebrate his life, to participate in practices and visit places associated with him, and to attempt to rationalize or explain his death. In addition, we need to take into consideration the pronounced volitional or intentional dimension of love as practised by Jesus and his followers. This is captured in what initially appears a rather incongruous requirement, namely, *the injunction to love* (Mark 12.28–31; also Matt. 5.43–8/Luke 6.27–36; cf. Deut. 6.4–5; Lev. 19.18). To a certain extent, this wilful component would counter the formlessness of grief and emotional trauma associated with loss by providing Jesus' followers with a discipline through which their love for him could be expressed and kept alive (cf. John 13.33–4; 14.15–27; 15.9–17).[26]

One final objection to Holy Saturday as a creative period within the life of the disciples relates to the question of continuity between the so-called Jesus of history and the Christ of faith. Surely, it could be argued, Jesus' death must have had the effect of dissipating the momentum of his ministry and disintegrating the community of faith that formed around him in order to explain the fundamentally new happening of the church born of resurrection and Pentecost. But is there really such a rift between the faith of Jesus and the faith of the church? Certainly, much early Christian preaching revolves around the person of Jesus, in contrast to the Kingdom of God, but this change in emphasis was a result of what he communicated about God and humanity when alive. That is to say, the reason why Jesus was proclaimed and worshipped as the risen and exalted one, who gave his life for our salvation, is not primarily because of what happened after his death, but because of who he was beforehand. It is precisely because he embodied the faith and did not simply teach it, that he could not readily be divorced from it or relegated into theological propositions about it.[27] The possibility of encountering God and discovering what it means to be one of God's children is not simply a matter of believing in Jesus, but of participating in his way of life. In this sense, resurrection becomes a *celebration of the transferability of Jesus' faith*.

For this reason, Jesus' followers continued in the pattern of life he established. We shall return to this observation later, but let us consider one example. We know that healing was an essential component of Jesus' ministry and witness to the Kingdom of God.[28] From what we can gather, he expected his followers to imitate him in this as in many other expressions of his faith (e.g. Mark 3.14–15; 6.12–13; cf. 16.17–18). What is significant, however, is the way in which healing continues to characterize the early church's evangelistic strategy. The author of Acts describes the therapeutic exploits of Peter, Paul and other disciples (Acts 3.10; 5.16; 9.32–42; 13.9–12; 14.8–10, 16–18; 20.7–12; 28.7–9), while a number of the epistles also attest this practice (2 Cor. 12.12; Gal. 3.5; Heb. 2.4). The inclusion of healing and other associated phenomena within Paul's list of spiritual gifts in 1 Corinthians (12.9–10), together with James's reference to its application in church life (Jas. 5.13–18), underlines in more general terms its place within the life of the church.[29] There can be little doubt that the reason why Christians practised healing in the name of Christ is because Jesus was a healer.

Hopefully, by anticipating a number of possible objections we have managed both to make space and to reinforce the need for Holy Saturday as a creative period for the disciples, of indeterminate length, following the crucifixion. Before bringing this chapter to a close, however, it is worth pausing for a moment to consider chapters 13 to 16 of John's Gospel from this perspective. Many scholars would recognize they represent a mature and nuanced reflection upon the implications of Jesus' death for his followers.[30] Although the current setting is of Jesus entrusting his last will and testament to his friends and commissioning them for service, it seems likely that additional material relating their post-crucifixion experiences can be discerned. If this is the case, then we may be able to identify within these chapters something of the Holy Saturday effect, namely, the process by which the disciples came to terms with Jesus' death and discovered his continuing impact upon their lives. A careful reading brings into focus a number of stages or characteristics of this transitional phase during which his mourners manage to dissociate Jesus' presence from his physical body and relocate it within the practice of sharing his faith, embracing his vocation and continuing his ministry. Consider the following components which can readily be identified within these chapters:

- Prior to death, the disciples are commissioned by Jesus to follow his example and to share his vocation.

  'You call me Teacher and Lord – and you are right, for that is what I am. So if I, your Lord and Teacher, have washed your feet, you also ought to wash one another's feet. For I have set you an example, that you also should do as I have done to you . . . Very truly, I tell you, whoever receives one whom I send receives me; and whoever receives me receives him who sent me.' (13.13–15, 20)

  'You did not choose me but I chose you. And I appointed you to go and bear fruit, fruit that will last, so that the Father will give you whatever you ask him in my name.' (15.16)

- At the time of Jesus' arrest or crucifixion, the group of disciples temporarily disintegrates.

  'The hour is coming, indeed it has come, when you will be scattered, each one to his home, and you will leave me alone.' (16.32)

- After Jesus' death, the disciples experience profound grief and long to be with him once more.

> 'Little children, I am with you only a little longer. You will look for me; and as I said to the Jews so now I say to you, "Where I am going, you cannot come." . . . Simon Peter said to him, 'Lord, where are you going?' Jesus answered, 'Where I am going, you cannot follow me now; but you will follow me afterward.' (13.33, 36)

> 'Do not let your hearts be troubled. Believe in God, believe also in me. In my Father's house there are many dwelling places. If it were not so, would I have told you that I go to prepare a place for you? And if I go and prepare a place for you, I will come again and will take you to myself, so that where I am, there you may be also . . . I will not leave you orphaned; I am coming to you.' (14.1–3, 18)

> 'But because I have said these things to you, sorrow has filled your hearts . . . Very truly, I tell you, you will weep and mourn, but the world will rejoice; you will have pain, but your pain will turn into joy. When a woman is in labour, she has pain, because her hour has come. But when her child is born, she no longer remembers the anguish because of the joy of having brought a human being into the world. So you have pain now; but I will see you again, and your hearts will rejoice, and no one will take your joy from you.' (16.6, 20–2)

- The disciples discover that by continuing in Jesus' pattern of love and service they remain close to him and, as a consequence, are able to participate in his relationship with God.

> 'Very truly, I tell you, the one who believes in me will also do the works that I do and, in fact, will do greater works than these, because I am going to the Father. I will do whatever you ask in my name, so that the Father may be glorified in the Son. If in my name you ask me for anything, I will do it. If you love me, you will keep my commandments . . . They who have my commandments and keep them are those who love me; and those who love me will be loved by my Father, and I will love them and reveal myself to them

. . . Those who love me will keep my word, and my Father will love them, and we will come to them and make our home with them. Whoever does not love me does not keep my words; and the word that you hear is not mine, but is from the Father who sent me . . . Peace I leave with you; my peace I give to you. I do not give to you as the world gives. Do not let your hearts be troubled, and do not let them be afraid.' (14.12–15, 21, 23–4, 27)

'Abide in me as I abide in you. Just as the branch cannot bear fruit by itself unless it abides in the vine, neither can you unless you abide in me. I am the vine, you are the branches. Those who abide in me and I in them bear much fruit, because apart from me you can do nothing. Whoever does not abide in me is thrown away like a branch and withers; such branches are gathered, thrown into the fire, and burned. If you abide in me, and my words abide in you, ask for whatever you wish, and it will be done for you. My Father is glorified by this, that you bear much fruit and become my disciples. As the Father has loved me, so I have loved you; abide in my love. If you keep my commandments, you will abide in my love, just as I have kept my Father's commandments and abide in his love. (15.4–10; cf. also 13.34–5; 14.6–14; 16.26–7)

- The disciples intuit a 'spiritual persona' or 'alter-ego', mediating Jesus' presence by acting as a source of guidance, inspiration and remembrance, discrete from themselves and capable of maintaining his accessibility for them.

'And I will ask the Father, and he will give you another Advocate, to be with you for ever. This is the Spirit of truth, whom the world cannot receive, because it neither sees him nor knows him. You know him, because he abides with you, and he will be in you. I will not leave you orphaned; I am coming to you. In a little while the world will no longer see me, but you will see me; because I live, you also will live. On that day you will know that I am in my Father, and you in me, and I in you . . . But the Advocate, the Holy Spirit, whom the Father will send in my name, will teach you everything, and remind you of all that I have said to you.' (14.16–20, 26)

'Nevertheless I tell you the truth: it is to your advantage that I go away, for if I do not go away, the Advocate will not come to you; but if I go, I will send him to you . . . I still have many things to say to you, but you cannot bear them now. When the Spirit of truth comes, he will guide you into all the truth; for he will not speak on his own, but will speak whatever he hears, and he will declare to you the things that are to come. He will glorify me, because he will take what is mine and declare it to you. All that the Father has is mine. For this reason I said that he will take what is mine and declare it to you.' (16.7, 12–15; cf. also 15.26–7)

- The disciples encounter opposition and persecution for continuing to follow Jesus, which has the effect of confirming their conviction that he is still with them and authenticating their commitment to following in his way.

'If the world hates you, be aware that it hated me before it hated you. If you belonged to the world, the world would love you as its own. Because you do not belong to the world, but I have chosen you out of the world – therefore the world hates you. Remember the word that I said to you, "Servants are not greater than their master." If they persecuted me, they will persecute you; if they kept my word, they will keep yours also. But they will do all these things to you on account of my name, because they do not know him who sent me.' (15.18–21)

'I have said these things to you to keep you from stumbling. They will put you out of the synagogues. Indeed, an hour is coming when those who kill you will think that by doing so they are offering worship to God. And they will do this because they have not known the Father or me . . . I have said this to you, so that in me you may have peace. In the world you face persecution. But take courage; I have conquered the world!' (16.1–3, 33)

It seems possible, then, that this section of John's Gospel affords access to an extraordinary chapter within the lives of the disciples which not only bears witness to their enduring love for him, but also generates a fresh sense of presence through their continuing to inhabit the spirituality and practice of his faith. Further, while the

Gospel concludes with traditions referring to the empty tomb and post-mortem appearances, these happenings form no part of Jesus' final words to his followers contained in the farewell discourses. It is difficult to escape the conclusion that the bodily resurrection of Jesus is neither the origin of nor a formative influence upon the 'Jesus-consciousness' reflected in these chapters. What is clear, however, is that his death and, to use John's terminology, departure are fundamental in triggering a grief process within the disciples which not only gives rise to their conviction about Jesus living on in the life of God, but also yields a sense of his continuing influence and impact upon their lives. This is the substance of Holy Saturday. The remaining pages are an attempt to understand the phenomenon more fully in order to appreciate what was taking place in the first generations of Jesus' disciples and, hopefully, to discover how their experiences can be shared by his followers today.

# NOTES

1 References to Jesus' post-mortem appearances include: Matt. 28.9–10, 16–20; [Mark 16.9, 12, 14–18]; Luke 24.13–35, 36–8; John 20.11–18, 19–23, 24–9; Acts 1.3; and to the empty tomb: Matt. 28.1–8; Mark 16.1–8; Luke 24.1–12, 22–4; John 20.1–10. Recent discussions of these texts, reflecting different views and theological positions, include: Avis (1993); Barton and Stanton (1994); Davis, Kendall and O'Collins (1997); C. F. Evans (1970); M. J. Harris (1983); Longenecker (1998); Lüdemann (1994); Lüdemann with Özen (1995); Lunny (1989); and Perkins (1984).

2 We find this 'on the third day/after three days' formula regularly repeated in the Synoptic Gospels, especially in the passion predictions (Matt. 16.21/Mark 8.31/Luke 9.22; Matt. 17.23/Mark 9.31; Matt. 20.19/Mark 10.34/Luke 18.33; cf. Matt. 27.63–4; Luke 13.32; 24:7, 21, 26), even though it cannot readily accommodate the timetable implicit within the evangelists' narrative portrayals of the resurrection. Interestingly, it is almost completely missing from John (cf. 2.19–20).

3 See the discussions of Lindars (1961), pp. 59–72; and Schillebeeckx (1979), pp. 526–32.

4 Harvey McArthur (1970–71) discusses later references to Hosea 6.1–2, pp. 81–6. Good surveys of Jewish belief in the resurrection can be found in Bauckham (1996), pp. 80–95; Cavallin (1974); and Nickelsburg (1972).

5 Consider also the Jewish belief that the soul of a deceased person remained associated with the body for a period of three days. This, presumably, accounts for the customs reflected in the following passages: 'And as soon as they brought the body [of Job] to the tomb, all the

widows and orphans circled about forbidding it to be brought into the tomb. But after three days they laid him in the tomb in a beautiful sleep, since he received a name renowned in all generations forever. Amen' (*T. Job* 53.5–8). 'And they tended the body of the righteous Abraham with divine ointments and perfumes until the third day after his death. And they buried him in the promised land at the oak of Mamre' (*T. Abr.* [Rec. A] 20.11). The following reference, now reflecting Christian interpolation, actually refers to the soul's reunification with the body: 'And after three days, his soul came into his body and he lifted up his voice in the midst of (them) all and said, "Glorify God with one voice! All (of you) glorify God, and the Son of God, who awakens us, Jesus Christ the light of the aeons, the inextinguishable lamp, the life of faith!' (*4 Bar.* 9.14). Consider, also, the views of the rabbis: 'R. Abba b. R. Pappai and R. Joshua of Siknin said in the name of R. Levi: For three days [after death] the soul hovers over the body, intending to re-enter it, but as soon as it sees its appearance change, it departs, as it is written, "When his flesh that is on him is distorted, his soul will mourn over him (Job 14.22)"' (*Lev. R.* 18.1; cf. also *Eccl. R.* 12.6).

6  I have discussed this in detail elsewhere, Wallis (1995a), pp. 175–221, and (1995c), pp. 10–17.

7  This would be a view held by many, whether liberal or conservative in outlook. For instance, Rudolf Bultmann, who was highly sceptical about the historical basis for Jesus' resurrection, could write thus: 'But Christian faith did not exist until there was a Christian kerygma; i.e. a kerygma proclaiming Jesus Christ – specifically Jesus Christ the Crucified and Risen One – to be God's eschatological act of salvation', Bultmann (1952), p. 3.

8  Marxsen (1970), and (1992), pp. 76–95, 96–116.

9  See Kim (1981), esp. pp. 269–311.

10  On this line of thinking, see, especially, Chilton (1997) and Sawicki (1994).

11  See the reviews of Carnley (1987) and Lorenzen (1995), Part 1.

12  Significantly, Jesus is rarely the object of belief in the Synoptics (cf. Matt. 18.6/Mark 9.42 [var.]; Matt. 18.10 [var.]; 27.42); rather than believing *in* Jesus, the reader is encouraged to believe *with* him.

13  In contrast to the Synoptic Evangelists, John's Jesus encourages belief in himself (John 1.12; 2.11, 23; 3.15, 16,18, 36; 4.39; 6.35, 40; 7.5, 31, 38, 39, 48; 8.30, 31; 10.42; 11.25, 26, 45, 48; 12.11, 37, 42, 44, 46; 14.12; 16.9, 17.20; cf. 9.35, 36).

14  The importance of narrative progression as the key to understanding Mark's Gospel has been recognized, at least implicitly, from the time of W. Wrede's (1971) interpretation of the messianic secret; recently, Jack Kingsbury (1983) has published a more explicit and thoroughgoing narrative Christology of the Second Gospel. It is in the area of Mark's understanding of discipleship, however, that the function of narrative

development has been most productive; see, for example, Best (1981); C. D. Marshall (1989); and Tannehill (1977), pp. 386–405.

15 Consider, for example, the approaches of Boff (1980); and Sobrino (1994).

16 Best (1983), pp. 72–8; and Marshall (1989), pp. 36–43. It is worth reflecting on the testimony of Paul as well. The apostle's awareness of Jesus' presence owes much to reflecting upon his own suffering in the light of Christ's (cf. 2 Cor. 4.7–15; Gal. 2.19–21; Phil. 2.1–11); see Kurz (1985), pp. 103–26, and the articles on Paul in Longenecker (1996), pp. 98–202.

17 The view that the behaviour of the disciples after the crucifixion is inexplicable without the resurrection has become known as the 'beaten men' theory; see the correspondence between Don Cupitt and Charlie Moule collected together in Cupitt (1979), pp. 27–41, and the discussion of Carnley (1987), pp. 167–72.

18 See, especially, Hengel (1981b), pp. 38–88; and Stanton (1974), pp. 13–27.

19 Chilton (1998), pp. 30–57; for an assessment of Jesus' experience of God, see Dunn (1975), pp. 11–92.

20 On the relationship between John and Jesus, see the magisterial treatment of Meier (1994), pp. 19–233.

21 Hollenbach (1982), esp. pp. 203–7.

22 We have followed John Meier's construction of the *Testimonium Flavianum* in Meier (1991), pp. 56–69.

23 This point is central to the creative and insightful exposition of N. P. Harvey (1985).

24 Dominic Crossan (1988, 1995), in particular, has drawn attention to (and probably overstated) the importance of the Gospel of Peter for understanding Jesus' death and his disciples' response to it.

25 Brown (1994), Vol. 1, pp. 264–92.

26 See the important study of Gary Anderson on grief and mourning in the Hebrew Scriptures, Anderson (1991), esp. pp. 1–18; also Walter Brueggeman's (1995b) article, pp. 84–97.

27 I offer a detailed discussion of this point in Wallis (1995a), esp. pp. 175–80, 194–200.

28 Meier (1994), pp. 509–1138.

29 There are many references to the practice of healing continuing beyond the period covered by the New Testament. For example, Arnobius, *Adversus Nationes* I.42–4; Athanasius, *De Incarnatione* 15; 18; Eusebius, *Historia Ecclesiastica* I.13; II.3; Gregory of Nyssa, *Oratio Catechetica* 23; 34; Irenaeus, *Adversus Haereses* II.32; Justin Martyr, *Dialogus cum Tryphone Judaeo* 69; *Apologia* I.30–3; Origen, *Contra Celsum* I.38; II.48; Tertullian, *Apologeticum* 23; cf. Exod. 4.5, 8, 9, 31; 14.31; 19.9; Num. 14.1. See E. Frost (1954); Lampe (1965), pp. 205–18; and Wiles (1965), pp. 221–34.

30 Ashton (1991), esp. pp. 443–84, provides a useful survey of opinion

and assessment. The question of whether chapters 14 to 16 contain two versions of the so-called 'farewell discourses' is not relevant to our concerns. See also the comments of Bornkamm (1997), pp.105–8.

# — 2 —

# Mourning Jesus:
# Theological Resources

The disciples did not mourn Jesus in a vacuum. They were part of
a tradition of faith possessing insights and practices capable of
giving form and expression to grief. Some of these grew out of
personal or communal experiences of being God's people through
faith-testing situations, whilst others were assimilated through contact with different cultures and religious traditions. Further, Jesus'
own teaching and approach to matters of life and death will have
remained with his followers long after the crucifixion. Together,
these constituted the resources at the disciples' disposal as they
were forced to carry on without their leader and friend. If we are to
appreciate how they responded to his death, we must begin by
reviewing these resources. This is the task of the next three chapters.

## Suffering Loss

No culture or society can escape the realities of human frailty, death
and bereavement.[1] Perhaps it was a strong sense of theological
identity, coupled with an equally profound awareness at different
times of divine abandonment,[2] which led to the integration of strategies for confronting mortality and coping with loss within the Jewish
practice of faith.[3] This had two significant and related implications.
First, it brought recognition to the experience of loss by locating it
within the contours of religious observance where mourners were
afforded status and given permission to grieve in public. To an
extent, this countered the disorientating effects of death in which
sustaining patterns of relationships are disrupted or destroyed.
Second, grief and mourning ceased to be individual pursuits, with
sufferers left to their own resources, and became the prerogative of
the community. One consequence of this was the emergence of
appropriate language, rituals and beliefs through which grief could
be channelled and the needful undertakings of mourning performed.

As a result, those suffering loss could draw on resources which not only gave form and expression to what had befallen them, but also provided safe passage through the ensuing period of transition and reorientation.[4]

It is no surprise, therefore, to find in one of the Jewish manuals of wisdom detailed instructions on how to respond to personal loss. Jesus ben Sirach, writing about 200 years before the Common Era, offers the following guidance:

> My child, let your tears fall for the dead,
>   and as one in great pain begin the lament.
> Lay out the body with due ceremony,
>   and do not neglect the burial.
> Let your weeping be bitter and your wailing fervent;
>   make your mourning worthy of the departed,
> for one day, or two, to avoid criticism;
>   then be comforted for your grief.
> For grief may result in death,
>   and a sorrowful heart saps one's strength.
> When a person is taken away, sorrow is over;
>   but the life of the poor weighs down the heart.
> Do not give your heart to grief;
>   drive it away, and remember your own end.
> Do not forget, there is no coming back;
>   you do the dead no good, and you injure yourself.
> Remember his fate, for yours is like it;
>   yesterday it was his, and today it is yours.
> When the dead is at rest, let his remembrance rest too,
>   and be comforted for him when his spirit has departed.

> (Ecclus. (Sirach) 38.1–23; cf. also
> 7.34; 22.11–22; Ps. 35.13–14)

As we should expect, the story of the people of God narrated in the Hebrew Scriptures contains many accounts of bereavement following death. Consider, for example, David's response to the demise of Saul and Jonathan: 'Then David took hold of his clothes and tore them; and all the men who were with him did the same. They mourned and wept, and fasted until evening . . . David intoned this lamentation over Saul and his son Jonathan' (2 Sam. 1.11–12, 17). Or that of Job on hearing of his children's fatal accident: 'Then Job arose, tore his robe, shaved his head, and fell on the ground and worshipped. He said, "Naked I came from my mother's

womb, and naked shall I return there; the Lord gave, and the Lord
has taken away; blessed be the name of the Lord"' (Job 1.20–1). A
more extended description is afforded by the Lamentations of
Jeremiah, including the following verses:

> The elders of daughter Zion
>   sit on the ground in silence;
> they have thrown dust on their heads
>   and put on sackcloth;
> the young girls of Jerusalem
>   have bowed their heads to the ground.
> My eyes are spent with weeping;
>   my stomach churns;
> my bile is poured out on the ground
>   because of the destruction of my people.
>                         (Lam. 2.10–11)[5]

Interestingly, in each of these cases, death is thought to result
from or indicate a falling from divine grace, confirming the intimate
link in Jewish faith between life and blessing. We can also glean from
these and other passages the types of behaviour associated with
loss.[6] Some responses, such as weeping, lamenting and the rending
of garments, clearly give expression to strong emotion, whilst others,
including deprivation, signal a desire to withdraw from life.

A particularly striking example of grief is David's reaction to
news of the critical condition and subsequent death of his love child
to Bathsheba.[7] Unusually, David's mourning precedes death and is
confined to the duration of the illness:

> David therefore pleaded with God for the child; David fasted,
> and went in and lay all night on the ground. The elders of his
> house stood beside him, urging him to rise from the ground; but
> he would not, nor did he eat food with them. On the seventh day
> the child died. And the servants of David were afraid to tell him
> that the child was dead; for they said, 'While the child was still
> alive, we spoke to him, and he did not listen to us; how then can
> we tell him the child is dead? He may do himself some harm.' But
> when David saw that his servants were whispering together, he
> perceived that the child was dead; and David said to his servants,
> 'Is the child dead?' They said, 'He is dead.' Then David rose from
> the ground, washed, anointed himself, and changed his clothes.
> He went into the house of the Lord, and worshipped; he then

went to his own house; and when he asked, they set food before him and he ate . . . Then David consoled his wife Bathsheba, and went to her, and lay with her; and she bore a son, and he named him Solomon. (2 Sam. 12.16–20, 24)

One of the striking features of this passage is David's dramatic change of mood and conduct once mourning is complete and he is able to return to normality. This period of mourning, characterized by the kinds of behaviour outlined above, usually following death and of varying duration,[8] was evidently an integral component within Jewish practice. Its purpose appears to be, at least in part, an attempt to identify with the dying or deceased through showing solidarity in their condition of being cut off from life and from the God of life. Various forms of abstinence and denial, together with withdrawal from relationships and social intercourse, characterize this transitory phase in which mourners embrace the disorientating and disintegrating effects of death, before re-engaging with life once more.[9]

Another element in the management of loss within the Jewish tradition relates to the corpse.[10] Burial was the normal means of disposal, even where Jews were executed for capital offences (Deut. 21.22–3). The Book of Tobit (third or fourth century BCE) underlines the importance of interment and the obligation of fellow Jews to ensure its performance (1.16–19; 2.4–8). Given the Eastern climate, a decomposing body would soon become a health risk, but the significance of the practice extends beyond this observation. Burial underlines the transient nature of existence and locates human being firmly within the processes of nature and the cycle of life. This is a theme regularly explored in the Psalms and wisdom literature (e.g. Ps. 90.3; Eccles. 3.20; 12.7; Ecclus. 14.16–19). And, although, as we shall see, such delimiting of life was in tension with other elements of faith, it does nonetheless establish the finality of death and so the completion of each particular investment of divine giftedness.[11] Furthermore, it is the responsibility of mourners not simply to bury the dead, but to bury them with their family and ancestors (e.g. Gen. 25.10; 47.30; 49.31; Josh. 24.32; 2 Sam. 2.32; 1 Kings 13.31; also *m. Sanh.* 6.5–6). Only in this way can the deceased be laid to rest as they take their rightful place within a continuum of existence – and so of divine graciousness – which gives significance to each life.[12]

As for mortals, their days are like grass;
    they flourish like a flower of the field;

for the wind passes over it, and it is gone,
   and its place knows it no more.
But the steadfast love of the Lord is from everlasting to
     everlasting
on those who fear him,
   and his righteousness to children's children,
to those who keep his covenant
   and remember to do his commandments.

                             (Ps. 103.15–18)

It would be difficult to overestimate the importance of kinship for
Jewish identity.[13] By belonging to a stream of vitality, reaching back
to Abraham and beyond (Gen. 12.1–3; 15.1–6; cf. 1.28; 9.1, 7–9),
each Jew is able both to enjoy and to participate in the divine vocation of blessing. As a consequence, once the prescribed period of
mourning is completed, it is the *obligation of Jews to re-affirm the gift
of life entrusted to them by God* through the agency of their parents.
This is signalled by the return of joy through the restoration of
sustaining and life-enriching relationships, principally with God but
also with other people. Hence, David's dramatic return to normality
in the passage from 2 Samuel cited above. This re-vitalizing of life
was celebrated and, most probably, ritualized in public worship where
the movement from mourning to joy found liturgical expression.[14]
Consider, for example, Psalm 30 which, although originally concerned with the loss of health and subsequent recovery, illustrates
this phenomenon:

I will extol you, O Lord, for you have drawn me up,
   and did not let my foes rejoice over me.
O Lord my God, I cried to you for help,
   and you have healed me.
O Lord, you brought up my soul from Sheol,
   restored me to life from among those gone down to
     the Pit.

Sing praises to the Lord, O you his faithful ones,
   and give thanks to his holy name.
For his anger is but for a moment;
   his favour is for a lifetime.
Weeping may linger for the night,
   but joy comes with the morning.

As for me, I said in my prosperity,
  'I shall never be moved.'
By your favour, O Lord,
  you had established me as a strong mountain;
you hid your face;
  I was dismayed.

To you, O Lord, I cried,
  and to the Lord I made supplication:
'What profit is there in my death,
  if I go down to the Pit?
Will the dust praise you?
  Will it tell of your faithfulness?
Hear, O Lord, and be gracious to me!
  O Lord, be my helper!'

You have turned my mourning into dancing;
  you have taken off my sackcloth
  and clothed me with joy,
so that my soul may praise you and not be silent.
  O Lord my God, I will give thanks to you for ever.

This return of joy and resurgence may seem rather artificial, but its significance resides in being part of a strategy for managing loss. Rather than leaving mourners to their own devices, grief is contained within a framework encompassing identification with the dead before facilitating reintegration into community and reaffirmation of life. Within this context, extended or indefinite preoccupation with mourning was tantamount to voluntarily cutting oneself off from God and opting for a 'living death'. Hence, Jacob's response to news of Joseph's demise: 'Then Jacob tore his garments, and put sackcloth on his loins, and mourned for his son many days. All his sons and all his daughters sought to comfort him; but he refused to be comforted, and said, "No, I shall go down to Sheol to my son, mourning"' (Gen. 37.34–5).

Significantly, the progression from death and mourning to life and rejoicing is harnessed by the exilic and post-exilic prophets to communicate, first, the sense of loss and abandonment[15] and, second, the hope that God will bless his people once more by restoring them to fullness of life.[16] God is portrayed as the great comforter (Isa. 40.1; Jer. 31.15) who will bring the days of mourning to an end (Isa. 60.3) and give God's people 'a garland instead of ashes, the oil of gladness instead of mourning, the mantle of praise instead of a faint spirit' (Isa. 61.3). Even the fortunes of the heartbroken Rachel will be transformed:

> Thus says the Lord:
> A voice is heard in Ramah,
> lamentation and bitter weeping.
> Rachel is weeping for her children;
> she refuses to be comforted for her children,
> because they are no more.
> Thus says the Lord:
> Keep your voice from weeping,
> and your eyes from tears;
> for there is a reward for your work,
> says the Lord:
> they shall come back from the land of the enemy;
> there is hope for your future,
> says the Lord:
> your children shall come back to their own country.
> (Jer. 31.15–17; cf. Matt. 2.16–18)

It would be incorrect, however, to think that one simply resumed life as before on emerging from the prescribed period of mourning. In most cases, death would bring new responsibilities and opportunities for the living, especially where familial or tribal relations existed. Inheritance could bring blessing in the form of added prosperity, possessions and status; but this, in turn, could be a source of strife and division (e.g. Gen. 21.1–10; 27.1–46; 1 Kings 1.15–20). Laws of inheritance regulated the distribution of a deceased person's estate (e.g. Num. 27.8–11; 36.1–12; Deut. 21.15–17) even to the extent of ensuring a male beneficiary[17] – where necessary, a man was required to marry his dead brother's wife and to procreate with her (Deut. 25.5–10; cf. Gen. 38; Ruth 4.5–10)![18]

More significant for our own investigations, however, is the entrusting not of material wealth, but of vocation. We touched in the first chapter on how charismatic leadership could be communicated through acts of commissioning (cf. Deut. 34.9; 2 Kings 2.9–11). What we witness in the last centuries before the Common Era, when the Jewish way of life was particularly under threat from foreign domination and religious syncretism, is a concerted effort to impress upon Jews the importance of allegiance to the God of Exodus and Sinai, of Covenant and Law. A number of literary genres flourished during this period, often embellishing stories found in the Hebrew Scriptures. The Testament or Last Will is one such example, where great figures of the faith gather their families together before death and entrust to them not principally material wealth, but the Jewish way of life which they had striven to embrace.[19] In some cases, whole books are devoted to this subject, in others, testamentary sections are included within larger works. But one common characteristic throughout is a strong ethical imperative *to live out the faith through lives of uprightness and moral integrity*.[20] Of all the virtues championed, it is striking how often readers are enjoined to love God, family, neighbour and even all humanity:

And he [Abraham to Ishmael and Isaac] commanded them that they should guard the way of the Lord so that they might do righteousness and each one might love his neighbour . . . 'I [Abraham] exhort you, my sons, love the God of heaven, and be joined to all of his commands.' (*Jub.* 20.2, 7)

'I call to witness the God of heaven that you do the truth, each to his neighbour, and that you show love, each to his brother.' (*T. Reub.* 69)

'And you, my children, each of you love his brothers with a good heart, and the spirit of envy will depart from you.' (*T. Sim.* 4.7)

'Keep the Law of God, my children; achieve integrity; live without malice, not tinkering with God's commands or your neighbour's affairs. Love the Lord and your neighbour; be compassionate toward poverty and sickness.' (*T. Iss.* 5.1–2; also 7.6–7)

'Whomever you see, do not harbour resentment, my children; love one another, and do not calculate the wrong done by each to his brothers.' (*T. Zeb.* 8.5)

'Throughout all your life love the Lord, and one another with a true heart . . . Love one another in deed and word and inward thoughts.' (*T. Gad* 5.3, 6.1; also 4.4–7)

'You, therefore, love one another and in patient endurance conceal one another's shortcomings.' (*T. Jos.* 17.2)

'Now, my children, love the Lord God of heaven and earth; keep his commandments; pattern your life after the good and pious man Joseph. Let your thoughts incline to the good, as you know to be so with me, because he who has the right set of mind sees everything rightly. Fear the Lord and love your neighbour.' (*T. Ben.* 3.1–3; also 8.1)[21]

If dying afforded a suitable opportunity to communicate the heart of the faith, the vocation of every Jew, then martyrdom provided an even more impressive setting.[22] The Book of Daniel, where Daniel and his companions risk death at the hands of their Babylonian overlords for their unwillingness to compromise the Jewish way of life, antecedes a thoroughgoing glorification of martyrdom as a noble fate and one worthy of emulation. What we find in books such as 2 and 4 Maccabees is the attempt to narrate the Maccabean uprisings against Seleucid domination and Temple corruption so as to portray martyrdom as the ultimate prize for faithfulness, which is amply rewarded in the next life with God's vindication of the righteous.[23] Significantly, the heroes of these books include ordinary Jews who distinguish themselves through the quality of their discipleship – Eleazar, the seven brothers and their mother. And as death brings them glory, it also visits a weighty moral imperative upon fellow Jews to honour their memory through similar lives of obedience:

So in this way he [Eleazar] died, leaving in his death an example of nobility and a memorial of courage, not only to the young but to the great body of his nation.' (2 Macc. 6.31)

'Imitate me, brothers . . . Do not leave your post in my struggle or renounce our courageous family ties.' (4 Macc. 9.23)

This burden of obligation visited upon the living by the martyrs of the faith grows out of the Jewish understanding of remembrance, which throughout the period covered by the Hebrew Scriptures and beyond is intimately associated with covenant.[24] When God promised to bless Abraham with offspring, wealth and real estate, and when he delivered his people from slavery in Egypt and entered into a covenant with them on Sinai, both parties became locked into a formal relationship with expectations and commitments. Within this context, remembrance becomes the means by which the conditions of the covenant continue to exert a formative influence upon the community of faith. To this end, remembrance is the discipline of appropriating the past in such a way that it interprets the present and informs the future. When God remembers his covenant or his faithful servants,[25] it is to act once more on their behalf; when he remembers their sin, it is to punish them for their failure to honour the covenant or to forgive them.[26] Similarly, when God's people remember it is to give thanks for what God has done for them through the years, to seek God's help in the present, or to repent of their failures.[27]

Within this scenario, few individuals are remembered for their own sake,[28] but those who serve God honourably are remembered by God and become absorbed within the momentum of faith that is entrusted to and constitutive of God's people in each generation.[29] Through remembrance, Jews find their place within the people of God as they learn of God's saving purposes, appreciate what God requires of them and draw inspiration from their faithful forebears so that they may learn to please God and bring honour upon God's name and the covenantal community. A particularly poignant example of how remembrance operates in this way to encourage faith and galvanize resolve is found on the lips of the dying Mattathias as he exhorts his sons, the Maccabees, to uphold the Jewish way at all costs:

'Now, my children, show zeal for the law, and give your lives for the covenant of our ancestors.

'Remember the deeds of the ancestors, which they did in their generations; and you will receive great honour and an everlasting name. Was not Abraham found faithful when tested, and it was reckoned to him as righteousness? Joseph in the time of his distress kept the commandment, and became lord of Egypt. Phinehas our ancestor, because he was deeply zealous, received the covenant of everlasting priesthood. Joshua, because he fulfilled the command, became a judge in Israel. Caleb, because he testified in the assembly, received an inheritance in the land. David, because he was merciful, inherited the throne of the kingdom for ever. Elijah, because of great zeal for the law, was taken up into heaven. Hananiah, Azariah, and Mishael believed and were saved from the flame. Daniel, because of his innocence, was delivered from the mouth of the lions.

'And so observe, from generation to generation, that none of those who put their trust in him will lack strength. Do not fear the words of sinners, for their splendour will turn into dung and worms. Today they will be exalted, but tomorrow they will not be found, because they will have returned to the dust, and their plans will have perished. My children, be courageous and grow strong in the law, for by it you will gain honour.' (1 Macc. 2.50–64; cf. also 4.9; 9.38)

## The Limits of God's Covenantal Faithfulness

For most of the period covered by the Hebrew Scriptures, Jewish faith was firmly focused on this life as the forum where God can be encountered and his presence felt.[30] Salvation, inspired by the great deliverance from Egypt, came in the form of rescue from various forms of danger, including illness, enemies and death.[31] Blessings were tangible and substantial: a large family, a long life, sound health and good reputation, together with wealth, possessions, peace and a share in the 'promised land'.[32] Various strategies were employed to ensure God's good favour (e.g. the sacrificial cult, obedience to Torah, pursuit of holiness or social justice) and to explain his absence (e.g. individual or corporate sinfulness, to test or purify faith, the presence of evil forces). Physical death was not thought to result in annihilation, but in a diminished 'shadowy' existence characterized by enduring separation from God, the source of life.

> For my soul is full of troubles,
>> and my life draws near to Sheol.
> I am counted among those who go down to the Pit;
>> I am like those who have no help,
> like those forsaken among the dead,
>> like the slain that lie in the grave,
> like those whom you remember no more,
>> for they are cut off from your hand.
> You have put me in the depths of the Pit,
>> in the regions dark and deep.
> Your wrath lies heavy upon me,
>> and you overwhelm me with all your waves.
>> (Ps. 88.3–7; cf. also Pss. 6.4–5; 30.9; 89.47–8; 143.7;
>>> Isa. 14.9; 26.14; Ecclus. 17.27–30)

This extreme form of exile was known as Sheol or Hades and located, at least metaphorically, somewhere in the bowels of the earth.[33] Thus, death was thought to prescribe the upper limit of God's covenantal faithfulness to the individual and, for this reason, was conceived in all but the most austere and godless circumstances (cf. Job 3.20–2; Tobit 3.6) as the inevitable – albeit undesirable – end for all flesh.[34]

During life, God could be petitioned to intervene to avert danger and postpone death.[35] Occasionally, God was thought to resuscitate the dead by breathing life back into them (1 Kings 17.17–24; 2 Kings 4.32–7; 13.20–1; cf. Ezek. 37.1–14), but only Enoch and Elijah managed to cheat death altogether (Gen. 5.24; 2 Kings 2.11–12). Contact with the dead was not impossible (cf. 1 Sam. 28.3–25; Isa. 8.19–20), but considered unhelpful and so forbidden (Lev. 20.27; Deut. 18.11). However, communication with God through inter-mediaries was generally recognized, not only in the sense of God inspiring the living, but also through heavenly messengers.[36]

In the light of these observations, it is clear that life after death was not inconceivable to the Jewish way of thinking, although the issue of whether God's blessings could extend beyond the grave remained largely unexplored. Presumably, this was because God's covenant related to Israel as a whole rather than individual Israelites in particular. Each Jew was invited to enjoy God's goodness through-out life, but at death divine generosity was extended to another; hence the importance of children, especially sons, as inheritors.[37] Within this scenario, life becomes the property and prerogative of God alone (Gen. 2.7; 1 Sam. 2.6; Eccles. 12.7), and each gift of life gains its significance through belonging to and participating within the covenantal community (Deut. 30.15–20). This understanding was sustainable so long as life on earth proved to be a source of blessing and no competing world-views challenged the status quo. However, from the time of the Babylonian exile in the sixth century, both of these foundations began to crumble.

Before we consider what expressions of faith emerged from advers-ity and exposure to other cultures, it is insightful to reflect upon the prayerful explorations contained within the Psalms. Many of these profound testimonies explore the limits of God's covenantal love and faithfulness towards his people. If God is able to rescue from death once, then why not time and time again?

> For you do not give me up to Sheol,
>     or let your faithful one see the Pit.
>
> You show me the path of life.
>     In your presence there is fullness of joy;
>     in your right hand are pleasures for evermore.
>         (Ps. 16.10–11; cf. also Pss. 6.4–5; 30.9; 63.3)

Other psalms communicate an inability to conceive of existence without God or of a place beyond God's reach.

Nevertheless I am continually with you;
   you hold my right hand.
You guide me with your counsel,
   and afterward you will receive me with honour.
Whom have I in heaven but you?
   And there is nothing on earth that I desire other than you.
                                                    (Ps. 73.23–5)

Where can I go from your spirit?
   Or where can I flee from your presence?
If I ascend to heaven, you are there;
   if I make my bed in Sheol, you are there.
                              (Ps. 139.7–8; cf. also Pss. 36.5–9;
                                             48.8–9; Tobit 13.1–2)

There are protests at the prospect of being abandoned by God and
even the acknowledgement that God is able to deliver from death.

Do you work wonders for the dead?
   Do the shades rise up to praise you?

Is your steadfast love declared in the grave,
   or your faithfulness in Abaddon?
Are your wonders known in the darkness,
   or your saving help in the land of forgetfulness?
                                              (Ps. 88.10–12)

But God will ransom my soul from the power of Sheol,
for he will receive me.
                                              (Ps. 49.15)

While we find here no clearly formulated beliefs about life after death,
we do nevertheless gain access to a source of spiritual exploration
capable of feeding such convictions should circumstances necessi-
tate and language make possible.

Nor should we overlook how the metaphors of renewal, revival
and resurrection were appropriated within the prophetic tradition to
communicate the hope that God would restore the fortunes of his
chosen people.[38] Hosea, an eighth-century prophet of the Northern
kingdom, utters the following oracle of salvation to a war-torn Judah:

'Come, let us return to the Lord;
   for it is he who has torn, and he will heal us;
   he has struck down, and he will bind us up.

After two days he will revive us;
　　on the third day he will raise us up,
　　that we may live before him.

(Hosea 6.1–2)

The Little Apocalypse of Isaiah, probably a theological response to the fall of Jerusalem in 587 BCE and subsequent Babylonian deportation of the Jewish intelligentsia, envisages a great banquet of feasting and communing with God when death and mourning will come to an end (Isa 25.6–10). The prophet's words of reassurance are bold and uncompromising:

Your dead shall live, their corpses shall rise.
O dwellers in the dust, awake and sing for joy!
For your dew is a radiant dew,
　　and the earth will give birth to those long dead.

(Isa. 26.19)

Ezekiel, ministering during the same traumatic period, looks forward to a time when God will perform revitalizing transplants and spiritual resuscitations ('A new heart I will give you, and a new spirit I will put within you . . .' [Ezek. 36.26]), a time when God will act in sovereign power to redeem his people:

Therefore prophesy, and say to them, 'Thus says the Lord God: I am going to open your graves, and bring you up from your graves, O my people; and I will bring you back to the land of Israel. And you shall know that I am the Lord, when I open your graves, and bring you up from your graves, O my people. I will put my spirit within you, and you shall live, and I will place you on your own soil; then you shall know that I, the Lord, have spoken and will act, says the Lord.' (Ezek. 37.12–14)

We move on, then, to consider the expressions of faith that came into being as a response to adversity, persecution and exposure to different belief systems during the final centuries before and first century of the Common Era. The fate of righteous Jews who had suffered greatly for their faithfulness and who had died without sharing in God's covenantal blessings had become a theological crisis demanding a major revision of traditional conceptions of salvation. Put simply, the resolution was to extend the limits of God's commitment to his people beyond the grave. As we have just noted with respect to the Psalms and the prophetic literature, the foundations for such a development were at least partially in place with a growing awareness of the unconditional nature of God's covenantal love and a conceiving of a future dispensation of salvation inaugurated by divine intervention. Add to these the demand for divine justice, together with insights drawn from other cultures, and we have assembled the principal resources giving rise to a rich and varied literature.[39]

Vindication of the righteous was thought to require at least a reversal of their fortunes and a reward for their faithfulness; but there was also a strong conviction that God should judge and punish the perpetrators of evil. These hopes tended to find expression in one of two ways. Either God would intervene to give life back to his righteous ones and, in some cases, to administer justice to the wicked, or the souls of the faithful, having been purified through adversity, would be worthy of inheriting the Kingdom of God's pleasure.[40] Resurrection and immortality – we find both of these approaches expounded in relation to Eleazar, the seven brothers and their mother who suffered ignominious persecution before execution under Antiochus Epiphanes during the Maccabean rebellions. In 2 Maccabees the emphasis is upon resurrection:

> 'One cannot but choose to die at the hands of mortals and to cherish the hope God gives of being raised again by him. But for you there will be no resurrection to life!' . . . Although she saw her seven sons perish within a single day, she bore it with good courage because of her hope in the Lord. She encouraged each of them in the language of their ancestors . . . 'Therefore the Creator of the world, who shaped the beginning of humankind and devised the origin of all things, will in his mercy give life and breath back to you again, since you now forget yourselves for the sake of his laws.' (2 Macc. 7.14, 20, 23; cf. also 7.9, 29, 36–8)

Whereas, in 4 Maccabees, the author affirms his belief in the existence of an immortal soul within each person capable of being purified through this life and so made worthy of sharing eternity with God:

> None of the seven youths proved coward or shrank from death, but all of them, as though running the course toward immortality, hastened to death by torture . . . For these crimes divine justice pursued and will pursue the accursed tyrant. But the sons of Abraham with their victorious mother are gathered together into the chorus of the fathers, and have received pure and immortal

souls from God, to whom be glory for ever and ever. Amen. (4 Macc. 14.4–5; 18.22–4)[41]

It is important not to overemphasize the differences between 'the resurrection of the body' and 'the immortality of the soul' for, as we have noted, Jewish faith rarely conceived of life ending in annihilation, but only in permanent separation from God. This outlook, which seems to imply the depositing in Sheol of a residual self, is not wholly incompatible with the Platonic idea of a vital component within each person constituting the essence of being and capable of transcending the passage of time.[42] However, the distinction can be sustained in that it highlights the particular roles anticipated for God within each scenario. In the case of resurrection, God or God's agent of salvation intervenes; in the case of immortality, the divine ordering of life follows its course.[43]

There is little question that by the first century CE, belief in a life beyond death was widespread among Palestinian as well as Diaspora Jews, even if there was considerable difference in opinion over what form it would take.[44] Josephus claims that both the Pharisees and the Essenes shared this view, but not the Sadducees (cf. Matt. 22.23–33/Mark 12.18–27/Luke 20.27–40);[45] in truth, the diversity of Jewish opinion is likely to have been a good deal greater. In some scenarios, life continues for the righteous without interruption:

> The Lord is faithful to those who truly love him, to those who endure his discipline, To those who live in the righteousness of his commandments, in the Law, which he has commanded for our life. The Lord's devout shall live by it forever; the Lord's paradise, the trees of life, are his devout ones. Their planting is firmly rooted forever; they shall not be uprooted as long as the heavens shall last, for Israel is the portion and inheritance of God. But not so are sinners and criminals, who love (to spend) the day in sharing their sin. Their enjoyment is brief and decaying, and they do not remember God. For the ways of men are known before him always, and he knows the secrets of the heart before they happen. Therefore their inheritance is Hades, and darkness and destruction; and they will not be found on the day of mercy for the righteous. But the devout of the Lord will inherit life in happiness. (*Pss. Sol.* 14.1–10)[46]

In other scenarios a hiatus follows death before imprisoned souls are released from Sheol or Hades:

In those days, Sheol will return all the deposits which she had received and hell will give back all that which it owes. And he shall choose the righteous and the holy ones from among (the risen dead), for the day when they shall be selected and saved has arrived. (*1 En.* 51.1–2)[47]

Certain books concentrate on how a worthy life on earth determines fate:

And as for the visitation of all who walk in this spirit, it shall be healing, great peace in a long life, and fruitfulness, together with every everlasting blessing and eternal joy in life without end, a crown of glory and a garment of majesty in unending light. (1QS 4.6–8)[48]

But others concentrate on God's sovereign power:

And it will happen after these things when the time of the appearance of the Anointed One has been fulfilled and he returns with glory, that then all who hope of him will rise. And it will happen at that time that those treasuries will be opened in which the number of the souls of the righteous were kept, and they will go out and the multitudes of the souls will appear together, in one assemblage, of one mind. And the first ones will enjoy and the last ones will not be sad. For they know that the time has come of which it is said that it is the end of times. But the souls of the wicked will the more waste away when they shall see all these things. For they know that their torment has come and that their perditions have arrived. (*2 Bar.* 30.1–5)[49]

Yet, uniting them all is the conviction that blessing continues to be the inheritance of Jews who keep the faith of their ancestors and refuse to compromise its demands in the face of political upheaval, economic adversity and religious syncretism.

## Redeeming Death

Before bringing this review to a close, we need to consider one further development which had antecedents in the Hebrew Scriptures, but which flourished during the intertestamental period. In the previous section, we explored how faith managed to accommodate the challenge posed by the persecution of righteous Jews and to reconcile it with God's covenantal faithfulness. However, there was another dimension to this 'redeeming of death' which related not so much to the deceased as to their Jewish contemporaries. The notion of intercession has a long pedigree in the Hebrew Scriptures.[50] From the beginning, Jewish faith recognized the essentially mediatory nature of divine presence. God works through chosen servants who enable the covenantal commitments of both parties to be fulfilled. Priests, prophets and the wise can all be understood in these terms: priests regulate access to God by facilitating reconciliation; prophets maintain God's relevance through interpreting the present theologically; sages demonstrate how the practice of wisdom is the embodiment of divine will. In addition to these established roles, there was a tacit recognition that human initiative could on occasion accomplish 'on God's behalf' what would otherwise have been impossible. Abraham's plea for the innocent of Sodom and Gomorrah in Genesis 18.23–32 is one example of this, where the patriarch's prayer averts disaster. Moses' intercessions for sinful Israel is another (e.g. Exod. 33.12–23; Num. 14.13–19). But surely the most striking incidence occurs in the fourth servant song of Isaiah, where the death of God's servant is invested with redeeming power to forgive and to heal:

> Surely he has borne our infirmities
>     and carried our diseases;
> yet we accounted him stricken,
>     struck down by God, and afflicted.
> But he was wounded for our transgressions,
>     crushed for our iniquities;
> upon him was the punishment that made us whole,
>     and by his bruises we are healed . . .
> For he was cut off from the land of the living,
>     stricken for the transgression of my people . . .
> When you make his life an offering for sin . . .
>     The righteous one, my servant, shall make many righteous,
>     and he shall bear their iniquities . . .
> because he poured out himself to death,
>     and was numbered with the transgressors;
> yet he bore the sin of many,
>     and made intercession for the transgressors.
>
> (Isa. 53.4–5, 8, 10, 11, 12)

The efficacy of intercession continued to be celebrated well into the Common Era. For instance, the healings and nature miracles

performed by first-century rabbis such as Hanina ben Dosa and
Honi are well attested:[51]

> They say about Rabbi Hanina ben Dosa that he used to pray over
> the sick and say, 'This one will live,' or 'That one will die.' They
> said to him, 'How do you know?' He said to them, 'If my prayer
> is fluent in my mouth, I know that he is accepted; and if it is
> not, I know that he is rejected.' (*m. Ber.* 5.5; cf. also *m. Ber.* 5.1;
> *b. Ber.* 34b; *t. Ber.* 3.20)

> Once they said to Honi the Circle-Drawer, 'Pray that rain may
> fall.' He said to them, 'Go out and bring in the Passover ovens
> that they may not be softened.' He prayed, but rain did not come
> down. What did he do? He drew a circle and stood within it and
> said, 'Lord of the universe, Your sons have turned their faces to
> me, for I am as a son of the house before You. I swear by Your
> great name that I will not move from here until You have mercy
> on Your sons.' Rain began dripping. He said, 'Not for this have I
> prayed, but for rain (that fills) cisterns, pits, and caverns.' It began
> to come down violently. He said, 'Not for this have I prayed,
> but for rain of goodwill, blessing, and plenty.' It came down in
> moderation until Israel went up from Jerusalem to the Mount of
> the House because of the rain. (*m. Ta'an.* 3.8; cf. also *b. Ta'an.* 23a;
> Josephus, *Ant.* 14.2.1 §22–4)

We also read in rabbinic sources of the saving potential of the faith
of the patriarchs.[52]

> Shema'yah [first-century CE rabbi] says: 'The faith with which
> their father Abraham believed in Me is deserving that I should
> divide the sea for them.' For it is said: 'And he believed in the
> Lord . . . And so also you find that our father Abraham inherited
> both this world and the world beyond only as a reward for the
> faith with which he believed, as it is said: 'And he believed in the
> Lord . . .' (*Mek.*, Beshallah on Exod. 14.15 and 14.31)

Particularly poignant for us, however, are the following comments of
the Diaspora Jew who wrote 4 Maccabees, which bear witness to
what is perhaps the ultimate redemption of death – a life sacrificed
for faith capable of saving not only the martyr, but others as well:[53]

> These, then, who have been consecrated for the sake of God, are
> honoured, not only with this honour, but also by the fact that
> because of them our enemies did not rule over our nation, the

tyrant was punished, and the homeland purified – they having become, as it were, a ransom for the sin of our nation. And through the blood of those devout ones and their death as an atoning sacrifice, divine Providence preserved Israel that previously had been mistreated. (4 Macc. 17.20–2; cf. also 6.29; 18.3–4)[54]

## Making Connections

Hopefully, this chapter has put us in touch with some of the resources at the disposal of Jesus' disciples as they responded to his death. A number of these are particularly significant and resonate with what we know of the period after the crucifixion:

- the observance of a prescribed period of mourning, when sufferers give expression to their grief and demonstrate solidarity with the deceased, followed by re-establishment of daily routines and reintegration into community life and worship;
- the practice, in the shadow of death, of entrusting the inheritance of faith to those under one's authority and charging them to follow in one's footsteps;
- the importance of remembrance as a means of appropriating the past into the present and enabling key figures and events in Israel's history to exert a formative influence on shaping the future;
- the belief that God will vindicate his righteous ones who suffer for the faith by raising them to new life or by purifying their souls so that they may share in the blessings of heaven;
- the moral obligation exerted by martyrs upon those required to honour their memory through lives of obedience and faithfulness;
- the power of the blood of the righteous to atone for sins and forge reconciliation with God.

## NOTES

1 Useful surveys are provided by D. J. Davies (1997); Holm and Bowker (1994); and Thomas (1987), pp. 450–8.
2 The most influential case of this must surely be the Babylonian Exile of the sixth century; see, especially, G. A. Anderson (1991), pp. 99–130; Brueggemann (1986); and Gowan (1998), pp. 10–16.
3 See the articles by A. P. Bender cited in the bibliography, together with

Rothkoff (1972), pp. 486–92; De Vaux (1961), pp. 56–61; Walters (1997), pp. 9–24; and Wolff (1974), pp. 99–118.

4 Brueggemann (1995b), pp. 84–97; and Turner (1995), pp. 125–30; also Gill (1994), pp. 17–24.

5 See, especially, Joyce (1993), pp. 304–20.

6 Weeping: Gen. 50.4; 2 Sam.19.2; Esth. 4.3; Job 30.31; lamentation: Gen. 50.10; 2 Sam.1.18; Esth. 4.3; Ps. 35.14; beating of breasts: Isa. 32.12; fasting: Deut. 26.14; 2 Sam. 3.35; Esth. 4.3; Ezra 10.6; Neh.1.4; rending of clothes: 2 Sam. 3.31; Esth. 4.1–3; wearing sackcloth: 2 Sam. 3.31; Ps. 30.11; Esth. 4.3; cf. 2 Sam. 14.2; imposition of dust or ashes: Josh 7.6; 2 Sam.13.19; Jer. 6.26; 25.34; Ezek. 27.30; Lam. 2.10; Esth. 4.1–3; refraining from washing and anointing: Exod. 33.4; 2 Sam. 14.2; donning mourning garments: 2 Sam.14.2; Ezek. 26.16; covering one's head: Esth. 6.12; cowering: Pss. 35.14; 38.6; employment of 'professional mourners': Jer. 9.17; Amos 5.16. See also *m. Ber.* 2.6–7; *Ter.*11.10; *Šab* 23.4–5; *Sanh.* 2.1–3; 5.6; 6.6; *Pes.* 8.6–8; *Meg.* 3.3; 4.3; *M. Qaṭ.* 1.5–6; 3.5; *Mak.* 3.5.

7 Another case of mourning for the dying, rather than the deceased, can be found in Job: 'Now when Job's three friends heard of all these troubles that had come upon him, each of them set out from his home – Eliphaz the Temanite, Bildad the Shuhite, and Zophar the Naamathite. They met together to go and console and comfort him. When they saw him from a distance, they did not recognize him, and they raised their voices and wept aloud; they tore their robes and threw dust in the air upon their heads. They sat with him on the ground seven days and seven nights, and no one spoke a word to him, for they saw that his suffering was very great' (Job 2.11–13).

8 Periods of three (*T. Job* 53.7–8), seven (Job 2.13; Ecclus. 22.12), thirty (Num. 20.29; Deut. 21.13; 34.8) and forty (*Jub.* 23.7) days are recorded; cf. 'If a man buried his dead three days before the Feast, the rule of seven [days' mourning] is annulled for him; if eight days before, the rule of the thirty days is annulled for him. For they have said: The Sabbath is included and does not interrupt; but Feasts interrupt and are not included' (*m.M. Qaṭ.* 3.5; the note of Herbert Danby is insightful: 'The rules for mourning were that the first three days should be given to weeping, and the first seven to lamenting the dead; the tokens of mourning were to be worn for thirty days').

9 Turner (1995), esp. pp. 129–30.

10 For more information, see De Vaux (1961), pp. 56–8; and O'Rahilly (1941a), pp. 123–35.

11 See the important study of A. R. Johnson (1964).

12 Conversely, the worst fate that could befall a Jew was to be denied burial in the family grave and left unattended. Consider the following curse visited upon Jeroboam by the prophet Ahijah: ' "I will cut off from Jeroboam every male, both bond and free in Israel, and will consume the house of Jeroboam, just as one burns up dung until it is all

gone. Anyone belonging to Jeroboam who dies in the city, the dogs shall eat; and anyone who dies in the open country, the birds of the air shall eat; for the Lord has spoken." Therefore set out, go to your house. When your feet enter the city, the child [i.e. Abijah] shall die. All Israel shall mourn for him and bury him; for he alone of Jeroboam's family shall come to the grave, because in him there is found something pleasing to the Lord, the God of Israel, in the house of Jeroboam' (1 Kings 14.10–13).

13  H. W. Robinson (1964); Rowley (1956), pp. 99–123; and Wolff (1974), esp. pp. 214–22.

14  Especially, G. A. Anderson (1991), pp. 87–97; and Brueggemann (1995a), pp. 67–83.

15  E.g. Isa. 22.12; Jer. 6.26; 48.38; Lam. 2.5; 5.15; Ezek. 2.10; Amos 5.16; 8.10; Mic. 1.8–16; Zech.12.11.

16  Brueggemann (1986); and now Gowan (1998), pp. 78–142.

17  Cf. 'When the father dies he will not seem to be dead, for he has left behind him one like himself, whom in his life he looked upon with joy and at death, without grief' (Ecclus. 30.4–5).

18  E. W. Davies (1981), pp. 138–44, 257–88; and L. R. Bailey (1979), pp. 49–51, draw attention to additional strategies used to ensure a male heir.

19  There is considerable scholarly debate about the dates of some of these works. We have restricted ourselves to those which tend to be dated no later than the first century of the Common Era: The Testaments of the Twelve Patriarchs, the Testament of Job, the Testament of Abraham, together with less controversial books, such as Jubilees and Tobit.

20  E.g. *Jub.* 20.1–10; 21.1–4; 22.10–16; *T. Jud.*14.1–8; 16.1–4; *T. Iss.* 4.1–6; 5.1–5; 7.1–9; *T. Zeb.* 5.1–5; 7.1–4; 8.1–6; 9.8; *T. Dan* 2.1; 4.5–7; *T. Gad* 4.4–7; 6.1; 8.1–4; *T. Ash.* 6.1–3; *T. Jos.*10.1–3; 17.1–3; *T. Ben.* 3.1–5; 4.1–5; 8.1–3; Tobit 4.3–11; 14.8–9.

21  Evidence of interpolation suggests that at least some of these Testaments were appropriated by Christian audiences (e.g. *T. Sim.* 6.7; *T. Lev.* 4.4; 14.2; *T. Ash.* 7.3).

22  Martyrdom has attracted considerable interest in recent years; see, for example, Droge and Tabor (1992); M. C. de Boer (1988); and Van Henten (1989 and 1997).

23  E.g. ' "You accursed wretch, you dismiss us from the present life, but the King of the universe will raise us up to an everlasting renewal of life, because we have died for his laws" ' (2 Macc. 7.9; cf. also 7.14, 20, 23, 29, 36–8). ' "You too must have the same faith in God and not be grieved. It is unreasonable for people who have religious knowledge not to withstand pain." By these words the mother of the seven encouraged and persuaded each of her sons to die rather than violate God's commandment. They knew also that those who die for the sake of God live to God, as do Abraham and Isaac and Jacob and all the patriarchs' (4 Macc. 16.22–5; cf. 17.20–2; 18.3–4, 23–4).

24  See Childs (1962); Clements (1980), pp. 64–8; and Verhey (1992), pp. 667–9.

25  Gen. 9.16; 19.19; 30.22; Exod. 2.24; 32.13; Lev. 26.42; Deut. 9.27; 1 Sam.1.19; 2 Kings 20.3; Neh. 5.19; 6.14; 13.14, 22, 29, 31; Job 7.7; Pss. 74.2; 98.3; 105.5, 42; Mal.3.16.

26  Ps. 25.7; 79.8; 109.14; Isa. 43.25; 64.9; Jer.14.10; 31.34; Ezek. 3.20; 18.22, 24; 33.13,16; 36.31; Hos. 8.13; 9.9; Tobit 3.3.

27  Exod.12.14; 13.3; 20.8, 24; Num. 5.15; 15.39–40; Deut. 5.15; 9.7; 15.15; Judg. 16.28; 1 Sam.1.11; 1 Chron 16.12–15; Pss. 77.11; 106.4; Isa. 38.3.

28  Cf. 'The people of long ago are not remembered, nor will there be any remembrance of people yet to come by those who come after them' (Eccles. 1.11; also Wisd. 2.4; cf. Job 18.17; Pss. 9.6; 109.15; Eccles. 9.5; Isa. 26.14; Wisd. 4.19; Ecclus. 10.17; 23.26; 44.9).

29  'For the righteous will never be moved; they will be remembered for ever' (Ps. 112.6; also Prov. 10.7; Ecclus. 39.9; 45.1; 46.11; 49.1, 13; 1 Macc. 3.7).

30  Pss. 90.9–17; 103.15–18; Eccles. 8.2; 12.1–8; Ecclus. 14.16–19; 17.27–30.

31  E.g. Exod. 15.1–19; Job 5.20; Pss.13.3–6; 18.3–6, 17–18; 30.1–12; 33.18–20; 40.1–3; 41.1–13; 51.1–5; 56.12–13; 69.13–16; 86.12–13; 103.1–5; 106.4–5, 47; 121.1–8; *5 Apoc. Syr. Pss.* 4; 5; Ecclus. 51.1–12. See the discussion of E. M. B. Green (1965), pp. 11–71.

32  Consider, for example, the blessings bestowed upon God's chosen ones (Gen.1.28; 9.1, 7–9; 12.1–3; 27.28–9; 48.3–4; Deut. 6.3; Ps.11.2) and the varying fortunes of Job (1.1—2.10; 42.10–17). See Westermann (1972), pp. 9–19.

33  See T. J. Lewis (1992), pp. 101–5.

34  Kaiser and Lohse (1981), esp. pp. 30–54.

35  P. D. Miller (1994), pp. 55–134, 244–61, offers a good overview.

36  See Newsom (1992), pp. 248–53.

37  'Sons are indeed a heritage from the Lord, the fruit of the womb a reward. Like arrows in the hand of a warrior are the sons of one's youth. Happy is the man who has his quiver full of them. He shall not be put to shame when he speaks with his enemies in the gate' (Ps.127.3–5). Cf. childlessness as a threat to the fulfilment of God's promise to form a chosen people (Gen.15.1–6; 18.1–15; 30.1–24), and as a curse or punishment (Lev. 20.20–1; 1 Sam.15.33; 1 Chron. 2.30, 32; Jer.18.21).

38  Brueggemann (1986); and Gowan (1998), pp. 24–142.

39  See, especially, the discussions of Nickelsburg (1972), and (1992a), pp. 680–91; also N. T. Wright (1992), pp. 280–338.

40  The best-known expression of this comes from the Book of Wisdom: 'But the souls of the righteous are in the hand of God, and no torment will ever touch them. In the eyes of the foolish they seemed to have died, and their departure was thought to be a disaster, and their going from us to be their destruction; but they are at peace. For though in the sight of others they were punished, their hope is full of immortality. Having been disciplined a little, they will receive great good, because

God tested them and found them worthy of himself; like gold in the furnace he tried them, and like a sacrificial burnt offering he accepted them. In the time of their visitation they will shine forth, and will run like sparks through the stubble' (3.1–8).

41  Also, 4 Macc. 9.9; 16.22–5; cf. Josephus' comments on Eleazar's martyrdom: 'For it is death which gives liberty to the soul and permits it to depart to its own pure abode, there to be free from all calamity; but so long as it is imprisoned in a mortal body and tainted with all its miseries, it is, in sober truth, dead, for association with what is mortal ill befits that which is divine. True, the soul possesses great capacity, even while incarcerated in the body; for it makes the latter its organ of perception, invisibly swaying it and directing it onward in its actions beyond the range of mortal nature. But it is not until, freed from the weight that drags it down to earth and clings about it, the soul is restored to its proper sphere, that it enjoys a blessed energy and a power untrammelled on every side, remaining, like God Himself, invisible to human eyes' (*War* 7.8.7 §344–6).

42  A. R. Johnson (1964), pp. 87–109; Kaiser and Lohse (1981), p. 41; Nickelsburg (1972), esp. pp. 177–80.

43  For further references, see 4Q521, Frag.1, Col. 2, lines 1–12; 1QS 4.6–14; *2 Bar.* 23.1–7; 30.1–5; 50.2—51.6; *1 En.* 50, 51; 100.1–6; *4 Ezra* 7.26–44; *Pss. Sol.* 3.11–12; 9.5; 12.6; 13.11–12; 14.1–10; 15.10–13; *T. Jud.* 25.1–5; *T. Gad* 4.4–7; *T. Ben.*10.2–11; *T. Abr.*17.5–8; *T. Job* 39.8–13; 52—3; Wisd. 3.1–13; 4.1–2, 10–11; 4.20—5.2; 5.14–15; 16.13; cf.1.12–15; 2.4–5.

44  'Individual immortality or resurrection is not a major topic of our literature, but it is probable that most Jews expected death not to be the end, though they may have conceived the future quite vaguely.' E. P. Sanders (1992), p. 298. The Eighteen Benedictions, in their ancient Palestinian form, are thought by many to reflect popular Jewish belief in the first century CE. The second benediction includes a reference to God raising the dead: 'Thou art mighty, bringing low the proud; powerful, judging the arrogant; ever-living, raising up the dead; causing the wind to blow and the dew to descend; sustaining the living, quickening the dead . . .' (the translation here and elsewhere is taken from Petuchowski and Brocke (1978), pp. 27–30).

45  'They [i.e. the Pharisees] believe that souls have power to survive death and that there are rewards and punishments under the earth for those who have led lives of virtue or vice: eternal imprisonment is the lot of evil souls, while the good souls receive an easy passage to a new life' (Josephus, *Ant.* 18 §14; cf. *War* 2.8.14 §163). 'The doctrine of the Essenes is wont to leave everything in the hands of God. They regard the soul as immortal and believe that they ought to strive especially to draw near to righteousness' (Josephus, *Ant.* 18 §18; cf. *War* 2.8.11 §154). Cf. 'The Sadducees hold that the soul perishes along with the body' (Josephus, *Ant.* 18 §16; War 2.8.14 §163).

46 Also, *Pss. Sol.* 3.11–12; 6.6; 9.5; 12.6; 13.11–12; 15.10–13; cf. 'The beginning of wisdom is the most sincere desire for instruction, and concern for instruction is love of her, and love of her is the keeping of her laws, and giving heed to her laws is assurance of immortality, and immortality brings one near to God; so the desire for wisdom leads to a kingdom. Therefore if you delight in thrones and sceptres, O monarchs over the peoples, honour wisdom, so that you may reign for ever' (Wisd. 6.17–21; cf. also 1.12–15; 2.4–5; 3.1–13; 4.10–11; 4.20—5.2; 5.14–15; 8.14; *T. Job* 52—3; *T. Abr.* [A] 20.1–15).

47 Also, 'For the earth will surely give back the dead at that time; it receives them now in order to keep them, not changing anything in their form. But as it has received them so it will give them back' (*2 Bar.* 50.2); and 'And the earth shall give up those who are asleep in it; and the chambers shall give up the souls which have been committed to them' (*4 Ezra* 7.32).

48 Also, 'After he had spoken these things to them he said, "You know then, my children, that I am dying. Do the truth, each of you to his neighbour; keep the Law of the Lord and his commandments, for I leave you these things instead of an inheritance. Give them, then, to your children for an eternal possession; this is what Abraham, Isaac, and Jacob did. They gave us all these things as an inheritance, saying, 'Keep God's commandments until the Lord reveals his salvation to all the nations.' And then you will see Enoch and Seth and Abraham and Isaac and Jacob being raised up at the right hand in great joy. Then shall we also be raised, each of us over our tribe, and we shall prostrate ourselves before the heavenly king"' (*T. Ben.*10.2–7; cf. *T. Gad* 4.4–7; Tobit 4.3–11).

49 Also *2 Bar.* 50.2—51.6; *3 Bar.* 11.1–9; *1 En.* 50—51; 100.1–6; *4 Ezra* 7.26–44; cf. 4Q521, Frag.1, Col. 2, lines 1–12.

50 See Bowker (1966), pp. 69–82; P. D. Miller (1994), esp. pp. 262–80; Muilenburg (1968), pp 159–81; and Rhodes (1977), pp. 107–28.

51 See Bokser (1985), 42–91; Büchler (1922), pp. 196–264; C. A. Evans (1995), pp. 213–50; W. S. Green (1982), pp. 619–47; and Vermes (1972), pp. 28–50. The most convenient collection of rabbinic traditions about Hanina and Honi is probably that of Francis Martin (1988).

52 On the so-called 'merits of the fathers', see Marmorstein (1968); Stewart (1961), pp. 127–33; and Urbach (1987), pp. 496–511.

53 On the development of this way of interpreting death and its influence upon how Jesus' crucifixion was understood, see Hengel (1981a); and S. K. Williams (1975).

54 Cf. 'In those days, the prayers of the righteous ascended into heaven, and the blood of the righteous from the earth before the Lord of the Spirits. There shall be days when all the holy ones who dwell in the heavens above shall dwell (together). And with one voice, they shall supplicate and pray – glorifying, praising, and blessing the name of the Lord of the Spirits on behalf of the blood of the righteous ones which

has been shed. Their prayers shall not stop from exhaustion before the Lord of the Spirits – neither will they relax forever – (until) judgement is executed for them' (*1 En.* 47.1–2; also 2 Macc.12.38–45; *Pss. Sol.* 6.7; *3 Bar.* 11.1–9).

# Mourning Jesus:
# Psychological Insights

The reality of death and the experience of loss belong to the universal currency of humanity.[1] In the previous chapter, we reviewed the kind of resources Jewish faith made accessible to Jesus' followers after his crucifixion. We must now start to consider how (if at all) they were used. Our concern at this stage is with those who felt his death most acutely, among whom must surely be numbered those disciples accompanying him throughout his ministry and, finally, to Jerusalem. And here the challenge begins, for our access to their response to Jesus' death is via documents, principally the Gospels, which were composed considerably later than the events they purport to narrate and which, in all probability, condense the vital period immediately after the crucifixion into a three-day scenario. These factors, however, need to be balanced against the proposal made earlier, namely, that the Gospels can be understood as expressions of loss communicating a desire to compensate for Jesus' absence by embodying his life and teaching. In other words, the need to remember Jesus and to facilitate the broadest access to his memory grew out of the grief of those who first loved him.

A further difficulty revolves around method. How are we to identify when the disciples are responding to Jesus' death? The question becomes even more demanding with the recognition that many of the relevant traditions now offer alternative interpretations revolving around the image of resurrection. But, as have seen, resurrection, especially resurrection of the righteous, belongs to the language of faith accessible to Jesus' followers at the time of his death. Thus, their conviction that Jesus had been raised from the dead may itself be an expression of grief; equally, the disciples' grief may have been transformed by encounters with their risen Lord. However, even this latter explanation is ambiguous for, as we shall see, appearances of the departed are not uncommon among the bereaved. To help us address these complex and extremely important issues, we need an interpretative framework capable of guiding our investigations.

45

Recent studies into grief have brought to light what each mourner discovers personally, namely, that there is an anatomy of loss, exhibiting certain characteristics and progressions, by which the sufferer responds to the death of a loved one and accommodates his or her absence.[2] An anatomy sufficiently detailed to afford genuine insight into the condition and sufficiently sophisticated to embrace natural variation while identifying complications. What is more, this anatomy appears to cross boundaries of culture, religion and time, although each of these contributes to how death is managed and loss is expressed.[3] We propose, therefore, to structure this part of our investigation around insights drawn from contemporary research into grief.[4]

## Denial, Guilt and Regret

We begin with the post-mortem appearances of Jesus to his followers and the observation that a similar phenomenon is not uncommon among the bereaved.[5] In some cases, these 'encounters' are precipitated or invoked, but more often than not they surprise the recipient and engender a mixed response, including shock, fear, reassurance and disbelief.[6] Whether these manifestations are identical in origin and form to those experienced by the disciples is a matter of controversy. What is interesting, however, is that they can be interpreted not so much as evidence for the afterlife as disbelief over whether death has taken place at all. That is to say, they are expressions of *denial* or mitigation by which the overwhelming reality of loss is temporarily eased or averted.[7] Significantly, the conclusion that Jesus had risen from the dead is rarely the response of those to whom he appeared![8] It is also striking how much emphasis is placed upon continuity. It is the *same Jesus* who is encountered: he can be seen and touched; he presides at meals, blessing the food; he eats and shares fellowship; he ministers God's forgiveness. These are all characteristics of Jesus' earthly ministry and would have preoccupied those struggling to accommodate the loss of one who had been at the centre of their lives.

Another aspect of denial and one closely associated with what has just been described is the practice of *searching*,[9] whereby the bereaved assume a restless disposition in which they become preoccupied with thoughts of the deceased as they revisit old haunts and rehearse behaviour associated with them. One implication of this can be incidents of mistaken identity, with a corresponding sense of disappointment, frustration and anger, where the mourner misinterprets sensory experience in favour of the deceased. Not infrequently, loved ones see, hear, smell and even feel the touch of one who is dead. In the light of this, it seems more than coincidental that much of the disciples' response to Jesus' death can be understood in this way: they physically look for him (John 20.11–13; cf. Matt. 28.1/ Mark 16.1–3/Luke 24.1–2/John 20.1–2); they hear his voice uttering familiar words (Matt. 28.9; John 20.16, 19, 26); they discern his presence in familiar actions (e.g. eating: Luke 24.30–1; John 21.9–14; Scripture: Luke 24.27, 45–7) and characteristic sensations (e.g. forgiveness: John 21.15–17; reassurance: Matt. 28.10; Matt. 28.6/ Mark 16.6–7/Luke 24.6–8). Whatever else may have generated these perceptions, they do seem to resonate with what we know of the grief process and, in particular, of the mechanisms by which we lessen the shock and gradually come to accept a major loss. Further, our review of Jewish belief in the afterlife confirms that Jesus' followers possessed a matrix in which to interpret these experiences. In addition, as we have already acknowledged implicitly, it would appear that denial of the finality of death, especially as a response to righteous Jews whose faithfulness had been left unrewarded in this life, was one of the formative influences giving rise to conceptions of resurrection or immortality in the first place.[10]

If denial of Jesus' death was one component in the disciples' grief, then *regret* may have been another.[11] It is striking, for example, how much coverage is given to Peter's denial of Jesus[12] – an incident the apostle must have dearly lamented and one which surely caused considerable embarrassment and difficulty, both personally and within the Jesus movement as a whole.[13] In the light of this, should we discern in Peter's encounter with Jesus by the lakeside (John 21.15–19) the yearning for a reconciliation that death prevented?[14] Again, reference to the women's attempt to anoint Jesus' corpse with spices (Mark 16.1–2/Luke 24.1–2), an initiative unlikely to succeed owing to the tomb being sealed or ignorance over the whereabouts of the body, may also reflect a need to perform rites associated with death that did not take place.[15] And surely the words of the disciples on the Emmaus road communicate a least a measure of disillusionment as the reality of unfulfilled expectations hits home: 'But we had hoped that he was the one to redeem Israel' (Luke 24.21).[16] In each of these cases, deeply personal expressions of grief have been canonized within the passion narratives and made the property of the community of faith.

A strong feeling of *guilt* can also be associated with regret.[17] This can have a debilitating effect, especially when the death of one of the parties means there is little hope of reconciliation. On occasion, guilt can become so preoccupying for the bereaved that it reaches pathological proportions; in its extremist forms, it finds expression in self-punishment. One wonders whether something of this outlook is not reflected in the Gospel presentations of both Peter's denial and, more particularly, of Judas' demise.[18] Although there is little doubt that Judas, known as Iscariot, was a follower of Jesus, it is questionable whether the portrayal of him as the one who receives just retribution for betraying his Lord is correct or, at least, the whole story.[19] Could it be that Judas was made into something of a scape-goat by grief-stricken disciples struggling to live with oppressive feelings of guilt and regret – feelings intensified by a tradition that emphasized uncompromising commitment to God's ways and solidarity with his faithful ones?

## Holding On and Letting Go

One set of circumstances complicating grief revolves around the body of the deceased being *missing*.[20] In such cases, there is no opportunity to prepare the corpse for death nor to take leave of the deceased on a personal basis. The bereaved can also be denied any rite of passage at which the dead person is formally commemorated, publicly mourned and officially bid farewell.[21] This, in turn, can be a source of distress or aggravation and lead to the conviction that something important has been left undone which prevents all parties from finding peace. Further, the absence of the body to underline the finality of death can even render mourners incapable of accepting what has taken place and leave them expecting their loved ones to return at any time. There is, in addition, the further complication of no special place associated with the deceased where they are known to have been laid to rest and where they can be mourned and commemorated.

We know from the Gospel records that the grief of Jesus' followers included ignorance over the whereabouts of his body. How this situation arose is a matter of considerable debate, revolving around, first, whether the disciples knew where Jesus had been buried and, second, if they did, whether the body was subsequently removed and, if so, by whom.[22] The empty tomb traditions (Matt. 28.1–8/ Mark 16.1–6/Luke 24.1–12; John 20.1–13) tend to be viewed as products of the resurrection either because they convey historical information about where Jesus could no longer be found or because they were created in order to emphasize the corporeal nature of Jesus' rising.[23] However, there are serious difficulties with both of these options. In the case of the former, whilst some first-century conceptions of the afterlife envisage the transformation of the body, an empty tomb does little to confirm this has taken place. Certainly, it was not obvious to the eyewitnesses who needed angelic assistance to interpret what it meant![24] In the case of the latter, we simply observe that Paul managed to convince himself and those in his care of Jesus' bodily resurrection without recourse to this consideration. Surely, if he had known about the empty tomb and had thought it relevant, he would have mentioned it.

In the light of this, an alternative explanation presents itself, namely, the significance of the empty tomb does not rest with the resurrection, but with the recognition that Jesus' body could not be located.[25] This is an historical reference noteworthy precisely because it meant that his disciples were unable to lay him to rest or to perform the prescribed post-mortem rituals and disciplines. It also denied them a focus for their mourning or, indeed, for future veneration.[26] Recalling what we noted earlier about the importance of being buried with one's ancestors, it would have been difficult enough for his followers to live in the knowledge that they had failed him on this count; but, add to this their uncertainty over whether he had been buried at all, and their burden would have been greatly increased.[27] These considerations, if correct, would undoubtedly have complicated their grief and made it more difficult to accept Jesus' death and mourn his passing.

Another factor influencing the ability of the bereaved to let go of the deceased concerns the *afterlife*.[28] Although beliefs of this nature can conceal the enormity of loss, they can also be a source of great comfort and strength whereby mourners are empowered to reaffirm life without feelings of betrayal or desertion. Quite simply, death takes on a very different significance when interpreted as an entrusting of loved ones into God's safe keeping. In the previous chapter, we reviewed the different understandings of post-mortem existence embraced by Jewish faith in the time of Jesus. In addition, we can be reasonably confident that Jesus himself entertained such beliefs and, presumably, encouraged his followers to do likewise.[29] There is, then, every probability that his disciples would have drawn upon these resources in their grief as they sought ways of giving expression to their love and form to their hopes. Such resources would affirm the resurrection and vindication of the righteous, their unending communion with God and a role in administering God's final judgement upon all people[30] – convictions characterizing belief in Jesus' resurrection.[31]

## Mitigation and Acceptance

The circumstances of death can greatly influence grief, especially when it was unexpected or could have been averted. In such cases, the bereaved have to cope with a range of additional complications associated with the ending of a life abruptly, prematurely and as a consequence of factors judged unworthy, unacceptable or avoidable.[32] One way in which mourners may seek to make sense of their loss is by attempting to 'redeem' the death through investing it with significance. Sentiments such as 'he did not die in vain', 'she died in the service of others', or 'he gave his life to bring us to our senses' reflect this process and, by rescuing death from meaninglessness and futility, reinforce the value of the deceased person and help mourners to accommodate their tragedy.

In the previous chapter we noted how a similar motivation gave expression during the Maccabean uprisings to notions of martyr-dom and of lives sacrificed for others. It should not surprise us, therefore, to find a similar process at work in relation to Jesus.[33] Consider, for example, the ancient tradition attested by Paul in 1 Corinthians 15: 'For I handed on to you as of first importance what I in turn had received: that Christ *died for our sins in accordance with the scriptures*, and that he was buried, and that he was raised on the third day in accordance with the scriptures . . .' (vv. 3–4; our emphasis). Two *mitigations* for Jesus' death are offered in verse 3: it is an atonement for sin and a part of the divine plan disclosed in God's word. Whatever additional factors may have informed these convictions, we must surely identify here a desire to redeem Jesus' death by locating it within God's saving purposes. Furthermore, this motivation informs the Gospel presentations at a number of points, including the so-called 'ransom' logion (Matt. 20.28/Mark 10.45), Jesus' agony over the cup in Gethsemane (Matt. 26.36–46/Mark 14.32–42/Luke 22.39–46), the institution of the Lord's Supper (Matt. 26.28/Mark 14.24; Luke 22.20–1), his words on the cross (Luke 23.34; Matt. 27.46/Mark 15.34), the rending of the Temple curtain (Matt. 27.51/Mark 15.38), the general resurrection of the

righteous following his death (Matt. 27.52–3) and John's presentation of Jesus as the sacrificial lamb of God (John 19.14, 36; cf. 1.29).[34]

## Remembering and Restructuring

If, as human beings, we develop and become ourselves within a
sophisticated web of sustaining relationships and meaningful interactions,[35] then the death of someone who has been formative within
this process results in at least a temporary diminishing of the self.[36]
This is often experienced by the bereaved as a sense of incompleteness and, although the passage of time may compensate for this loss
through the forming of new associations or the reinforcement of
existing ones,[37] there may be certain elements of the original relationship or of the dead person's character that are considered unique
and irreplaceable. Where this is the case, mourners may purposefully
endeavour to keep their loved ones alive, so to speak, through various
forms of remembering and recollection.[38]

Remembering in such circumstances embraces both retrospective
and prospective dimensions. The former because particular encounters with the deceased are recalled and relived – things they did
and said, how they looked and felt and, equally importantly, how
they made the mourner feel. But more so, in addition to mediating
impressions of times together and fragments of a life once shared,
memory can also allow the 'glory' of the deceased person to shine
through.[39] It seems that, by enabling someone to be appreciated
outside of the intensity of personal encounter, remembering establishes a measure of detachment, making it easier for the overall
worth and impact of that person to be discerned. This, in turn, can
be a source of gratitude, appreciation and, on occasion, veneration
as the worth of the deceased is recognized and celebrated.

Equally, remembering can perform a forward-looking function
through which the dead continue to occupy a significant place in
the lives of their mourners and to be influential in the unfolding of
their futures. This need not be a morbid, oppressive or debilitating
affair in which the living are 'haunted' by memories of the dead,[40]
but a more dynamic and creative operation whereby the inspiration
and insights of the deceased are sustained. If memory mediates
presence, in whatever form, then as long as memory permits and
mourners wish to recollect, the departed can be significant and,
indeed, accomplish in death what they were unable to do in life.
Not only in the conservative sense of their values and convictions

being preserved and maintained, but also in a more heuristic way whereby these characteristics are freshly applied, generating new opportunities.[41]

The practice of remembering the dead can also become associated with specific triggers or rituals: particular places, objects, expressions or activities which when revisited or rehearsed enable mourners to gain a heightened awareness of their deceased and an increased sense of intimacy and presence.[42] In one way, these triggers give access to memories which might otherwise have been forgotten or repressed; in another, they can act as 'hooks' on which memories, feelings and emotional responses can be 'hung' in order to facilitate association and recall. And while remembering is often a very private and personal affair, it nonetheless has a pronounced social dimension. As with the 'wake', the rehearsing of memories together not only provides a fuller picture of the deceased, but also legitimizes the grief of mourners through the recognition that there are others who share their sense of loss. Further, the communication of memories to those who have never known the dead person is a way of enabling the deceased to be influential on a broader basis and across future generations.[43]

What light, then, does all this throw on how the disciples responded to Jesus' death? We have already touched on the importance of remembrance within Jewish faith and noted how it supplied a constituting medium by which members were able to locate themselves within a paradigmatic story defined by particular events and figures. A story that can be understood as a corporate memory made up of multiple layers of 'lived in' remembrance, each narrating how a generation appropriated the past into the present, and contributing a fresh stratum. As we should expect for a people whose identity resides within a confluence of faith stretching over a considerable period, remembrance was translated into a way of life for Jews. Patterns of worship and celebration, rituals of initiation and participation, definitions of behaviour and conduct, methods of instruction and communication, structures of authority and mediation, articulations of privilege, responsibility and hope. Through these and other means, each Jew was helped to appreciate what it means to belong to the people of God – to commemorate the past, to be faithful in the present and to be hopeful for the future.

It is not difficult to envisage, therefore, how Jewish faith furnished Jesus' mourners with various disciplines, insights and practices which would have encouraged them to remember him and enabled them to do so. Three areas are worthy of note. First, the need to remember helps to explain why Jesus' followers continued to meet together after the crucifixion. They came together both to mourn the death of someone who had made a profound impact upon them and to support one another as they worked out how life would go on without him.[44] Integral to this will have been a 'sharing of their stories' as they reminisced over times spent with Jesus. This, in turn, will have helped them to appreciate how influential a figure he had become for them and to explore ways of sustaining his influence. Further, it is through the process of remembering that the true significance of Jesus will have started to emerge as the profundity of his ministry and the quality of his humanity were reflected upon and appreciated. One implication of this will have been a desire to relate Jesus to the story of faith remembered in the Scriptures.[45] With these observations, we may well have identified one of the key motivating factors for exploring Jesus' theological significance and, in due course, for his veneration.

Second, the need to remember explains why testimonies about Jesus survived and were gradually brought together and embellished.[46] If remembering informs the process of mourning by keeping absent ones present, then the collection of stories about Jesus is surely evidence of how deeply his loss was felt and, by implication, of how influential he had become during his ministry. Further, if habitual recollection reflects a desire for that presence to be sustained by those who knew the deceased and communicated to those who did not, then the Gospels, largely consisting of such traditions, furnish evidence of this practice. What is more, the very fact that we have Gospels points towards the existence from the outset of those who were committed to maintaining Jesus' continuing influence – who, through oral and then written transmission, kept him accessible and influential.[47] This also explains why existing traditions about Jesus betray signs of reinterpretation and embellishment, tendencies reflecting the processes of application and appropriation by which the memories of Jesus are put to work by those seeking to follow him.[48]

A third area where the role of remembering in grief is insightful concerns the place certain practices of Jesus came to occupy within the lives of his followers. We shall expand on this in the next chapter, but for the present we simply need to acknowledge that this phenomenon can be understood as a natural expression of mourning through which the bereaved seek to draw close to the deceased.

For example, one reason why the sharing of a meal established itself at the heart of Christianity was its centrality within the common life Jesus shared with his disciples. And it was precisely because of this that Jesus invited his followers to remember him in this way![49]

## Revisioning and Restoration

In cases where the deceased were exponents of a vocation or cause, mourners may come to believe the best way of remembering them and, if they died as martyrs, of honouring their death is to keep their vision alive.[50] This resolve assumes a new impetus when survivors are commissioned to act in this way by the departed (cf. Matt. 28.18–20; Mark 16.14–18; Luke 24.44–9; John 20.21–3). Such a response not only provides a constructive channel for expressing grief, but also gives the bereaved both a reason – if not a mandate – for engaging with life once more. Further, it can greatly reduce the disorientating effects of loss by providing a medium through which affection for the departed can be expressed, together with a supportive framework in the form of solidarity with like-minded people, a pattern of life and a common goal.

It is interesting, therefore, to recall how popular a literary form the *testament* had become by the beginning of the Common Era and how this and other genres, such as the *encomium* (e.g. 1 Macc. 2.50–64; Ecclus. 44.1—50.24; cf. Heb. 11.4—12.2) and *eulogy* (e.g. *4 Macc.* 6.1—18.24; cf. Phil. 2.6–11), inspired Jews to emulate the faith-filled lives of their predecessors. This suggests that the practice of honouring the dead through following their example and keeping their vision alive was well established when Jesus lived and, more importantly, was executed. We may even possess examples of this with John the Baptist and, to a lesser extent, the so-called Teacher of Righteousness. Despite the transfer of allegiance of some of John's number during his ministry (John 1.35–7; 3.22–30; 4.1–2), there is good reason to believe that he was buried by his followers (Matt. 14.12/Mark 6.29) and that his disciples were encountered by Paul, Priscilla and Aquila during their missionary work (e.g. Acts 18.24–8; 19.1–7).[51] Although it is remarkably difficult to reconstruct the history of the Qumran settlement from the Dead Sea Scrolls, it does seem likely that the one referred to as the Teacher was the founder[52] and that after his death, possibly at the hands of a high-priestly rival, the community continued in his interpretation of what God required.[53]

In the light of these observations, it cannot be without significance that, after a formal period of mourning, we hear of Jesus' disciples continuing in his pattern of life and ministry. Again, this is something we shall return to later, but for the moment let us note how, according to the Gospels, the Acts of the Apostles and other early Christian sources, Jesus' followers continued to meet together for meals, prayer and worship and, quite possibly, maintained the discipline of his teaching and common life.[54] What is equally significant is that they actively engaged in a form of ministry practised by Jesus – preaching, teaching, healing, exorcising and being martyred for their beliefs.

Another observation from contemporary grief studies throws light on this movement of Jesus' followers back into discipleship and ministry. It is commonplace today to hear grief described as a journey through a number of definable phases, each characterized by a set of responses and adjustments, to a predictable destination.[55] Undertaking such a journey is the work of grief and if mourners manage to complete the course, in their own way and at their own pace, they will find themselves engaging with life once more. Although an approach such as this can sound rather impersonal and artificial, studies do suggest grief has form and, in most cases, adheres to a pattern. This, in turn, resonates with our earlier investigations into the management of grief within Jewish expressions of faith. We should not expect religious texts to supply us with a detailed psychology, but we can discern a number of stages and, in particular, a movement towards resolution signified by a return to joyous living which, as we have seen, corresponds to a particular definition of behaviour and social expectation.[56] That is to say, the return of joy we noted in the Psalms, in David's grief and elsewhere is not initially an emotional response, but an indication that the mourner has been drawn back into the life of the community with all that implies in terms of blessing, privilege and responsibility.

One wonders whether something of this background and understanding is communicated though Jesus' final words in John 16, which seem to afford us a privileged insight into the disciples' grief:

'Very truly, I tell you, you will weep and mourn, but the world will rejoice; you will have pain, but your pain will turn into joy. When a woman is in labour, she has pain, because her hour has come. But when her child is born, she no longer remembers the anguish because of the joy of having brought a human being into the world. So you have pain now; but I will see you again, and your hearts will rejoice, and no one will take your joy from you.' (John 16.20–2)

Mourning and pregnancy are both life experiences of set term and predictable course. They remove the 'sufferer' from normality for a season, but return them with joy. It is true that the passage just cited also links joy with new life and fresh encounter; however, the farewell discourses make it abundantly clear that the disciples' relationship with Jesus can only be sustained through their commitment to service and willingness to indwell the love commandment (e.g. John 13.12–20, 31–5; 14.15–24; 15.1–17). In which case, the predicted return of joy after the crucifixion may reflect their re-engagement with the 'normal' pattern of discipleship defined by Jesus during his life. This insight also throws light on Luke's presentation of the birth of the church in Acts 1 and 2, together with other references to the joy of the disciples (e.g. Matt. 28.8; Luke 24.52).

## Interim Remarks

In this and the previous chapter, we have attempted to open up a new perspective on how Jesus' closest followers responded to his death. In the next chapter, we shall consider this further in the light of Jesus' legacy. What we hope has become clear at this juncture is, first, how rich a resource Jewish faith would have been for the grieving disciples and, second, how transforming and potentially innovative an experience grief can be. When these two realities are brought together in ways we have outlined above, an unfamiliar picture of the disciples begins to emerge, namely of grief-stricken men and women, mourning the loss of someone who had won their devotion, and drawing on their faith to redeem the irredeemable by giving form, meaning and direction to their sense of loss. What is, perhaps, even more striking is that now we entertain such a picture it seems so remarkably uncontroversial. But can it be sustained? Or did the resurrection prevent the development of the disciples' grief? Or was their grief the seedbed from which resurrection blossomed? Certainly, we have seen how grief draws mourners into a particularly receptive and, in certain respects, creative mode of being.

## NOTES

1 An earlier version of this chapter was presented at a meeting of the Durham Centre for Theological Research. I am grateful for comments received on that occasion.

2 The seminal studies in this sphere are Bowlby (1981); Kübler-Ross (1970); and Parkes (1986). These works have generated a substantial literature; see Littlewood (1992); Raphael (1984); and Worden (1991).

3 Especially, Rosenblatt, Walsh and Jackson (1976). The contribution of religion and culture to mourning is a highly controversial issue, with certain anthropologists and sociologists (e.g. Durkheim (1952), pp. 397–401) maintaining the experience of grief is a social construct and not a universal human response (also G. A. Anderson (1991), pp. 1–18). However, there is a growing body of empirical psychological research identifying the phenomenon of grief which, when studied across cultures and religions, exhibits common characteristics. It is these characteristics we wish to draw on in the current chapter.

4 A comparable approach has been adopted by Walter Brueggemann and Paul Joyce in relation to the Psalms and Lamentations (Brueggemann (1995b), pp. 84–97; and Joyce (1993), pp. 304–20).

5 Consider, for example, the treatment of Peter's Easter vision by Gerd Lüdemann (1994), pp. 97–100; also Spong (1994), pp. 233–60.

6 D. J. Davies (1997), pp. 146–63; and Rosenblatt, Walsh and Jackson (1976), pp. 51–66, offer thorough reviews of this phenomenon.

7 Parkes (1986), pp. 77–82; however, a continuing sense of the presence of the deceased can be beneficial, see Bowlby (1981), Vol. 3, pp. 96–100.

8 It is announced by an angelic intermediary (e.g. Matt. 28.2–7/Mark 16.5–7/Luke 24.4–10; cf. John 20.13–14) or explained by Jesus himself (e.g. Matt. 28.16–20; [Mark 16.14–18]; Luke 24.13–35, 38–49; John 20.15–18,19–23, 24–9; cf. Matt. 28.9–10). The response of those who encounter Jesus ranges from incredulity (Matt. 28.17; [Mark 16.11, 13]; Luke 24.11, 38, 41; John 20.25), through mistaken identity (Luke 24.16; John 20.15), to belief that they had seen an apparition (Luke 24.37); but see [Mark 16.9–10] and John 21.1–14.

9 Bowlby (1981), Vol. 3, pp. 86–93; Parkes (1986), pp. 60–76; and Spiegel (1978), pp. 207–15.

10 On this, see Collins (1974), pp. 21–43; and Walters (1997), esp. pp. 73–109.

11 Jackson (1985), esp. pp. 88–101; and Parkes (1986), pp. 97–106; clearly, the level of guilt felt by the bereaved is greatly influenced by the circumstances surrounding the death and the state of their relationship at that time.

12 Matt. 26.30–5/Mark 14.26–31/Luke 22.31–4; Matt. 26.57–75/Mark 14.53–72/Luke 22.54–71/John 18.15–18, 25–7. Brown (1994), Vol. l, pp. 587–626, offers a thorough exegesis of these passages.

13 The following account from the second- or third-century *Acts of Peter*

reflects something of this: 'Dearest brethren, I denied our Lord Jesus Christ, and not once only, but three times. For there were wicked dogs who came about me, as said the prophet of the Lord. But the Lord did not lay it to my charge; he turned to me and had compassion on the weakness of my flesh, so that afterwards I wept bitterly and lamented the weakness of my faith, because I was made senseless by the devil and did not keep my Lord's word in mind' (7).

14 Cf. the reconstruction by John Spong (1994), pp. 242–57.

15 Perhaps a similar motivation can be discerned behind the anointing at Bethany traditions (Matt. 26.6–13/Mark 14.3–9).

16 Walters (1997), pp. 31–2.

17 Bowlby (1981), Vol. 3, esp. pp. 204–6, 358–61; Parkes and Weiss (1983); Raphael (1984); and Worden (1991), esp. pp. 93–115.

18 Esp. Matt. 27.3–10 and Acts 1.16–22; also Matt.10.4/Mark 3.19/ Luke 6.16; Matt. 26.14–16/Mark 14.10–11/Luke 22.3–6; Matt. 26.20–5/Mark 14.17–21/Luke 22.21–3/John 13.21–30; Matt. 26.47–56/Mark 14.43–52/Luke 22.47–53/John 18.2–12; John 6.71; 12.4; 13.2.

19 Useful summaries of the problems surrounding the Judas traditions can be found in Brown (1994), Vol. 2, pp. 1394–418; and Klassen (1992), pp. 1091–6. See also Klassen (1996), for a highly suggestive presentation.

20 Ainsworth-Smith and Speck (1982), pp. 92–3; Raphael (1984), pp. 34–7; and Worden (1991), esp. pp. 66–7.

21 On the function and importance of mourning ceremonies, see D. J. Davies (1997), pp. 1–22; Jackson (1985), pp. 122–9; Littlewood (1992), pp. 20–39; Rosenblatt, Walsh and Jackson (1976), pp. 86–98; and Spiegel (1978), pp. 101–33.

22 A well-informed review of opinion is offered by Carnley (1987), pp. 44–62; also Lindars (1993), pp. 116–35.

23 Lorenzen (1995), pp. 167–81.

24 See Matt. 28.1–10/Mark 16.1–8/Luke 24.1–12; the reaction of Mary Magdalene in John 20.1–2 is particularly insightful: 'Early on the first day of the week, while it was still dark, Mary Magdalene came to the tomb and saw that the stone had been removed from the tomb. So she ran and went to Simon Peter and the other disciple, the one whom Jesus loved, and said to them, "They have taken the Lord out of the tomb, and we do not know where they have laid him."'

25 This also explains why Paul does not mention it – the empty tomb was not traditionally associated with the resurrection and, as a consequence, was irrelevant in that context.

26 Significantly, there is no evidence of veneration of the tomb of Jesus before the fourth century when it was 'rediscovered'; see, Lüdemann (1994), pp. 115–21.

27 Lüdemann and Özen (1995), pp. 17–24.

28 'Almost all societies, it seems, believe that, despite a bodily death, the

person not only lives on but continues his relationship with the living, at least for a time.' Bowlby (1981), Vol. 3, p. 128; also Walters (1997); and Parkes (1986), pp. 96, 177–8.

29  The strongest case for this is probably Jesus' controversy with the Sadducees about the resurrection (Matt. 22.23–33/Mark 12.18–27/ Luke 20.27–40). But consider also the parable of the rich man and Lazarus (Luke 16.19–31), and the prophecy concerning the coming of the Son of Man (Matt. 24.29–31/Mark 13.24–7/Luke 21.25–8). See, Strawson (1959), esp. pp. 203–20; and Riches (1980), pp. 158–67.

30  *1 En.* 51; *4 Ezra* 7.26–44; *Pss. Sol.*14.1–10; 1QS 4.6–14; *T. Ben.*10.2–7; Wisd. 3.1–13.

31  E.g. Acts 2.33; 4.11–12; 1 Cor. 15.20–8, 50–8; Phil. 2.9–10; 1 Thess. 4.13–18; 1 Peter 1.21; 3.21–2; Heb. 1.3–4; Rev. 1.18–19. It is unlikely that the appearance traditions can be accounted for in these terms. By locating Jesus' risen form on earth, rather than in heaven, they have the effect of impeding the process of acceptance of death and letting go of the deceased – the very issues where belief in the afterlife can help! It is worth noting that the resurrection appearances do not remove the need for the disciples to mourn, but only postpone it until after the ascension – one way or the other, they still have to confront his loss.

32  Bowlby (1981), Vol. 3; Littlewood (1992), pp. 122–47; Raphael (1984), pp. 28–32, 320–51; Spiegel (1978), pp. 230–85; and Worden (1991), pp. 93–115. This can be exacerbated where the dead person is thought to have been instrumental in the death (e.g. suicide).

33  For a thorough exploration of the antecedents, see Hengel (1981a); and S. K. Williams (1975).

34  On the presentation of the sacrificial understanding of Jesus' death in these texts, see R. E. Brown (1994), Vol. 2, pp. 1445–67; Grayston (1990), esp. pp. 164–228; and Weber (1979), esp. pp. 30–63, 95–134. Lindars (1961) offers a helpful introduction to how the Hebrew Scriptures inform the Gospel passion narratives; for a more radical approach, see Crossan (1988).

35  Much of John Bowlby's work on 'attachment theory' is informed by this insight; see Bowlby (1979), esp. pp. 126–60. For a review of the different psychological models informing this understanding, see Raphael (1984), pp. 3–32. Relational understandings of human being have greatly influenced much recent theological discussion. For instance, Brümmer (1993); Greenwood (1994); McFadyen (1990); Schwöbel and Gunton (1991); Thatcher (1993); Zizioulas (1985); but see H. A. Harris (1998), p. 214–34; and White (1996).

36  This is often spoken of in terms of loss of identity or social context: Bowlby (1981), Vol. 3, pp. 173–8; and Parkes (1986), pp. 107–23.

37  Cf. 'gaining a new identity', Parkes (1986), pp. 107–23; also Jackson (1985), pp. 75–87; and Spiegel (1978), esp. pp. 324–42.

38  On the importance of remembering within the grief process, especially, Spiegel (1978), pp. 301–42. We are familiar with these processes in

other aspects of life. Consider, for example, anniversaries of birth and marriage – occasions when we remember formative experiences and seek to celebrate them with people who have been important in our personal becoming. It is also interesting how often people who have gone through a particularly profound experience – war, natural disaster, miscarriage or serious illness, to name but a few – often wish to meet together to remember and, where appropriate, to give thanks.

39 Parkes (1986), pp. 88–90; and Spiegel (1978), pp. 316–24.

40 Cf. Rosenblatt, Walsh and Jackson (1976), pp. 51–85, explore this phenomenon, including methods of 'tie-breaking' whereby the hold of the deceased on the living is released.

41 Familiar phrases such as 'I wonder what he would have done?' or 'I'll do it the way we always used to' are straightforward illustrations of this phenomenon.

42 D. J. Davies (1997), pp. 157–63.

43 This is particularly important for families and other associations where the integrity or coherence of the grouping is rooted in key founder figures. In such cases, a tradition may form which originates in the memories of those who knew the deceased and is appropriated, re-interpreted and augmented by subsequent generations.

44 This point is made by Spong (1994), esp. pp. 247–9.

45 Cf. 'For I handed on to you as of first importance what I in turn had received: that Christ died for our sins *in accordance with the scriptures*, and that he was buried, and that he was raised on the third day *in accordance with the scriptures*, and that he appeared to Cephas, then to the twelve' (1 Cor.15.3–5).

46 On the importance of remembering Jesus, see Carnley (1987), pp. 266–368; Dahl (1976), esp. pp. 38–60; and Knox (1963), esp. pp. 38–79.

47 See Werner Kelber's comments of 'social identification' as the key to the oral transmission of traditions about Jesus, in Kelber (1983), esp. pp. 1–43.

48 This, of course, is one of the fundamental presuppositions of form and redaction criticism; see the excellent introduction of Sanders and Davies (1989); and Theissen (1992).

49 Lunny (1989), pp. 105–38; and Spong (1994), pp. 198–209.

50 Parkes (1986) describes this kind of reaction as a form of identification with the deceased, pp. 116–23; see also Spiegel's (1978) comments on 'Incorporation', pp. 316–24.

51 There is some evidence to link John with the Mandaean sect; Dodd (1953), pp. 115–30.

52 Cf. 'Interpreted, this concerns the Priest, the Teacher of [Righteousness whom] God chose to stand before Him, for He established him to build for Himself the congregation of . . .' (4Q171 on Ps. 37.23–4); and 'And God observed their deeds, that they sought Him with a whole heart, and He raised for them a Teacher of Righteousness – to guide

them in the way of His heart' (4QD 1.11). For a summary of what we know about the Teacher, see Murphy-O'Connor (1992), pp. 340–1, and the works cited there.

53 For a helpful review of the Dead Sea Scrolls and of the history of the (Essene?) community that produced them, see Collins (1992), pp. 85–101.

54 Blue (1994), pp. 119–222; Horsley (1989), esp. pp. 105–8; Johnson (1981); and Johnson (1986), pp. 114–41.

55 E.g. Bowlby (1981), Vol. 3, pp. 85–103; Kübler-Ross (1970); Parkes (1986); and Spiegel (1978), pp. 59–83.

56 G. A. Anderson (1991), pp. 19–57, 82–97.

# —4—

# The Legacy of Jesus

In attempting to discover what happened to Jesus' followers after his death, we have reviewed relevant aspects of their Jewish heritage and explored ways in which these may have been appropriated with the help of insights from the understanding of grief. We must now move on to our third area of investigation, namely, the legacy of Jesus himself. Our concern here is with the following set of questions. What resources did Jesus make available to those he influenced that would have sustained them in faith whether he was with them or not? What insights, practices and disciplines did he share with those he encountered that enriched their humanity through opening up new ways of seeing themselves and relating to God, other people and creation? If the legacy of John the Baptist was a radical social ethic, a baptism of repentance, and a call to righteous living in the shadow of imminent judgement, and if the legacy of the Teacher of Righteousness was the establishment of a community and a rule of common life, what was Jesus' legacy?

One presupposition of this approach is that the canonical Gospels and, to a lesser extent, other sources purporting to give information about Jesus are not wholesale products of the early church, but bear witness to deposits of faith laid down in the lives of those to whom he ministered:[1] experiences of healing and forgiveness, insights into prayer and daily living, practices of fellowship and common life, treasuries of wisdom and perception, words of admonition and challenge, mediations of divine presence and vocations to discipleship. These traditions account for the majority of our sources about Jesus and were only accessible to the evangelists (writing a generation removed) because of their preservation by those who received from him something of *immediate worth*:[2] something valuable to the recipients which maintained its value when communicated to others. For example, recent investigations into Q, a body of predominantly non-Marcan sayings and stories common to Matthew and Luke, postulate a community drawing inspiration from Jesus' teaching and approach to life.[3] We can also identify other collected remembrances within the Gospels[4] and, with the help of insights from the social sciences, we now have a much fuller picture of first-century Palestinian life which, in turn, enables us to appreciate Jesus' impact upon different groups together with the ways in which his influence was preserved and communicated.[5]

What we are suggesting, therefore, is that our sources, especially those represented by the Synoptic Gospels and John, give us access to the legacy of Jesus and that through careful evaluation we can identify at least some of the principal characteristics. Before we attempt to do this, however, three observations are noteworthy. The first concerns the nature and extent of Jesus' following during his life. Because the Gospels present the traditions about him in the form of a narrative with temporal progression, we tend to identify with those who journeyed with him, with the inner circle of disciples, including 'the twelve', who had been engaged by Jesus to share in his ministry or to support in some way. The composition and size of this group is difficult to determine and may have been purposefully imprecise to allow a measure of coming and going. But, in addition, a closer study of the texts reveals other interested parties who were influenced by Jesus.[6] These include members of the crowds who received his teaching and witnessed his mighty acts, his debating partners and those he challenged, needy people who found a measure of wholeness in his presence, those he invited to share his table, children who were given privileged attention, together with relations and friends who looked after him. The vestiges of these relationships and interactions, together with those of his co-workers and companions, are contained in the Gospels, and it is here that we should expect to find evidence of his legacy. Equally, the very existence of these traditions reflects something of the nature and extent of Jesus' impact, together with the scale of indebtedness to his ministry and humanity.

Our second observation concerns the nature of Jewish faith. One of the remarkable characteristics of this phenomenon is that, prior to the emergence of the rabbinic tradition in the first century CE, it is communicated via an ongoing story of a people who find identity and coherence through being inextricably linked to God. The Hebrew Scriptures give access to the emergence of this confluence of faith and narrate how successive generations sought to live it out or, indeed, to misappropriate it. Along the way, particular events assume normative status in defining relationship with God, other Jews and non-Jews. For example, the experiences of Exodus and Sinai, of liberation from captivity and oppression in Egypt, followed by entry into a covenant of service and blessing, occupy a central position in Jewish consciousness. Similarly, the deportation and subsequent Babylonian exile precipitated a radical reassessment and, aided by access to other cultures and religious traditions, generated fresh expressions of Jewish identity.

Within this experientially driven approach, great prominence is given to those figures who embody the faith by the inspiration of their insights, the quality of their example or the strategic role they fulfilled:[7] figures such as Abraham, Moses, David, Solomon and Elijah who mediate defining moments in the story of God's people and whose impact is maintained through various associations. For instance, Abraham, the founder of monotheism and friend of God, was thought to be honoured each time God is blessed or his blessings received. The legacy of Moses was sustained through the centrality of Torah, considered his handiwork, and through observance of the rituals and cultus contained therein. David continued to lead his people in worship through the Psalms and to carry their longings for the future through messianic hope. Solomon's legendary sagacity lived on in the wisdom traditions, while the Temple commemorated the glory of Israel realized under his rule and that of his father. The spirit of prophecy empowering Elijah was visited upon those who followed in his wake. These formative events, figures and traditions constitute the authorities of Jewish faith which, in turn, vested authority in those responsible for maintaining the respective areas of influence (e.g. priests and Temple personnel, interpreters of the Law, prophets and seers, sages).

The critical insight here is that Jewish faith up to the time of Jesus was neither expressed nor conceived primarily in propositional terms, but by *embodiment*. God acting through people, with faith defined by paradigmatic events and inspirational exemplars. If we were able to ask Jesus' Galilean contemporaries to define faith, the chances are they would not have echoed the words of the author of the letter to the Hebrews: 'Now faith is the assurance of things hoped for, the conviction of things not seen' (Heb. 11.1). Rather, they would have recited the Shema (Deut. 6.4–9) and extended an invitation to remember Abraham and Moses, and to celebrate the Passover! Further, we know that a number of competing expositions of Jewish faith were prevalent in first-century Palestine.[8] The

Temple was still standing with its clergy administering the sacrificial cult and hosting the great pilgrim festivals. Local synagogues, with a diet of prayer, Scripture reading and exposition, sustained a manageable covenantal fidelity for those who needed to survive in an environment necessitating interaction with Gentiles and exposure to Hellenistic culture.[9] The Pharisees offered a more uncompromising approach through extending the teaching of Torah to cover all aspects of life and through limiting social intercourse to those who followed suit. The Dead Sea community was committed to sanctification through separation and observance. In addition, we know of the existence of various holy men, resistance movements, messianic pretenders and prophets who offered their regimes, interpretations and giftings to those who would listen and follow.[10] Palestine in the first century, therefore, was a place of experimentation and exploration. Further, we know that this diversity was not restricted to Jerusalem and its environs, but extended into Galilee;[11] in fact, the Temple may have exerted a normalizing effect in this respect. Whatever else may be deduced from this climate, it reflects a yearning for and openness to new embodiments of faith and paradigms for Jewish identity.[12]

Third, and following on from this, a review of Jewish literature originating around the time of Jesus reveals a strong desire to experience God's blessings once more:[13] for a time of liberation and healing, of feasting and celebration, of justice and peace, of creativity and abundance. A number of examples afford us some insight to this mood. A (priestly?) Palestinian Jew of the second century BCE expresses his convictions in this way:

> And in those days, children will begin to search the law, and to search the commandments and to return to the way of righteousness. And the days will begin to increase and grow longer among those sons of men, generation by generation, and year by year, until their days approach a thousand years, and to a greater number of years than days. And there (will be) no old men and none who is full of days. Because all of them will be infants and children. And all of their days they will be complete and live in peace and rejoicing and there will be no Satan and no evil (one) who will destroy, because all of their days will be days of blessing and healing. And then the Lord will heal his servants, and they will rise up and see great peace. And they will drive out their enemies,

and the righteous ones will see and give praise, and rejoice forever and ever with joy; and they will see all of their judgements and all of their curses among their enemies. (*Jub.* 23.23–30)

Devout Jews of first-century CE Jerusalem (Pharisees?) look forward to the raising up of God's messiah:

See, Lord, and raise up for them their king, the son of David, to rule over your servant Israel in the time known to you, O God. Undergird him with the strength to destroy the unrighteous rulers, to purge Jerusalem from gentiles who trample her to destruction; in wisdom and in righteousness to drive out the sinners from the inheritance; to smash the arrogance of sinners like a potter's jar. To shatter all their substance with an iron rod; to destroy the unlawful nations with the word of his mouth. At his warning the nations will flee from his presence; and he will condemn sinners by the thoughts of their hearts. He will gather a holy people whom he will lead in righteousness; and he will judge the tribes of the people that have been made holy by the Lord their God. He will not tolerate unrighteousness (even) to pause among them, and any person who knows wickedness shall not live with them. For he shall know them that they are all children of their God. He will distribute them upon the land according to their tribes; the alien and the foreigner will no longer live near them. He will judge peoples and nations in the wisdom of his righteousness. And he will have gentile nations serving him under his yoke, and he will glorify the Lord in (a place) prominent (above) the whole earth. And he will purge Jerusalem (and make it) holy as it was even from the beginning, (for) nations to come from the ends of the earth to see his glory, to bring as gifts her children who had been driven out, and to see the glory of the Lord with which God has glorified her. And he will be a righteous king over them, taught by God. There will be no unrighteousness among them in his days, for all shall be holy, and their king shall be the Lord Messiah. (*Pss. Sol.* 17.21–32)

The (Essene?) community of Qumran gives expression to the hope that God's saving presence will be known again:

These are their ways in the world for the enlightenment of the heart of man, and that all the paths of true righteousness may be made straight before him, and that the fear of the laws of God may be instilled in his heart: a spirit of humility, patience, abundant charity, unending goodness, understanding, and intelligence; (a spirit of) mighty wisdom which trusts in all the deeds of God and leans on His great loving-kindness; a spirit of discernment in every purpose, of zeal for just laws, of holy intent with steadfastness of heart, of great charity towards all the sons of truth, of admirable purity which detests all unclean idols, of humble conduct sprung from an understanding of all things, and of faithful concealment of the mysteries of truth. These are the counsels of the spirit to the sons of truth in this world. And as for the visitation of all who walk in this spirit, it shall be healing, great peace in a long life, and fruitfulness, together with every everlasting blessing and eternal joy in life without end, a crown of glory and a garment of majesty in unending light. (1QS 4.2–8)

Visionaries of the period anticipate God's salvation in powerful pictures and vivid language:

. . . the Anointed One will begin to be revealed . . . The earth will also yield fruits ten thousandfold. And one vine will be a thousand branches, and one branch will produce a thousand clusters, and one cluster will produce a thousand grapes, and one grape will produce a cor of wine. And those who are hungry will enjoy themselves and they will, moreover, see marvels every day. For winds will go out in front of me every morning to bring the fragrance of aromatic fruits and clouds at the end of the day to distil the dew of health. And it will happen at that time that the treasury of manna will come down again from on high, and they will eat of it in those years because these are they who will have arrived at the consummation of time. (*2 Bar.* 29.3–8)

The righteous and elect ones shall be saved on that day; and from thenceforth they shall never see the faces of the sinners and the oppressors. The Lord of the Spirits will abide over them; they shall eat and rest and rise with that Son of Man forever and ever. The righteous and elect ones shall rise from the earth and shall cease being of downcast face. They shall wear the garments of glory. These garments of yours shall become the garments of life from the Lord of the Spirits. Neither shall your garments wear out, nor your glory come to an end before the Lord of the Spirits. (*1 En.* 61.13–16)

The Palestinian recension of the Tephillah or Eighteen Benedictions, a set of bidding prayers repeated thrice daily, may reflect the convictions not only of post-70 CE, rabbinic Judaism, but also of popular piety around the time of Jesus:[14]

(7) Look at our affliction, and champion our cause, and redeem us for the sake of Your Name. You are praised, O Lord, Redeemer of Israel. (8) Heal us, O Lord our God, of the pain of our hearts. Remove from us grief and sighing, and bring healing for our wounds. You are praised, O Lord, who heals the sick of His people Israel. (9) Bless, O Lord our God, this year for us, and let it be good in all the varieties of its produce. Hasten the year of our redemptive End. Grant dew and rain upon the face of the earth, and satiate the world out of the treasuries of Your goodness; and grant a blessing to the work of our hands. You are praised, O Lord, who blesses the years. (10) Sound the great horn for our freedom, and lift up a banner to gather in our exiles. You are praised, O Lord, who gathers in the outcasts of His people Israel. (Benedictions 7–10)

If these texts are in any sense representative of Jewish life in first-century CE Palestine, then they speak of a spiritual vacuum, feeding hope that God would be a source of blessing once more and inspiring faith to persevere and prepare for that time. We mentioned in Chapter 2 that the exilic prophets drew on the experience of grief and the passage of mourning to communicate their convictions about how God would restore Israel's fortunes. In the light of what has just been said, it is surely not unreasonable to conclude that many Jews of Jesus' time struggled to sustain the optimism generated by their predecessors' return to the promised land and the re-establishment of the Temple. For them, it must have seemed as if the period of mourning had been extended indefinitely; but, as we have just noted, at least some continued to entertain the hope that joy would return. With these observations in mind, let us turn to the Gospels and other sources to discover what resources Jesus made accessible to those fellow Jews who were open to his ministry and pattern of life.

## Forgiveness and Opportunity

As we have seen, a number of strategies for investing the present with theological significance were current in first-century Palestine. The Temple in Jerusalem, supported by the family and local synagogue communities, maintained a pattern of covenantal fidelity rooted in the traditions of the past and mediating access to God through attention to Scripture, the offering of worship and service, and the observance of rituals and disciplines such as circumcision, sacrifice, Sabbath and festivals. Other approaches were more demanding. The Qumran community and the Pharisees advocated withdrawal from society, either through physical relocation or restricted participation, and sought to prescribe God's will for all of life through defining a common rule or through extrapolating God's commandments in Torah. Other movements, again, sceptical of whether God's covenantal blessings and saving presence could ever be realized within the limits set by the prevailing political and religious regimes, attempted to disturb the status quo in order to prepare for or indeed precipitate divine intervention. John the Baptist, with his demand for social justice and righteous living in response to God's impending judgement, belongs within this category, as do various political insurrectionists and freedom fighters.[15]

All these approaches were Jewish in origin, composition and appeal with the result that a climate of sectarianism emerged characterized by a measure of suspicion, antagonism and competing claims to be the true Israel. The existence of these various strands must have challenged non-participating Jews to consider embracing the additional undertakings of membership. It appears that Jesus, in addition to practising his faith in relation to the recognized structures of family, synagogue and Temple, committed himself to the radical repentance movement of John. We may deduce from this that he perceived an inadequacy in conventional embodiments of faith and was at least sympathetic towards the Baptist's convictions.[16] At some juncture they parted company; whether this was forced upon them by John's arrest and execution or whether it resulted from differences of opinion is now difficult to assess. What is clear, however, is that Jesus' ministry as narrated in the Gospels cannot readily be accommodated within the Baptist's emphasis upon imminent, punitive judgement for Jewish infidels who refused to repent and pursue morally upright lives. On the contrary, Jesus conceived of and mediated the intensifying of God's presence in an altogether different way. For him, the period of mourning precipitated by God's perceived absence was coming to an end and being replaced by a dispensation of divine generosity experienced as various forms of forgiveness and giving expression to manifestations of joyous living.

Significantly, the Gospels are packed with testimonies of how this perception could transform human experience. Further, while the provenance of certain traditions can be questioned, there seems little reason to doubt that the cumulative witness of this material communicates something of the substantial impact of Jesus upon those whom he encountered. In addition, with respect to their preservation and transmission, the most likely candidates are those whose experiences of Jesus resonated with or indeed were in some sense facilitated by these testimonies. What evidence are we referring to here? Principally, to accounts of release from various forms of oppression (e.g. disease, evil, sin) together with their attendant consequences (e.g. guilt, curse, rejection, isolation, ritual impurity, unemployment, ostracism, hunger, destitution).[17] Often the overall implications of these happenings are not spelt out, but once we appreciate the inadequate level of medical provision and welfare support, together with the economic necessities of paying taxes, meeting rents and survival, and the religious protocols regulating social intercourse, the overall impact of Jesus' healings, exorcisms and so forth begins to emerge.[18]

For example, recovery from leprosy would not only return sufferers to wholeness, but would also, after verification, lead to reintegration into family, community and religious life.[19] Or, again, the suffering of a woman plagued with internal bleeding from the womb would stretch far beyond debilitating weakness and embarrassment to include managing ritual uncleanness, restricted social interaction and the frustration of her motherly potential.[20] On top of this, the question of whether disease was a consequence of or punishment for sin remained unresolved in the minds of many.[21] To experience release from oppressive constraints and associations such as these can only have been a profoundly transforming experience, changing the status of the recipient in relation to family, society, religious authorities and God. And with these transitions would come a revised and greatly enhanced sense of personal value and worth.

Another collection of traditions bears witness to experiences of liberation from a rather different and, perhaps, more subtle range of constraints and limitations. Consider Jesus' table-fellowship with sinners.[22] While the identity of those referred to in this manner remains a matter of debate,[23] there can be little doubt the term communicates a value judgement by those in positions of authority upon others whose conduct was considered inappropriate or unacceptable. Jesus, it seems, refused to restrict his relationships to those whose lifestyles or allegiances conferred respectability; on the contrary, he made a point of keeping 'bad company'.[24] This was a highly significant gesture and one likely to have precipitated something of an identity crisis for those deemed 'sinners' as well as to have challenged prevailing definitions of what it meant to be Jewish.[25] In a similar way, Jesus' encouragement of women and uneducated men to see themselves as disciples capable of understanding God's ways and competent in communicating them to others, together with his transgression of protocols associated with boundaries of age, gender, social class and, possibly, nationality would have disturbed existing patterns of expectation and enabled those involved to gain a revisioned perspective on life.

*Experiences of forgiveness* seems an appropriate description for these traditions because of their gratuitous and liberating quality. Although it is impossible to be certain about what happened in each case, we can be confident that they bear witness to people encountering in Jesus a concentration of divine giftedness and human resourcefulness capable of catalysing release from oppressive or restrictive constraints and facilitating a return to joyous living.[26] The resulting expansiveness of humanity afforded recipients new opportunities in terms of self-perception and engagement within society. What also seems to have been the case is that, while these experiences of forgiveness were not mediated through the recognized religious practices or authorities, they were nonetheless interpreted theologically as distillations of divine presence and located within the co-ordinates of the fulfilment of God's covenantal promises.[27] We do not know what became of the many beneficiaries of this kind of phenomenon, but the preservation of their stories points towards the transforming quality of the encounters described. Furthermore, it suggests these traditions came to fulfil a canonical function in communicating a class of experience associated with Jesus.

## Prayer and Performance

Experiences of forgiveness, realized in relation to Jesus, were occasions of opportunity flowing from a new or revised identity. From what we can gather, Jesus did not require beneficiaries to demonstrate a change of heart beforehand or subscribe to a set of beliefs or practices afterwards. It also appears that forgiveness engendered a variety of responses: for instance, some opted or were invited to indwell their new identity in relation to Jesus, others were encouraged to do so within their own communities, others we must assume retreated into the safety of the known and predictable.[28] In addition, it appears that those who accompanied Jesus as disciples benefited not only from his public ministry, but also from private instruction and time spent in his company.[29]

What resources, then, did Jesus offer to sustain the life of forgiveness? Our investigations begin with what has become known as the Lord's Prayer. It has been preserved in three forms:[30]

| *Matthew 6:9b–13* | *Luke 11:2b–4* | *Didache 8* |
|---|---|---|
| Our Father in heaven hallowed be your name. | Father, hallowed be your name. | Our Father in heaven, hallowed be your name. |
| Your kingdom come. | Your kingdom come. | Your kingdom come. |
| Your will be done, on earth as it is in heaven. | | Your will be done, on earth as it is in heaven. |
| Give us this day our daily bread. | Give us each day our daily bread. | Give us this day our daily bread. |
| And forgive us our debts, | And forgive us our sins, | And forgive us our debt, |
| as we also have forgiven our debtors. | for we ourselves forgive everyone indebted to us. | as we forgive our debtors. |
| And do not bring us to the time of trial, but rescue us from the evil one. | And do not bring us to the time of trial. | And do not bring us to the time of trial, but rescue us from the evil one. |
| *For the kingdom and the power and the glory are yours for ever. Amen.* | | *For power and glory are yours for ever.* |

We need not concern ourselves with the original wording for it is sufficient to note that the substance of the prayer is consistent across all three recensions.[31] What is significant for us, however, is why it was preserved within a Christian community which came to understand Jesus' role with respect to prayer in a radically different way.[32] The answer must surely be because it was *Jesus' prayer*, not simply in the sense that he composed it, but far more significantly because he used it. That is to say, the Lord's Prayer was remembered precisely because it was the prayer of Jesus himself; as such, it provides one of our most reliable conduits into his faith. Questions, therefore, about whether the Lord's Prayer summarizes Jesus' teaching or provides a programmatic agenda for prayer become secondary to the insight it affords into how Jesus perceived himself in relation to God and appreciated the implications of this perception for life. As a result, the value of the prayer resides not primarily in the guidance it offers, *but in the invitation it extends to experience faith in a particular way.*[33]

This is confirmed when the contents of the Lord's Prayer are compared with other Jewish prayers current in the first century CE.[34] Consider, again, biddings from the Tephillah:

(3) Holy are You, and awe-inspiring is Your Name; and beside You there is no God. You are praised, O Lord, the holy God. (6) Forgive us, our Father, for we have sinned against You. Blot out and remove our transgressions from before Your sight, for Your mercies are manifold. You are praised, O Lord, who abundantly pardons. (9) Bless, O Lord our God, this year for us, and let it be good in all the varieties of its produce. Hasten the year of our redemptive End. Grant dew and rain upon the face of the earth, and satiate the world out of the treasuries of Your goodness; and grant a blessing to the work of our hands. You are praised, O Lord, who blesses the years.

Or from the Kaddish, another proto-rabbinic prayer:

Exalted and hallowed be His great Name in the world which He created according to His will. May He establish His kingdom [and cause His salvation to sprout, and hasten the coming of His messiah,] in your lifetime and in your days, and in the lifetime of the whole household of Israel, speedily and at a near time. And say: Amen. May His great Name be praised forever and unto all eternity. Blessed and praised, glorified and exalted, extolled and honoured, magnified and lauded be the Name of the Holy One, praised be He although He is beyond all blessings and hymns, praises and consolations which may be uttered in the world. And say: Amen. May the prayers and supplications of the whole household of Israel be acceptable before their Father in heaven. And say: Amen. May there be abundant peace from heaven, and life, for us and for all Israel. And say: Amen. May He who makes peace in His high heavens make peace for us and for all Israel. And say: Amen.

It is clear that the Lord's Prayer belongs within this climate of theological discourse and expectation, attesting no radical points of departure except, perhaps, the linking of divine and human forgiveness.[35] The significance of the prayer, however, does not reside in the sphere of doctrinal innovation, *but in the identity it bestows upon those who pray it and come to inhabit its world*. It is first and foremost a testimony to Jesus' experience of God and to the effects of that experience for living out the faith. A mode of intercession accessible through a personal, dynamic and reciprocal relationship with God,[36] which resources a particular embodiment of faith through which God's presence and purposes are communicated. When we unpack both the contents of the prayer and its underlying spirituality, we discover Jesus:

- relates to God as to a father;
- acknowledges his dependence upon God for the gift of life and trusts him for sustenance and protection;
- embraces the responsibilities of sonship and the commensurate authority thereby entrusted to him;
- commits himself to honouring his heavenly Father's name through walking in his ways and upholding his causes.

Quite simply, the Lord's Prayer encapsulates Jesus' faith in a handful of succinct lines, inviting repetition and participation in a similar experience of God.

We have already drawn attention to the existence in the first century CE of other effective intercessors (pp. 35–8). Hanina ben Dosa, a Galilean rabbi who lived near to Nazareth, is probably the most celebrated for his ministry as a healer. A number of traditions relating to him are preserved in later Jewish literature. The following one is particularly interesting because it reports one of the principal architects of rabbinic Judaism acknowledging a Galilean charismatic, noted neither for exposition nor for interpretation of Torah, as possessing a privileged relationship with God:

> The deed happened again when Rabbi Hanina ben Dosa went to study Torah with Rabbi Yohanan ben Zakkai, that the son of Rabbi Yohanan ben Zakkai became ill. He said to him, 'Hanina my son, pray for him that he may live.' He put his head between his knees and prayed for him and he lived. Rabbi Yohanan ben Zakkai said, 'If ben Zakkai had stuck his head between his knees for the whole day, no notice would have been taken of him.' His wife said to him, 'Is Hanina greater than you?' He said to her,

'No; but he is like a servant before the king, and I am like a noble-man before the king.' (*b. Ber.* 34b) [37]

There can be little doubt Jesus was also recognized as a gifted inter-cessor possessing a special relationship with God which enabled him to translate the will of God into human experience.[38] Further, it can be no coincidence that Jesus is remembered, first, for associating prayer and faith (cf. Matt. 21.22/Mark 11.24)[39] and, second, for emphasizing how these human responses are intimately linked with the experience of forgiveness.[40] Jesus looks for faith among those coming to him for help[41] and celebrates the faith of those who find it – 'Your faith has made you well.'[42] Perhaps, most strikingly of all, Jesus draws his disciples' attention to faith as the medium through which God's powerful presence is communicated:[43]

'For truly I tell you, if you have faith the size of a mustard seed, you will say to this mountain, "Move from here to there," and it will move; and nothing will be impossible for you.' (Matt. 17.20)

'Truly I tell you, if you have faith and do not doubt, not only will you do what has been done to the fig tree, but even if you say to this mountain, "Be lifted up and thrown into the sea," it will be done.' (Matt. 21.21)

'Have faith in God. Truly I tell you, if you say to this mountain, "Be taken up and thrown into the sea," and if you do not doubt in your heart, but believe that what you say will come to pass, it will be done for you.' (Mark 11.22–3; cf. Luke 17.6)

I have explained elsewhere how the levelling of mountains, especially Mount Zion, was a metaphor for the manifestation of God's power.[44] In the same context, I presented the evidence in support of the view that during the intertestamental period faith was increasingly identified as one, if not the, essential human disposition not simply for maintaining covenantal fidelity, but also for translat-ing eschatological hope into reality. Interestingly, the author of 1 Maccabees identifies faith as one of the distinguishing character-istics of Simon, son of Mattathias, which resulted in his election to lead the Jewish people against their Seleucid rulers (140–134 BCE):

The people saw Simon's faith (*ten pistin*) and the glory that he had resolved to win for the nation, and made him their leader and high priest, because he had done all these things and because of the justice and faith (*ten dikaiosunen kai ten pistin*) that he had maintained toward his nation . . . The Jews and the priests have resolved that Simon should be their leader and high priest for ever, until a faithful prophet should arise. (1 Macc. 14.35, 41)[45]

And faith will be required of God's messiah to equip him for his divine responsibilities of ministering justice and salvation:

The Lord himself is his king, the hope of the one who has a strong hope in God . . . His hope (will be) in the Lord. Then who will succeed against him, mighty in his actions and strong in the fear of God? Shepherding the Lord's flock in faith and righteousness (*en pistei kai dikaiosune*), he will not let any of them stumble in their pasture. (*Pss. Sol.* 17.34, 39–40)[46]

In the light of these associations, we can readily appreciate the significance of the Lord's Prayer for those who received forgiveness through Jesus' ministry – it encapsulated his faith. And when he invited them to make this prayer their own (Matt. 6.9; Luke 11.1–2), he was, in effect, inviting them to share that faith and, through it, his experience of God.

## Wisdom and Discernment

If Jesus changed lives through a ministry of intercession and forgiveness, then, judging from the Gospels, he was no less effective as a teacher and preacher. The importance of God's word within Jewish faith needs no defending. By Jesus' time, the canonical status of the Torah was established, with the ancillary collections of Prophets and Writings reaching fixed form.[47] Although the rabbinic approach to biblical exegesis found in the Mishnah, Talmud, Midrash and other literature was still in the process of formulation, the importance of understanding and applying the Scriptures was generally recognized.[48] There were biblical interpreters (e.g. Gamaliel, Hillel and Shammai) and, quite possibly, schools where Torah was taught.[49] Observant Jews would repeat the Shema (Deut. 6.4–9; 11.13–21; Num. 15.37–41) twice a day. A reading from the Torah and, probably, the Prophets (cf. Luke 4.17; Acts 13.15) was a central component of synagogue worship,[50] and through the early Targumim, Aramaic paraphrases for non-Hebrew-speaking Jews, we gain insight to how the Scriptures were appropriated.[51] The Dead

Sea Scrolls also bear witness to a number of interpretative approaches, as do other works originating in the period between the Testaments (e.g. Septuagint, Book of Jubilees).

Jesus taught in a number of venues – established religious institutions such as the Temple[52] and the synagogue,[53] together with various outdoor locations.[54] No doubt, he received some form of schooling in the Scriptures as a child, both at home and through involvement in the life of his local synagogue.[55] However, he is not remembered principally as a biblical interpreter, but as a sage – a teacher of wisdom. Jesus' preferred forms of communication were the *aphorism* and the *parable*. The first, a compact, poignant and memorable saying; the second, a narrative metaphor inviting engagement and interpretation through participation. In recent years, a great deal has been written on the form and content of Jesus' teaching,[56] together with its relation to conventional Jewish wisdom, Hellenistic strains such as Cynic philosophy, and rabbinic disputation.[57] Our concern here is not with the detail of what Jesus taught,[58] but with the simple observation that much of his wisdom relates to the life of faith, that is, to the rooting of faith within human being; as such, it possesses a self-authenticating quality when appropriated in this way.

Insights into God's presence and purposes through contemplating the natural order, explorations into the contours of divine forgiveness through the fabric of daily living and human relationships, challenges to prejudice, bigotry and complacency, warnings against religiosity and observance without spiritual content, distillations of what is essential and of true worth, exhortations to vigilance, discernment and fruitfulness, invitations to live as children of God within a dispensation of grace – Jesus' teaching possesses a practical relevance and comprehensiveness that all but guaranteed its preservation, especially when communicated through vivid language and memorable turns of phrase. And perhaps the scale and compass of this body of teaching reflects a motivation which, in a different way, informs the corpus of rabbinic literature referred to above, namely, to interpret life theologically. At the risk of oversimplification, the different approaches can be summarized in these terms. Guided by a set of hermeneutical principles,[59] the rabbis elucidated the Scriptures and extrapolated their influence to situations not directly mentioned; the approach is definitive and prescriptive. In contrast, Jesus interpreted the Scriptures through his own experience of God and offered a collection of axioms, insights and observations which needed to be appropriated as circumstances required; the approach is empowering, participatory and generative.

The wisdom of Jesus, therefore, represents a substantial repository of lived-in faith. Collections of his sayings almost certainly existed prior to the composition of the Gospels and it is possible that the desire to preserve and practise Jesus' sapiential legacy was the impetus behind some of the earliest Christian communities.[60] But perhaps the most significant point to make at this juncture concerns Jesus' relationship to wisdom:

> They [Jesus and his disciples] went to Capernaum; and when the sabbath came, he entered the synagogue and taught. They were astounded at his teaching, for he taught them as one having authority, and not as the scribes. Just then there was in their synagogue a man with an unclean spirit, and he cried out, 'What have you to do with us, Jesus of Nazareth? Have you come to destroy us? I know who you are, the Holy One of God.' But Jesus rebuked him, saying, 'Be silent, and come out of him!' And the unclean spirit, convulsing him and crying with a loud voice, came out of him. They were all amazed, and they kept on asking one another, 'What is this? A new teaching – with authority! He commands even the unclean spirits, and they obey him.' (Mark 1.21–7)

The issue is one of authority. As books such as Proverbs, Ecclesiasticus and the Wisdom of Solomon make clear, wisdom was held in the highest esteem by many Jews. It kept the closest company with God, being of divine origin and intimately involved in creation.[61] Thus, the truly wise were those whose wisdom communicated divine authority. It is striking, therefore, that Jesus is remembered as one whose wisdom is confirmed not by his abilities in exegesis or disputation, but *by his authority to effect God's forgiveness*, an association reaching back through Solomon to King David.[62] That is to say, Jesus' practice of wisdom was thought to possess a certain transparency, translating divine presence into human experience.[63]

## Meals and Joyous Living

On a number of occasions, the Gospels record Jesus blessing God for food before sharing it with the gathered company.[64] The substance of what he said is not recorded, presumably, because he was reciting a familiar formula.[65] From what we can gather, food and mealtimes possessed a pronounced sacramental quality for Jews throughout the period covered by the Hebrew Scriptures and New Testament.[66] For this reason, what was eaten, how it was consumed and with whom were significant issues.[67] The underlying conviction being that God is the author of all life and that each living form is an expression of divine vitality and must be respected as such.

Food, therefore, was seen as a gift from God and a tangible demonstration of divine generosity and covenantal faithfulness. God created the world to yield an abundant supply (Gen. 1.28–31; 2.15–17) and miraculously provided sustenance for Israel in the wilderness (Exod. 16), before leading them into a bountiful land of 'milk and honey' (Exod. 3.8; Lev. 20.24; Deut. 6.3). This conviction established another link, namely, between eating and covenant, with food constituting an expression of divine hospitality and shared meals communicating reconciliation, friendship and mutual commitment (Exod. 24.9–11). Furthermore, as beneficiaries of God's blessings, Jews were expected to extend hospitality not only to their own, but especially to foreigners (Gen. 18.1–8).[68]

In these and other ways, subsistence was translated into the currency of grace, with feeding an experience of divine goodness and eating together a means of participating in God's covenantal blessings. Because of this, mealtimes and, especially, feasts were occasions for remembering God's goodness through participation and, as such, were esteemed as one of the principal definitions of joy.[69] We noted when discussing Jewish mourning customs, how fasting and isolation were two of the defining characteristics facilitating solidarity with the deceased in their exile from God; similarly, the ending of the period of mourning signalled return to the dispensation of grace where food and community were to be enjoyed. We also drew attention to the ways in which the exilic prophets appropriated the language of grief to communicate what it means to live in God's absence and to anticipate God's presence. With this in mind, the following description of how the covenant was renewed after return is significant:

And Nehemiah, who was the governor, and Ezra the priest and scribe, and the Levites who taught the people said to all the people, 'This day is holy to the Lord your God; do not mourn or weep.' For all the people wept when they heard the words of the law. Then he said to them, 'Go your way, eat the fat and drink sweet wine and send portions of them to those for whom nothing is prepared, for this day is holy to our Lord; and do not be grieved, for the joy of the Lord is your strength.' So the Levites stilled all the people, saying, 'Be quiet, for this day is holy; do not be grieved.' And all the people went their way to eat and drink and to send portions and to make great rejoicing, because they had understood the words that were declared to them. (Neh. 8.9–12)

What is equally striking is the way in which the abundance of food and feasting come to symbolize God's blessings in the future.[70] Isaiah, from exile in Babylon, envisages a time when God will host a great banquet for his people on mount Zion:

> On this mountain the Lord of hosts will make for all peoples
>     a feast of rich food, a feast of well-matured wines,
>     of rich food filled with marrow, of well-matured wines
>         strained clear.
> And he will destroy on this mountain
>     the shroud that is cast over all peoples,
>     the sheet that is spread over all nations;
> he will swallow up death for ever.
> Then the Lord God will wipe away the tears from all faces,
>     and the disgrace of his people he will take away from all
>         the earth,
>     for the Lord has spoken.
>
> (Isa. 25.6–8)

In a similar fashion, the image of the banquet of God or his messiah is employed by visionaries to encapsulate a similar hope. For instance, the author of *1 Enoch* envisages a time when God's righteous and elect ones will be robed with 'garments of glory' and feast in God's presence: 'The Lord of the Spirits will abide over them; they shall eat and rest and rise with that Son of Man forever and ever' (62.14). Another seer conceives of the world being transformed into a cornucopia of divine munificence:

> The earth will also yield fruits ten thousandfold. And on one vine will be a thousand branches, and one branch will produce a thousand clusters, and one cluster will produce a thousand grapes, and one grape will produce a cor of wine. And those who are hungry will enjoy themselves and they will, moreover, see marvels every day. For winds will go out in front of me every

morning to bring the fragrance of aromatic fruits and clouds at the end of the day to distil the dew of health. And it will happen at that time that the treasury of manna will come down again from on high, and they will eat of it in those years because these are they who will have arrived at the consummation of time. (*2 Bar.* 29.5–8)

*Joseph and Aseneth*, a fictional romance from the turn of the eras narrating the marriage of the patriarch to the daughter of an Egyptian priest (cf. Gen. 41.45), also deserves mention. Of particular interest is the way Aseneth's conversion to Jewish faith is depicted. Initially, when they meet, Joseph refuses to have dealings with Aseneth because of her pagan practices:

It is not fitting for a man who worships God, who will bless with his mouth the living God and eat blessed bread of life and drink a blessed cup of immortality and anoint himself with blessed ointment of incorruptibility, to kiss a strange woman who will bless with her mouth dead and dumb idols and eat from their table bread of strangulation and drink from their libation a cup of insidiousness and anoint herself with ointment of destruction. (*Jos. Asen.* 8.5)[71]

Aseneth, having fallen in love with Joseph, undergoes a period of mourning when she dons sackcloth and ashes, refuses to wash or eat, and weeps incessantly for her sinfulness (10—13). At the conclusion, an angel appears and announces her acceptance: 'Behold, from today, you will be renewed and formed anew and made alive again, and you will eat blessed bread of life, and drink a blessed cup of immortality, and anoint yourself with blessed ointment of incorruptibility' (15.5). After partaking in divine hospitality (16.1–16), she marries Joseph when, at last, they are able to feast and commune together (18.1—21.9). Aseneth's joy is complete as she thanks God for being able to share in the 'bread of life' and the 'cup of wisdom' (21.21). The author's use of the process of mourning to symbolize conversion, together with food and eating together to communicate divine blessing and communion, is pertinent.

In a not dissimilar way, access to the 'pure meal of the congregation' at the heart of community life at Qumran was thought to confer blessing (1QS 5.7–20; 6.14–23; 7.18–21).[72] Participation was restricted to those who had served their probationary period and been judged worthy of belonging to God's elect. To take one's place at the table, therefore, was to experience the privileges of salvation and to anticipate their fulfilment when God's priest and messiah would preside:

> And [when] they shall gather for the common [tab]le, to eat and [to drink] new wine, when the common table shall be set for eating and the new wine [poured] for drinking, let no man extend his hand over the first-fruits of bread and wine before the Priest; for [it is he] who shall bless the first-fruits of bread and wine, and shall be the first [to extend] his hand over the bread. Thereafter, the Messiah of Israel shall extend his hand over the bread, [and] all the congregation of the Community [shall utter a] blessing, [each man in the order] of his dignity. (1QSa 2.17–21)

There is good reason to believe at least some of the Pharisees of the first century CE, similarly concerned to preserve God's covenantal community in a state of uprightness and purity, committed themselves to strict observance of tithing laws and of those protocols moderating the preparation of food and its consumption at meals.[73] Among other ramifications, this had the effect of restricting table-fellowship to those of similar discipline and this, by implication, led to value judgements being made about who should be considered a faithful Jew and a worthy recipient of God's favour.

All this constitutes the background against which we need to interpret Jesus' understanding of food and of sharing meals together. The Gospels report many occasions when he eats in the company of various groups. As one would expect, he dines with friends and disciples,[74] but possibly also with debating-partners and opponents.[75] Even more surprisingly, he offers hospitality to those considered unworthy company,[76] as well as to vast crowds gathered in his name.[77] In the light of what has been said about the Qumran community and the Pharisees, Jesus' indiscriminate practice of eating with all and sundry is itself insightful, suggesting that *he saw meals as a source of inclusion and not exclusion*.[78] This clearly caused controversy, especially with the Pharisees:

> And as he sat at dinner in Levi's house, many tax-collectors and sinners were also sitting with Jesus and his disciples – for there were many who followed him. When the scribes of the Pharisees saw that he was eating with sinners and tax-collectors, they said to his disciples, 'Why does he eat with tax-collectors and sinners?' When Jesus heard this, he said to them, 'Those who are well have

no need of a physician, but those who are sick; I have come to call not the righteous but sinners.' (Mark 2.15–17; cf. Matt. 9.9–13/ Luke 5.27–32; also Matt. 11.19/Luke 7.34; Luke 15.1–2)

As we have already mentioned, the epithet 'sinner' in this and other Gospel passages denotes a value judgement applied to those deemed to have transgressed the prerequisite conditions of membership. The attitude of Pharisees towards those who refused to observe their tithing and purity regulations is one possible setting for this.[79] Another and more arresting one is to identify 'sinners' with 'the wicked', namely with 'those who sinned wilfully and heinously and who did not repent'.[80] In this scenario, Jesus sat at table not only with ordinary Jews who lacked the opportunity or inclination to embrace the strictures of sects such as the Pharisees, but also with those who knowingly ignored God and refused to modify their lifestyles according to the teaching of Torah. The poignancy of this is reinforced by the recognition that Jesus evidently invested meals with immense theological significance.[81]

We have noted already how Jesus was remembered as a great intercessor who communicated God's forgiveness. For a Jew, however, forgiveness was not the substance of salvation, but a necessary precursor – a conviction rooted in the archetypal Exodus story where liberation from Egypt is not an end in itself, but a prerequisite to covenant. In a comparable way, Jesus' ministry of forgiveness is part of the in-breaking of God's Kingdom, constituting a demonstrative invitation to enjoy the blessings and responsibilities associated with divine presence and favour.[82] Meals provided the opportunity and the context for this to take place. *For Jesus, the inclusiveness of his table-fellowship, in conjunction with the highly symbolic and sacramental nature of eating, drinking and communing together, embodied essential characteristics of God's vision for humanity (e.g. reconciliation and peace, generosity and abundance, trust and openness, equality and justice, belonging and mutual obligation, worship and joy), and enabled others tangibly to participate in that vision.*

Given meals and feasting were already very much a part of theological currency and debate, Jesus could hardly have chosen a more appropriate and, at the same time, provocative expression of God's presence. By rooting divine encounter within human experience in this way, he was establishing another means of access to God – perhaps even an alternative 'altar', not mediated by religious professionals nor restricted to those judged pure or worthy; but open to all Jews whose faith (or lack of it!) would allow them to partake.[83] Further, if Jesus invited and welcomed unrepentant Jews who wilfully disobeyed God's commandments, he was, in effect, challenging the foundations of Jewish soteriology and undermining the gatekeepers of the prevailing religious institutions.

All this enables us to make sense of why Jesus earned a reputation for excess (cf. 'a glutton and a drunkard', Matt. 11.19/Luke 7.34) and why he used the imagery of banquets in parables when teaching about the Kingdom (Matt. 22.1–14/Luke 14.15–24; Luke 15.11–32). Similarly, it explains Jesus' refusal to observe ritual purity at meals or the practices of mourning (e.g. fasting). If God wishes to shower blessings upon the people, joy can be their only response! And if God's blessings are given without discrimination or condition, why engage in human inventions devised to ensure worthy acceptance?

> Now John's disciples and the Pharisees were fasting; and people came and said to him, 'Why do John's disciples and the disciples of the Pharisees fast, but your disciples do not fast?' Jesus said to them, 'The wedding guests cannot fast while the bridegroom is with them, can they? As long as they have the bridegroom with them, they cannot fast.' (Mark 2.18–19; cf. Matt. 9.14–15/Luke 5.33–4)

## Motivation and Discipline

So far in this chapter we have identified how Jesus communicated a sense of God's presence through forgiveness, prayer, wisdom and eating together, as vital components of his own faith were made accessible to others. However, each of these is an expression of an underlying spirituality or fundamental orientation to life, and it is to this that we now turn. Jesus, it seems, like every observant Jew, was familiar with the Shema. When asked by a religious official about the premier commandment, he responded:[84]

> 'The first is, "Hear, O Israel: the Lord our God, the Lord is one; you shall love the Lord your God with all your heart, and with all your soul, and with all your mind, and with all your strength." The second is this, "You shall love your neighbour as yourself." There is no other commandment greater than these.'(Mark 12.29–31; Matt. 22.37–40/Luke 10.27–8; cf. Deut. 6.4; Lev.19.18)

Evidently, Jesus' answer was greeted with approval, as we should expect given the centrality of love of God within Jewish piety.[85]

Controversy centred, however, not on the principle, but on its application, namely, on what loving God meant and how it should be
expressed. Judging from the different expressions of Jewish faith in
existence in the first century CE, there was considerable latitude in
interpretation; hence, the question to Jesus noted above.

In certain respects, it seems that Jesus followed the normative
religious practices of his community: daily prayer, regular worship in
the local synagogue, observance of the great pilgrim feasts in
Jerusalem and so forth. In other areas, such as keeping the Sabbath,
he departed from conventional practice.[86] What is particularly striking, however, is the way in which the nature of his relationship with
God is remembered and given significance. During our discussion
of the Lord's Prayer, we noted how it was informed by a dynamic
and personal relatedness to God. Although implicit throughout the
Gospels, this insight is highlighted in a number of key passages,
including Jesus' baptism, the transfiguration, the parable of the
wicked tenants, and the garden of Gethsemane. The first two
include heavenly affirmation in the form of voice: 'You are my Son,
the Beloved; with you I am well pleased' (Mark 1.11; Matt. 3.17/
Luke 3.22), and 'This is my Son, the Beloved; listen to him!' (Mark
9.7; Matt.17.5/Luke 9.35). Both of these traditions raise major
interpretative problems, but what is beyond question is that they
bear witness to Jesus being remembered as *one who knew himself to
be loved of God*. Further, the parable (Mark 12.1–12; Matt. 21.33–6/
Luke 20.9–19), which may well be one of our surest guides to Jesus'
self-understanding,[87] has 'a beloved son' being commissioned by his
father to further his causes and being murdered in the process of
doing so. Gethsemane, once again, gives access to an intense sense
of divine presence and personal intimacy. What is more, the author
of John's Gospel places great stress upon Jesus' experience of being
loved of God as the generative core from which both his identity and
ministry emanated: 'As the Father has loved me, so I have loved you;
abide in my love. If you keep my commandments, you will abide in
my love, just as I have kept my Father's commandments and abide
in his love' (John 15.9–10).

From what we can gather, this way of 'being-in-relation-to-God',
characterized by an existential intensity and dynamic reciprocity,
distinguished Jesus from many of his contemporaries. It stands in
stark contrast to permutations of the prevailing derived and indirect
religious consciousness, where each Jew is born into a covenantal
relationship with God mediated by ritual, regulated by laws and

administered by professionals. Within such a scenario, identity is a function of belonging to a privileged people, God's elect, and relating to God is expressed in terms of observance and obedience. Even with groups such as the Pharisees and Essenes, we simply find a more demanding version of this applied and prescriptive form of love where the responsibilities of covenantal membership defined in Torah are extended to embrace all of life.

It appears that Jesus' perception of being loved by God engendered a radically different embodiment of faith. For one thing, his pattern of ministry and lifestyle clearly did not draw their significance from existing models of piety or structures of authority; rather, their itinerant and nonconformist nature suggest a charismatically inspired and existentially determined paradigm, where the appropriate response to God's love emerged through attending to the needs and demands of each situation, albeit within certain parameters.[88] This is captured particularly well by those traditions narrating Jesus ministering forgiveness on the Sabbath:

> Again he entered the synagogue, and a man was there who had a withered hand. They [the Pharisees] watched him to see whether he would cure him on the sabbath, so that they might accuse him. And he said to the man who had the withered hand, 'Come forward.' Then he said to them, 'Is it lawful to do good or to do harm on the sabbath, to save life or to kill?' But they were silent. He looked around at them with anger; he was grieved at their hardness of heart and said to the man, 'Stretch out your hand.' He stretched it out, and his hand was restored. The Pharisees went out and immediately conspired with the Herodians against him, how to destroy him. (Mark 3.1–6; cf. Matt. 12.9–14/Luke 6.6–11)[89]

What is striking is the way in which Jesus is remembered as one whose conduct was not restricted to existing canons of covenantal fidelity, but who was motivated by an overriding compunction to communicate divine blessing. We encounter here a form of faith-filled living capable of *investing the present with theological intensity through interpreting each moment as an opportunity to respond to God.* Evidently, this proved to be a source of controversy and animosity, raising questions about the source of Jesus' authority for his radical performance of what loving God both requires and makes possible;[90] however, it also mediated a profound sense of God's will being done. A similar conviction that faith is not principally a matter of keeping laws or applying commandments, but of pursuing a life of

trust in God and of dynamically translating his priorities and purposes into day-to-day living, can be seen in his exchange with the
wealthy Jewish inquirer[91] and in much of the teaching gathered
together in Matthew's sermon on the mount.[92]

It is unclear whether Jesus was the first Jewish teacher explicitly
to link love of God with love of neighbour and even of one's enemies
(Matt. 5.44/Luke 6.27).[93] However, there can be little doubt that
human relationships constituted an integral component within his
spirituality and a reliable measure of a person's openness to God.
Rather than associating God's presence with particular places (e.g.
Temple), possessions (e.g. Torah) or practices (e.g. sacrifice, Sabbath
observance), his ministry reflects a commitment to encountering
God in the midst of authentic human being. To this end, Jesus coun-
tenanced no strategies of withdrawal by restricting the compass of
human interaction to those judged worthy or acceptable. On the
contrary, his investment in ministering the blessings associated with
God's presence to those whose lifestyles, circumstances or conditions
placed them on the margins of community life was extraordinary.
And while there can be little doubt that Jesus practised his vocation
among Jews, he may well have recognized the potential of faith for
transcending boundaries of nationality and culture.[94]

It seems that in Jesus' profoundly personal experience of being
loved by God and of living in his presence we have identified the
nucleus of his faith, which gave rise to the discipline of love informing his entire ministry. A discipline that was essentially *a reciprocity
of love – a response to God which translated the vitality and vibrancy of that
relationship into a life of intercession communicating divine blessing.*
Whatever else Jesus meant by the Kingdom of God, it included this
conviction about divine glory – of God's presence being felt with
transforming effect.[95]

## Entrusting and Vocation

Jesus did not conceive of his vocation in exclusive terms. This much
is clear from the way he identified a small sub-set of sympathizers
and involved them in the practice of his faith and vocation. It
appears that Jesus constituted a group of twelve disciples from a
much larger body of support. The number, one for each tribe of
Israel, suggests a programmatic ministry of restoration and renewal
among the Jewish people as a whole.[96] How the disciples were
selected and trained continue to be matters of debate, although a

form of apprenticeship provides a suitable interpretative model for their induction.[97] There are strong grounds for maintaining 'the twelve' found themselves in active service during Jesus' lifetime, preaching and performing acts of forgiveness. The Gospels attest different versions of their mission charge,[98] together with a disputation about their relative importance and incidental references relating their progress or attitudes towards other practitioners.[99] The scale of their missionary activities prior to the crucifixion is difficult to establish, but we can be confident that at least some of Jesus' followers had become co-workers.[100] This is a significant observation suggesting they had already begun to embody his faith, through indwelling his discipline of love characterized by forgiveness, prayer, wisdom and hospitality, and to share his experience of God. We encounter here an early demonstration of what we referred to in the opening chapter as the *phenomenon of transferability* whereby the faith of Jesus becomes accessible to others. Further, the strategic importance of this pattern of *dissemination through participation* comes into focus with Jesus' awareness of the likelihood of his imminent death.

This is nowhere clearer than in the traditions narrating Jesus' final meal with his followers. It is probable that the framing of this occasion as a Passover celebration reflects a later interpretative stratum concerned to emphasize the sacrificial nature of Jesus' death,[101] although there is little reason to doubt it occurred around the time of this great Jewish feast of liberation.[102] We draw closer to the original significance of the occasion when we view it as the last in a series of meals characterizing Jesus' ministry and communicating his convictions about the nature and proximity of the blessings associated with God's presence.[103] Earlier in the chapter, we explored the significance of food and meals for Jesus and noted their central role within the experience of joy. Whether Jesus was sufficiently sensitive to the machinations of those who orchestrated his crucifixion so that he accurately predicted the time of his arrest, or whether he precipitated his demise in some way, need not detain us here. What is clear, however, is that his followers remembered a particular meal or, perhaps, meals, when Jesus spoke about his death and of how he wished them to respond to it. Judging from the traditions about this Last Supper, at least three components of that meal were extraordinary.

First, in addition to the blessing of bread and wine, which was commonplace, Jesus associated himself with these provisions in particular ways:

> 'Take, eat; this is my body . . . Drink from it, all of you; for this is my blood of the covenant, which is poured out for many for the forgiveness of sins.' (Matt. 26.26–8)

> 'Take; this is my body . . . This is my blood of the covenant, which is poured out for many.' (Mark 14.22–4)

> 'This my body, which is given for you . . . This cup that is poured out for you is the new covenant in my blood.' (Luke 22.19–20)

> 'This is my body that is for you . . . This cup is the new covenant in my blood.' (1 Cor. 11.24–5)

A number of preliminary observations help us to appreciate what Jesus intended by these words. Bread and wine were not neutral symbols for Jews, even less so for Jesus' disciples. They belonged to the currency of grace. Bread was the fundamental food for Jews and, as such, came to symbolize all that was necessary for life. In consequence, to pray, as Jesus did, that God would 'give us this day our daily bread' (Matt. 6.11) was to express the conviction that the God who gave life would provide what was necessary for its sustenance. Wine, by contrast, symbolized the richness and fruitfulness of life. While water was the essential counterpart to bread,[104] wine communicated a sense of abundance and, as such, characterized joyous living. To drink wine, therefore, was to celebrate life in its fullness. As we have seen, meals performed a particular function within Jesus' ministry as a locus where God's blessings could be enjoyed. In this context, the sharing of bread and wine became defining characteristics of his practice and intimately associated with the experience of God's presence mediated by him.

It seems highly improbable that Jesus used 'body' and 'blood' complementarily in this context to represent or equate to the entirety of his person.[105] If this had been his intention we should have expected either 'flesh' and 'blood',[106] a common juxtaposition in the Hebrew Scriptures, or 'body' and 'soul',[107] which captures the vital component of human being while removing the scandalous and forbidden prospect of a Jew consuming blood.[108] The situation is complicated because the Greek word translated here as 'body' (*soma*) could conceivably render an Aramaic original meaning either 'flesh' or 'body'. However, as Greek vocabulary enables this distinction to be drawn more adequately, we should have expected to find *sarx* and not *soma* if Jesus' meaning was the former rather than the latter. Perhaps more significant is the observation that *soma* and its most probable Aramaic equivalent (*gupa*) can both denote a person as a whole, suggesting a translation for the eucharistic words over the bread along the lines of 'this is me'.[109]

Although the Matthean and Marcan versions of Jesus' eucharistic words reflect a similar relation between 'bread/cup of wine' and 'body/blood', the tradition attested in Luke and Paul associates the 'cup of wine' directly with 'covenant' and only indirectly with 'blood'. This suggests a link between sharing the cup of wine and participating in the blessings of God associated with Jesus and extended to those who share his company. The connection between wine and divine favour was already established in the Hebrew Scriptures[110] and it is clear from traditions such as his disputation with John's disciples, the parable of the wine and the wineskins, and the wedding at Cana, together with the reputation he earned for being 'a glutton and a drunkard',[111] that Jesus located his own ministry within the dispensation of fulfilment characterized by an outpouring of God's abundant generosity. And while he sees arrest and death as a temporary exile from the community of celebration that had formed around him, he nonetheless looks forward to renewing the covenant with his followers and friends at the consummation of God's Kingdom: 'Truly I tell you, I will never again drink of the fruit of the vine until that day when I drink it new in the kingdom of God' (Mark 14.25; also Matt. 26.29; Luke 22.18).

All this suggests that Jesus' eucharistic words, although now harmonized in Matthew and Mark, should be understood in significantly different ways. It is interesting how Luke and Paul imply that those associated with the cup were uttered after the meal (cf. 'after supper', Luke 22.20; 1 Cor. 11.25); perhaps Jesus uttered them on a separate occasion. Certainly, we know some of the earliest post-crucifixion celebrations were simply described as 'the breaking of bread'.[112] And what of their respective meanings? In the case of the bread, Jesus encourages his followers to see this gift of God as embodying himself ('this is me'), something which would readily have commended itself, given the centrality of meals within his ministry; in the case of the cup of wine, the association is not with Jesus per se, but with the new relationship with God mediated by his

presence and characterized by joyous living. To share in the cup,
therefore, communicated participation in this community of blessing,
which Jesus inaugurated or re-established through his ministry and
which, in some way, required his death before coming to fulfilment.

The second distinguishing feature of the Last Supper relates to
remembrance. We have already drawn attention to the importance of
remembering for Jews. In brief, to remember was to be reconstituted
within the story of God's people, a story shaped by key figures and
events, and informed by certain insights, practices and disciplines
that embodied faith. To remember, therefore, was to appropriate the
past in such a way that it shaped one's response to the present and
gave substance to one's hopes for the future. What, then, did Jesus
intend when he included the injunction to remember along with the
invitation to share in the bread and the wine?

> 'This is my body, which is given for you. Do this in remembrance
> of me.' (Luke 22.19)

> 'This is my body that is for you. Do this in remembrance of me
> . . . This cup is the new covenant in my blood. Do this, as often
> as you drink it, in remembrance of me.' (1 Cor. 11.23–5)

One possible solution is suggested by the Graeco-Roman practice of
holding memorial meals in honour of a founder-figure.[113] However,
although remembering Jesus would become an important component
in post-crucifixion eucharistic observance,[114] it is doubtful whether
this adequately conveys Jesus' intention – his concern was principally with encountering God, rather than with his own significance.
A more promising proposal is suggested by the testamentary material reviewed in the second chapter in which key figures from Israel's
past gather their families around them before death, sometimes in
the context of a meal, and entrust to them the inheritance of faith
they sought to embody. Given that Jesus' practice of meals and
table-fellowship encapsulated so much of his vision for God's people,
and in the light of the importance of remembrance as a means of
maintaining the momentum of a formative past and appropriating it
into the present, is it not more likely that when Jesus, in the shadow
of his imminent death which he believed would be instrumental
within the fulfilment of God's purposes, took bread and said, 'This
is my life', broke it and offered it to his disciples and friends with the
words, 'Do this in remembrance of me', *he was entrusting to them his
vocation and commissioning them to continue to embody the faith which*

*he had embodied and which had informed their common life and ministry?* And is it not probable that when Jesus took the cup of wine and invited them to consume it with him, using words forging a link between the cup and the new relationship with God they had shared together and communicated to others, *he was sealing that relationship and entrusting it to them until the time in God's future when they would be reunited and able to renew the covenant together?*[115]

The precise form of Jesus' words over the bread and the cup will perhaps always remains matters of conjecture. However, it does seem likely that the sharing of bread and wine in the context of the associations outlined above *constituted a symbolic executing of Jesus' last will and testament through which he entrusted his vocation, the embodiment of his faith, to the disciples.* Significantly, in John's Gospel, where the foot-washing ceremony and farewell discourses replace the distribution of bread and wine, this is precisely what we find. Jesus invites his followers to emulate his example and reassures them that it is by continuing to embody his faith through lives of service and obedience that his presence will be felt and their relationship with God, mediated by him, will be sustained:

> 'You call me Teacher and Lord – and you are right, for that is what I am. So if I, your Lord and Teacher, have washed your feet, you also ought to wash one another's feet. For I have set you an example, that you also should do as I have done to you . . . Very truly, I tell you, whoever receives one whom I send receives me; and whoever receives me receives him who sent me.' (John 13.13–15, 20)

> 'If you abide in me, and my words abide in you, ask for whatever you wish, and it will be done for you. My Father is glorified by this, that you bear much fruit and become my disciples. As the Father has loved me, so I have loved you; abide in my love. If you keep my commandments, you will abide in my love, just as I have kept my Father's commandments and abide in his love.' (John 15.7–10; cf. also 13.34–5; 14.6–15, 21, 23–4, 27; 15.4–6, 16; 16.26–7)

The third and final characteristic marking the Last Supper out from other celebrations follows on from the previous one. While Jesus commits himself to abstinence until reunited with the disciples in God's Kingdom after his death, he enjoins his followers to continue their practice of meals and table-fellowship:

'Then he took a loaf of bread, and when he had given thanks, he broke it and gave it to them, saying, "This is my body, which is given for you. Do this in remembrance of me."' (Luke 22.19)

'This is my body that is for you. Do this in remembrance of me ... This cup is the new covenant in my blood. Do this, as often as you drink it, in remembrance of me.' (1 Cor. 11.23–5)

This is a remarkable request, especially as it appears to go against his teaching elsewhere.[116] We cannot say whether Jesus wished his followers completely to ignore Jewish mourning disciplines, but what does seem clear is that *he expected them to maintain those aspects of their common life associated with joyous living which were an integral component of the vocation and embodiment of faith he was entrusting to them.* If he refused to let his disciples fast when alive because he thought it inappropriate in the light of their experience of divine blessing, evidently he did not intend that his death should diminish their participation in this dispensation of grace; perhaps he even thought his death would intensify or precipitate its fulfilment in some way.

## NOTES

1 Although assessments of the reliability of the Gospels continue to vary enormously (see Witherington, 1995) a number of recent studies identify a significant body of material which is likely to originate in the ministry of Jesus: A. E. Harvey (1982); Meier (1991 and 1994); Meyer (1979); Riches (1980); E. P. Sanders (1985 and 1993); Vermes (1976); and N. T. Wright (1996). See also Aune (1987); and Burridge (1992).

2 See the discussions of Ebeling (1963), pp. 201–46; Marxsen (1992), pp. 76–95; and Schürmann (1962), pp. 342–70.

3 See, for example, Kloppenborg (1987); and Mack (1988 and 1993).

4 Consider, for example, attempts to reconstruct collections of pre-Gospel miracle traditions in Mark: e.g. Achtemeier (1970), pp. 265–91, and (1972), pp. 198–221; and in John: see the helpful review of Fortna (1992), pp. 18–22.

5 E.g. Freyne (1998); Horsley (1989); Malina (1981); and Theissen (1978 and 1992).

6 See Riesner (1991), pp. 193–6, and the literature cited there.

7 Brueggemann (1987), pp. 7–26; Hermisson and Lohse (1981), pp. 10–46; and Wallis (1995a), pp. 9–12.

8 See the helpful reviews of Rowland (1985), Part II; and N. T. Wright (1992), Part III.

9 The extent of hellenization within first-century Galilee is a matter of

considerable controversy; see, for example, the varying assessments of Crossan (1998); and Horsley (1996).

10  Good reviews can be found in Borg (1998), pp. 43–87; C. A. Evans (1995), Part I; Horsley (1987); and Horsley and Hanson (1985).

11  See, for example, the studies of Freyne (1998); and Horsley (1995 and 1996).

12  N. T. Wright (1992 and 1996) recognizes this as one of the key insights for understanding the impact of Jesus.

13  See N. T. Wright's review (1992), pp. 280–338; and the more detailed collections of studies in Charlesworth (1992b); and Neusner, Green and Frerichs (1987).

14  Charlesworth (1986), pp. 419–21, and (1992a), pp. 36–55.

15  In addition to the works of Hanson and Horsley cited earlier, see Bammel and Moule (1984).

16  See the thorough discussion of Meier (1994), Vol. 2, pp. 100–233. Hollenbach makes the interesting suggestion that the emphasis in Jesus' ministry changed with the discovery of his gifting for charismatic healing (1982), pp. 196–219; also Chilton (1998), pp. 31–57.

17  Detailed expositions of Jesus' healing ministry can be found in Loos (1968); Meier (1994), Vol. 2, Part III; and Twelftree (1993). Goppelt (1981), pp. 139–57; Jeremias (1971), pp. 85–96; Richardson (1941); Suhl (1968); and Wallis (1992), pp. 42–5, explore the theological significance.

18  The following discussions are particularly sensitive to the socio-economic, as well as the medical and theological implications of Jesus' miracles: Crossan (1998), pp. 337–82; Kee (1986); and Theissen (1983).

19  Matt. 8.1–4/Mark 1.40–5/Luke 5.12–16; Luke 17.11–19; cf. Matt. 11.5/Luke 7.22; Matt. 10.8. Wright and Jones (1992), pp. 277–82. Bruce Chilton maintains Jesus' healing ministry consisted essentially of extending levitical purity to some previously excluded conditions: Chilton (1998), pp. 58–97.

20  Matt. 9.20–2/Mark 5.25–34/Luke 8.43–8. Selvidge (1984), pp. 619–23, and (1980).

21  Cf. Luke 13.10–17 and John 9.1–3; also the link between healing and forgiveness in Pss. 32.3–5; 103.1–5; Mark 2.1–12; Jas. 5.13–18 and 4QprNab. See Seybold and Mueller (1981), esp. pp. 112–14.

22  E.g. Matt. 9.9–13/Mark 2.13–17/Luke 5.27–32; Luke 7.31–5; 15.2; also Luke 7.36–50; 19.1–10. See Hofius (1967), pp. 16–26; Koenig (1985), pp.15–51; and Mackey (1979), pp. 142–59.

23  See Chilton (1988), pp. 1–18; Dunn (1990), pp. 71–81; Neale (1991), pp. 40–67; and E. P. Sanders (1983), pp. 5–36.

24  On this aspect of Jesus' ministry, see Malina and Rohrbaugh (1992); Moltmann-Wendel (1993); Nolan (1977); Schüssler Fiorenza (1983); and Witherington (1984).

25  On the revolutionary implications of Jesus' table-fellowship in relation to Jewish identity and definitions of purity, see, especially, Borg (1998),

pp. 88–134.

26 See, especially, Schillebeeckx (1979), pp. 179–229; also Borg (1993), pp. 57–75.

27 Jesus' ministry of forgiveness constituted an integral component of his communication of God's saving presence. Like his preaching, prayer life and table-fellowship, it represents a performance of the Kingdom facilitating divine encounter. The Kingdom of God is clearly the climate within which Jesus practises forgiveness (Matt. 9.1–8/Mark 2.1–12/Luke 5.17–26; Matt.12.9–14/Mark 3.1–6/Luke 6.6–11; Matt. 4.17/Mark 1.15; Matt. 11.2–6/Luke 7.18–23; Matt.12.28/Luke 11.20; Luke 4.14–21; cf. Matt.10.1/Mark 6.7/Luke 9.1–2; Mark 3.14–15; Luke 10.1–12); but see also the response of participants (Matt. 9.8/ Mark 2.12/Luke 5.25–6; Matt. 14.33; 15.31; Luke 7.16; 13.13; 17.15–18), the testimony of the evil spirits (Matt. 8.29/Mark 5.7/Luke 8.28; Mark 1.24/Luke 4.34; Mark 3.11/Luke 4.41; Matt. 8.29) and editorial comments (e.g. Matt. 8.17; Mark 1.38–9; 3.7–12). We know that many expressions of Jewish hope for the re-establishment of God's Kingdom included miraculous acts of healing, resuscitation and other phenomena (e.g. Isa. 26.19; 29.18; 35.5–6; 53.5; 61.1–2; Jer. 30.17; 31.7–9; Ezek. 37.12–14; Dan.12.2; Joel 2.28-32; Mic. 7.15; Mal. 4.2; 2 Bar. 73.1–2; 4 Ezra 7.123; 9.6; 13.50; Jub. 23.29-30; T. Zeb. 9.8; 4Q521). See Wallis (1995a), pp. 48–53.

28 Cf. the structural analysis of Gerd Theissen with respect to Jesus' miracles (1983), pp. 47–80; also E. P. Sanders (1985), pp. 157–241.

29 See, for example, the call and ministering of the disciples (Matt. 4.18–22/Mark 1.16–20; Matt. 10.1–4/Mark 3.13–19/Luke 6.12–16; Matt 10.4–15/Mark 6.6–13/Luke 9.1–6), their special instruction (Matt.13.10–15/Mark 4.10–12/Luke 8.9–10; Matt. 17.19–20/Mark 9.28–9), sharing in profound experiences (Matt. 8.18, 23–7/Mark 4.35–41/Luke 8.22–5; Matt 14.22–33/Mark 6.45–52; Matt.17.1–8/Mark 9.2–8/Luke 9.28–36; Matt. 24/Mark 13/Luke 21; Matt 26.6–13/Mark 14.3–9; Matt. 26.17–29/Mark 14.12–25/Luke 22.7–23), and other times together (Matt 14.13/Mark 6.31–2/Luke 9.10; Mark 1.35–8/Luke 4.42–3).

30 Literature on the Lord's Prayer is substantial: for an exposition in sympathy with what follows, see Chilton (1997), pp. 24–51; for further study, see the extensive bibliography of Mark Harding in Charlesworth (1994), pp. 186–201.

31 Jeremias (1967), pp. 66–107, discusses the earliest version and probable Aramaic original. This begs the question, however, of whether there ever was one definitive form, rather than a number of nonidentical performances.

32 The classic trinitarian form of prayer was to pray to the Father, through the Son, and in the Spirit. See Jungmann (1965); also T. F. Torrance (1975), pp. 139–214; and J. B. Torrance (1981), pp. 127–47.

33 'The distinctiveness of the prayer is nothing other than that conscious-

ness of God and of one's relationship to him which is implied, and which is recapitulated whenever one prays in this way. Such an awareness of God and of oneself is what Christians kindle when they pray the Lord's Prayer. And at the same time, the prayer is nothing other than the Lord's; whatever the merits of such a consciousness, it is ours only because it was Christ's first. That is why the filial consciousness of praying in this manner is as strong as it is: one is God's child and Jesus' sister or brother in the same instant' (Chilton (1997), p. 50; cf. also McDonald (1980), p.106).

34  See Bradshaw (1992), pp. 1–29; the articles by Deissler, Graubard, Heinemann, Lauer, and Petuchowski, in Petuchowski and Brocke (1978); and the bibliographical entries in Charlesworth (1994), pp. 140–78. The following translations of the Tephillah and Kaddish are taken from Petuchowski and Brocke (1978), pp. 21–44.

35  Moule (1978), pp. 68–77.

36  Much debate has focused on the nature of Jesus' address to God in the Lord's Prayer, 'Our Father', and whether it reflects the Aramaic, *Abba*, used by Jesus elsewhere (Mark 14.36) and taken up within the language of prayer adopted by the post-crucifixion community of faith (cf. Rom. 8.15; Gal. 4.6). Jeremias maintained Jesus' use of *Abba* was almost unprecedented in Jewish prayer literature of the time, communicating a very intimate and childlike way of relating, similar to that reflected in the form 'daddy' (Jeremias (1967), pp. 11–65; (1971), pp. 61–8). While many scholars maintain Jeremias overemphasized the innovative nature of Jesus' address and its childlike quality, few would question he correctly identified the importance of Jesus' filial consciousness and personal way of relating to God (Barr (1988), pp. 28–47; and Charlesworth (1994), pp. 1–14).

37  Translation from C. A. Evans (1995), p. 232. On Hanina's way of relating to God in comparison to Jesus', see Vermes (1976), pp. 58–82.

38  I have developed this further in Wallis (1995b), pp. 225–50; also Borg (1993), pp. 39–75.

39  See Ebeling (1963), p. 230; and Jeremias (1971), pp. 191–2.

40  Goppelt (1981), pp. 127–38.

41  Matt. 8.26/Mark 4.40/Luke 8.25; Matt. 9.2/Mark 2.5/Luke 5.20; Mark 5.36/Luke 8.50; Matt. 9.28; 14.31; 16.8; Mark 9.23–4.

42  Matt. 9.22/Mark 5.34/Luke 8.48; Mark 10.52/Luke 18.42; Luke 7.50; 17.19; also Matt. 8.10/Luke 7.9; Matt. 8.13; 9.29; 15.28.

43  On Jesus' understanding of faith, see Buber (1951); Ebeling (1963), pp. 201–24; Hahn and Klein (1982); Mackey (1979), pp. 159–72; Marxsen (1979), pp. 57–68; Perrin (1967), pp. 130–51; and Sobrino (1978), pp. 79–145.

44  Wallis (1995a), esp. pp. 48–53; on the relationship between Matt.17.20, 21.21, Mark 11.22–3 and Luke 17.6, see *op. cit.*, pp. 46–8.

45  Cf. *4 Macc.* 15.24; 16.22; 17.2. The translation of the NRSV has been modified to reflect the Greek original more adequately.

46  NRSV translation revised; also 1 Sam. 2.35; Isa.11.5; 16.5; 42.3; *1 En.* 39.6; 83.8; *Eccl. R.* III.9.1; *Targ. Isa.* 11.4.

47  See the excellent article of J. A. Sanders (1992), esp. p. 843.

48  Daniel Patte (1975) offers a comprehensive review; Loewe (1990), pp. 346–54, offers a more accessible introduction.

49  Cf. 'I am a Jew, born in Tarsus in Cilicia, but brought up in this city at the feet of Gamaliel, educated strictly according to our ancestral law, being zealous for God, just as all of you are today' (Acts 22.3). See Hengel with Deines (1991), esp. chs 2–4; and Townsend (1992), pp. 312–17; also Crenshaw (1998).

50  Bradshaw (1992), pp. 21–4; and Petuchowski (1978), pp. 45–57.

51  See, for example, Chilton (1983). On Jesus' use of the Scriptures, Chilton (1984); and Young (1989).

52  E.g. Matt. 26.55/Mark 14.49/Luke 22.53/John 18.20; Matt. 21.23/ Mark 11.27/Luke 20.1; Luke 2.46; 19.47; 21.37–8; John 7.28; 8.2, 20.

53  E.g. Matt. 4.23/Mark 1.39/Luke 4.44; Matt.12.9/Mark 3.1/Luke 6.6; Matt. 13.54/Mark 6.2; Mark 1.21–8/Luke 4.31–7; Mark 9.35; Luke 4.4–14; 13.10; John 6.59; 18.20.

54  E.g. Matt. 5.1–2; 7.28–9; 11.1; Mark 2.13; 4.1; 6.6, 34; 10.1–2; Luke 5.3; 13.22, 26; 23.5.

55  Meier (1991), Vol. 1, pp. 253–315; Riesner (1984), pp. 123–206. Patte observes that Scripture was used in four distinct ways in the synagogue: it was read, preached, translated and used in prayers (1975), pp. 31–47.

56  Aphorisms: Aune (1991), pp. 211–65; and Crossan (1983). Parables: K. E. Bailey (1976); Crossan (1973); Jeremias (1972); Perrin (1976); and Scott (1989).

57  Jewish background: Flusser (1981); Gerhardsson (1961); McArthur and Johnston (1990); Riesner (1984), and (1991), pp. 185–210; Young (1989). Hellenistic background: Crossan (1991); Downing (1988 and 1992); and Mack (1988 and 1993).

58  A good summary of Jesus' teaching is provided by Borg (1992), pp. 804–12. For a thorough discussion in relation to Jewish and hellenistic wisdom traditions, consult Witherington (1994). A helpful collection of extracanonical sayings of Jesus has been compiled by William Stroker (1989).

59  John Bowker (1969) conveniently lists the seven principles (*middoth*) of Rabbi Hillel and the thirteen of Rabbi Ishmael, pp. 315–18.

60  Some scholars (e.g. Crossan, Kloppenborg and Mach) maintain that the community behind the Q tradition came into being around Jesus' wisdom sayings.

61  See the surveys in Kuschel (1992), pp. 177–221; and Witherington (1994), Part 1.

62  Cf. 1 Sam. 16.23; see *T. Sol.* esp. 20; also Ps.-Philo, *Bib. Ant.* 60; Josephus, *Ant.* 8.2.5; 11Q11; Wisd. 7.15–23. The link between exorcism and Davidic descent is explored by Berger (1973–74), pp. 1–44; and Duling (1975), pp. 235–52, and (1977–78), pp. 392-410.

63 This helps to explain why Jesus came to be seen as God's wisdom incarnate (cf. John 1.1–18). On the place of wisdom in christological development, see Dunn (1980); Kuschel (1992), Part 2; Witherington (1994), Part 2.

64 This occurs in the feeding miracles (Matt.14.19/Mark 6.41/Luke 9.16; Matt. 15.36/Mark 8.6–7), the Last Supper (Matt. 26.26–7/Mark 14.22–3/ Luke 22.17–19), and the meals after the crucifixion (Luke 24.30; John 6.11).

65 Cf. *Jub.* 22.6; *Aristeas Exeg.* 184–5; *m. Ber.* 3.4; 6.1–8; see Charlesworth (1986), p. 420.

66 Valuable discussions of the importance of food, meals and hospitality can be found in Feeley-Harnik (1994); Jenks (1992), pp. 250–4; L. T. Johnson (1998), pp. 137–79; and Malina (1981), pp. 122–52.

67 Schramm (1992), pp. 648–50.

68 Koenig (1985), pp. 1–20, and (1992), pp. 299—301.

69 Cf. 2 Sam.12.16–20; see G. A. Anderson (1991), esp. pp. 19–26.

70 There is a useful discussion in Priest (1992), pp. 222–38.

71 See the suggestive comments of Lindars (1987), pp. 181–99, concerning links between this work and Christian eucharistic practices; also Burchard (1987), pp. 109–34.

72 Schiffman (1979), pp. 45–56.

73 Part of the problem here is knowing what characterized pre-70 CE Pharisaism and, specifically, whether Pharisees of this period observed the laws concerning tithing and ritual purity defined in later rabbinic literature. Jacob Neusner maintains they did (e.g. (1971), pp. 301–19, and (1973), pp. 64–71) and, while this view has found considerable support, it has also been challenged repeatedly by Ed Sanders (esp. (1992), pp. 413–51). We know from Josephus that Pharisees were influential in the first century and were reputed to be the strictest of the Jewish sects or ways of life, accurately interpreting and living out the ancestral laws, including those not recorded in the laws of Moses (*Ant.* 13.171–2, 297–8; 18.12–15; *War* 1.110; 2.162; *Life* 191). We know from rabbinic sources that the *haberim*, or members of a *haburah*, practised special standards of tithing and ritual purity (e.g. *m. Dem.* 2.2–3; *t. Dem.* 2.2–3), the very things which according to the Synoptic Gospels were the prerogative of the Pharisees (e.g. Matt. 23.23–6; Mark 7.1–8; Luke 18.9–14; cf. Mark 2.16; Matt. 11:18–19; Luke 15.1–2). It seems likely, therefore, that at least some of the Pharisees around the time of Jesus were *haberim*, a conclusion which, given the link between pre-70 CE Pharisaism and rabbinic literature, is supported by the amount of discussion in the latter on associated matters.

74 Matt. 26.17–29/Mark 14.12–25/Luke 22.14–38/John 13.2–30; Matt. 8.15/Mark 1.31/Luke 4.39; Matt. 9.10/Mark 2.14; Matt. 15.1/Mark 7.1; Matt. 26.6-13/Mark 14.3–9; Luke 10.38–42; John 12.2–8; cf. Mark 16.4; Luke 24.13–35; 24.36–49; John 21.9–14.

75 Luke 7.36–50; 11.37–52; 14.1–14. Whether these passages reflect

Jesus' practice remains a matter of debate; in the light of Matt.15.1–20/ Mark 7.1–23, it is difficult to envisage how Jesus and the Pharisees could have shared the same table.

76  Matt. 9.10–11/Mark 2.15–16/Luke 5.29–30; Luke 19.1–10.

77  Matt. 14.13–21/Mark 6.30–44/Luke 9.10–17/John 6.1–14; Matt. 15.32–9/ Mark 8.1–10.

78  Both Marcus Borg (1998, pp. 88–134) and Bruce Chilton (1994, pp. 13–92) see the issue of purity as holding the key to many aspects of Jesus' ministry, including his practice of table-fellowship. Jesus celebrated the purity of all God's people and opposed attempts to use purity as a means of introducing sectarianism within Jewish faith.

79  See Dunn (1990), pp. 71–81.

80  E. P. Sanders (1983), pp. 5–36, and (1985), pp. 174–211; cf. Chilton (1988), pp. 1–18.

81  See the discussions of Chilton (1994); Fuchs (1964), pp. 219–28; Hofius (1967), pp. 16–26; L. T. Johnson (1998), pp. 137–79; Koenig (1985), pp. 15–51; Mackey (1979), pp. 142–59; Moloney (1997), pp. 1–150; and Riches (1980), pp. 105–9.

82  I have developed this line of thinking in Wallis (1992), pp. 42–5.

83  Bruce Chilton believes Jesus established through his table-fellowship a 'sacrifice of sharings' for all those whose purity was a function of their being born a Jew, rather than upon any additional requirements (1992), pp. 473–88, (1994), pp. 13–74, (1997), pp. 52–75.

84  On Jesus' understanding of the love commandment, see Chilton and McDonald (1987); Furnish (1973), pp. 22–69; A. E. Harvey (1990), esp. pp. 92–115; Klassen (1992b), pp. 385–9; and Schrage (1988), esp. pp. 68–87.

85  E. P. Sanders (1992), pp. 192–212. The Shema of rabbinic Judaism included Deut. 6.4–9; 11.13–21 and Num.15.37–41, together with additional morning and evening blessings (*m. Ber.* 1.1–4). Whether this was the recognized form in Jesus' time remains unclear.

86  Cf. 'The sabbath was made for humankind, and not humankind for the sabbath; so the Son of Man is lord even of the sabbath' (Mark 2.27–8). On Jesus' attitude to the law and its interpreters, see Banks (1975), Part 2, and Westerholm (1978) Part 2.

87  Charlesworth (1988), pp. 139–64.

88  Borg (1993), pp. 25–75; Chilton and McDonald (1987); Vermes (1993 and 1983).

89  Also Luke 13.10–17; 14.1–6; John 5.1–18; 7.23; 9.1–34; Mark 1.21–8/Luke 4.31–7; cf. Matt.12.1–8/Mark 2.23–8/Luke 6.1–5.

90  Cf. 'They were astounded at his teaching, for he taught them as one having authority, and not as the scribes' (Mark 1.22; Matt. 7.29/Luke 4.32); and 'They were all amazed, and they kept on asking one another, "What is this? A new teaching – with authority! He commands even the unclean spirits, and they obey him" ' (Mark 1.27/Luke 4.36; plus Matt. 9.6/Mark 2.10/Luke 5.24; Matt. 8.9/Luke 7.8). See also

the debate recorded in Matt. 21.23–7/Mark 11.27–31/Luke 20.1–8, where Jesus identifies himself with John the Baptist as one possessing charismatic rather than institutionalized authority.

91 Matt.19.16–30/Mark 10.17-31/Luke 18.18–30.

92 Cf. the aphorisms introduced with the saying (Matthaean?), 'You have heard that it was said . . .' (Matt. 5.21, 27, 33, 38, 43).

93 In addition to the works cited above, see the thorough discussion of Piper (1980).

94 Cf. Matt. 15.21–8/Mark 7.24–30; Matt. 8.5–13/Luke 7.1–10/John 4.46–54; John 4.1–26; contra Neusner and Chilton (1996), pp. 93–117.

95 See, especially, the writings of Bruce Chilton (e.g. 1979 and 1996).

96 See Meyer (1979), pp. 153–4; E. P. Sanders (1985), pp. 98–106; and N. T. Wright pp. 299–301.

97 Comparable forms of apprenticeship can be found within rabbinic schools as well as Hellenistic mimetic traditions revolving around figures such as Apollonius of Tyana. See Hengel (1981b), esp. pp. 16–37; Riesner (1984), esp. pp. 408–98; and Weder (1992), pp. 207–10.

98 For a detailed analysis of the relationship between the different versions (Mark 6.6b–13/Luke 9.1–6; Luke 10.1–16/Matt. 9.37–8; 10.7–16; 11.21–3; cf. Mark 3.13–19/Luke 6.12–16; Matt. 10.1–4) and a review of current scholarly thinking, see Catchpole (1993), pp. 151–88.

99 Matt. 17.16/Mark 9.18/Luke 9.40; Matt. 20.20–8/Mark 10.35–45; Mark 6.12-13/Luke 9.6; Mark 9.38/Luke 9.49; Mark 6.30; cf. Luke 10.17–20.

100 Hengel (1981b), esp. pp. 73–83; and Twelftree (1993), pp. 122–7.

101 The most comprehensive study of the changing significance of Jesus' table-fellowship, including the Last Supper, as witnessed in the New Testament literature is that of Bruce Chilton (1994), who identifies six phases. See also the 'double origin' theory championed by Hans Lietzmann and others (1979); cf. Fuller (1963), pp. 60–72; and Higgins (1952), pp. 56–63.

102 Although the Synoptic Gospels place the Last Supper at the time when the Passover meal was celebrated (Matt. 26.17/Mark 14:12/Luke 22.7), John's Gospel locates it 24 hours earlier (13.1; 18.28). None of the accounts mentions those symbolic foods essential for the Passover (e.g. lamb, bitter herbs) and it is highly improbable that Jesus would have encouraged fellow Jews to contemplate, let alone participate in, drinking blood.

103 'Quite outside the context of what became known as "the last supper", the practice of fellowship at meals within Jesus' movement in its formative period forged a link with the kingdom, such that the promise of God's final disclosure on behalf of his people was as ardently and carelessly anticipated as the next dinner . . . Within Jesus' movement, the bread which sustains us and the wine which rejoices us are taken as a foretaste and a warrant of the kingdom

which transforms us' (Chilton (1994), p. 39).

104 'The necessities of life are water, bread, and clothing, and also a house to assure privacy' (Ecclus. 29.21; also Gen. 21.14; Exod. 23.25; 34.28; Deut. 9.9, 18; 1 Sam. 25.11; 30.11–12; 1 Kings 18.4, 13; 22.27; 2 Chron. 18.26; Ezra 10.6; Neh. 9.15; 13.2; Job 3.24; 22.7; Ps. 78.20; Prov. 9.17; 25.21; Isa. 3.1; 30.20; Ezek. 4.16–17; 12.18–19; Hos. 2.5; Amos 8.11; 1 Esd. 9.2; 2 Esd. 15.58).

105 It should also be noted that the copula 'is' in 'this *is* my body/blood', although present in the Greek (*estin*), has no Aramaic equivalent.

106 'Only, you shall not eat flesh with its life, that is, its blood, (Gen. 9.4); 'For the life of the flesh is in the blood; and I have given it to you for making atonement for your lives on the altar; for, as life, it is the blood that makes atonement' (Lev. 17.11; also Lev. 6.27; Num.19.5; Deut. 32.42; Ps. 50.13; Isa. 49.26; Jer. 51.35; Ezek. 33.25; 39.17–18; Zeph. 1.17; Wisd.12.5; Ecclus.14.18; 17.31; 2 Esd. 15.58; 1 Macc. 7.17; 4 Macc. 6.6; 9.20; 10.8). It should be noted, however, that the Hebrew *basar* can mean either 'flesh' or 'body', although the context usually determines which is the most appropriate rendering; cf. 'When a woman has a discharge of blood that is her regular discharge from her *body*, she shall be in her impurity for seven days, and whoever touches her shall be unclean until the evening' (Lev. 15.19).

107 'Pleasant words are like a honeycomb, sweetness to the soul and health to the body' (Prov. 16.24; also Pss. 16.9; 31.9; Isa. 10.18; Mic. 6.7; Wisd. 1.4; 9.15; 2 Macc. 6.30; 15.30; 2 Esd. 5.14; 4 Macc.1.20, 28). Again, Jesus may have used this juxtaposition himself 'Do not fear those who kill the body but cannot kill the soul; rather fear him who can destroy both soul and body in hell' (Matt. 10.28).

108 Gen. 9.4; Deut.12.15–28; cf. 'I will make your oppressors eat their own flesh, and they shall be drunk with their own blood as with wine. Then all flesh shall know that I am the Lord your Saviour, and your Redeemer, the Mighty One of Jacob' (Isa. 49.26) 'Those who are in the mountains and highlands shall perish of hunger, and they shall eat their own flesh in hunger for bread and drink their own blood in thirst for water' (2 Esd. 15.58; Ezek. 33.25; 39.17–18; Wisd.12.5).

109 For references and technical discussions, see Behm (1965), pp. 735–7; Casey (1990), pp. 1–12; Gundy (1976), esp. pp. 3–23, 117–34; Schweizer (1971a), pp. 98–124, (1971b), pp. 1026, 1058–9, (1992), p. 768.

110 'The time is surely coming, says the Lord, when the one who ploughs shall overtake the one who reaps, and the treader of grapes the one who sows the seed; the mountains shall drip sweet wine, and all the hills shall flow with it' (Amos 9.13–14; also Jer. 31.12; Hos.14.7; *1 En.* 10.19; *2 Bar.* 29.5–6). See Brown (1981), p.105.

111 Matt. 9.14–17/Mark 2.18–22/Luke 5.33–9; John 2.1–11; Matt.11.19/ Luke 7.34.

112 'They devoted themselves to the apostles' teaching and fellowship, to

the breaking of bread and the prayers . . . Day by day, as they spent much time together in the temple, they broke bread at home and ate their food with glad and generous hearts' (Acts 2.42, 46; also Luke 24.30–1, 35).

113  E.g. Lietzmann (1969), pp. 56–9, 91–4; see also the discussion of Klauck (1993), pp. 67–9; and, more fully, Klauck (1986); and cf. Jeremias (1964), pp. 237–55.

114  See Chenderlin (1982).

115  For a similar line of thinking, see Stacey (1994), pp. 65–76.

116  'Now John's disciples and the Pharisees were fasting; and people came and said to him, "Why do John's disciples and the disciples of the Pharisees fast, but your disciples do not fast?" Jesus said to them, "The wedding guests cannot fast while the bridegroom is with them, can they? As long as they have the bridegroom with them, they cannot fast. The days will come when the bridegroom is taken away from them, and then they will fast on that day' (Mark 2.18–20).

# —5—

# Living the Legacy:
# The Early Years

In the previous three chapters, we attempted to demonstrate how the disciples possessed both the motivation and the resources to continue in the faith of Jesus after his death. A faith Jesus embodied himself and which was communicable to his followers precisely because it was embedded within a habitus of life:[1]

- an experience of forgiveness;
- a way of praying;
- a treasury of wisdom;
- an exposition of joyous living;
- a discipline of love;
- a vocation to pursue.

In brief, this is the substance of Jesus' legacy to his disciples and there is good reason to believe they embraced it. For one thing, they had already served some form of induction or apprenticeship. For another, Jesus specifically entrusted it to them when gathered for what has become known as the Last Supper. And, finally, maintaining the habitus of faith will have brought structure and direction to their mourning by providing a means of honouring Jesus and maintaining his significance in their lives. We should also remember that, more generally, deposits of faith will have been formed within those whom Jesus encountered during his life and ministry, those who were influenced by him even if they did not become his personal followers.

In response to Jesus' death, the disciples were also able to draw on a rich and creative tradition constituting their Jewish identity and inheritance. This furnished them with convictions relating to God's righteous martyrs which will have brought significance to Jesus' execution and helped them to articulate their hopes for him. For example, insights about how death can be redemptive or how God's covenantal love and passion for justice are not limited to this life, are likely to have been particularly formative within their reflections. Without question, Jesus' execution plunged his followers into a deep crisis where they discovered whether faith, rooted in their Jewish past and innovatively expounded by Jesus, was able to sustain them personally, maintain a common life and give expression to fresh initiatives of ministry in his name. We should not be surprised, therefore, to find the cross occupying a central place within Christian thought.[2] By drawing a line under Jesus' life, it precipitated assessments of him and of his contribution to our experience of God, together with creating an opportunity for his disciples to determine whether his embodiment of faith remained accessible to them and through them to others.

Whether the faith of Jesus and Jewish tradition were the only resources available to the disciples after the crucifixion or whether the resurrection narratives of the Gospels bear witness to an altogether independent impetus is beyond the scope of the present study. We have noted how phenomena similar to Jesus' post-mortem appearances can be precipitated by grief. Alternatively, the conviction that Jesus was raised from the dead could be an expression of, rather than a stimulus for, faith. What has become clearer, however, is that the faith of Jesus as outlined in the previous chapter, together with insights drawn from the Hebrew Scriptures and intertestamental literature discussed in Chapter 2, may have provided *a sufficient resource* for the disciples to interpret their grief, manage their mourning and sustain their ministry. At this juncture, it is important to remember where the significance of Jesus, both before and after his death, resided – namely, in a capacity to draw others into his experience of faith where they discovered new ways of perceiving themselves and relating to God, other people and creation. Furthermore, this *phenomenon of transferability*, as we have called it, was not mediated primarily through theological assessments about him, but through the opportunity to indwell a particular habitus which gave rise to a quality of human being exemplified by Jesus himself. It is in this sense that Jesus continued to be influential as his faith was remembered in the lives of his disciples and beyond.

This recognition is important because it identifies one of the major reasons why Jesus receives such exaltation and veneration after his death. Unlike Moses or David, he did not perform mighty acts of liberation which fundamentally changed the material fortunes of God's people en masse; what he did, however, was *mediate a particular experience of faith which enabled others to enjoy the blessings of God within the changing circumstances of life and, on the basis of this, to anticipate a glorious future within the fulfilment of God's purposes.* As more people came to share this experience and as those responsible for its communication sought to appreciate how the faith of one man could become accessible to many, so the enduring contribution of Jesus began to emerge.[3] The honouring of Jesus, which started during his life with those who found in him a source of blessing, and picked up new impetus in the grief of his closest followers, gathered momentum as, first, Jews and, then, Gentiles discovered for themselves the faith of Jesus. And with the growing impact of Jesus upon Jewish and Mediterranean life, the importance of being able to authenticate this habitus of faith in an appropriate way began to emerge – if it was no longer possible to be addressed by Jesus in person or by those who knew him, then he continued to demand attention as crucified Messiah, powerful Lord, Son of God, Word of the Father, Giver of the Spirit, and so forth.[4] Further, even the affirmations that God raised Jesus from the dead and enthroned him in the heavenly places can be understood as endorsements of his ministry and invitations to discover the difference he can make to life.

Our task in the following pages, then, is to establish whether the contours of Jesus' faith outlined in the previous chapter continued to make him accessible and a formative influence after his death. This undertaking should be distinguished from attempts to chart christological developments in the early church or to account for the many epiphenomena emerging out of the dissemination and continuing practice of Jesus' faith. We should also be prepared for variety in how particular components within the habitus were appropriated and expounded. For instance, we know the vitality of joyous living celebrated in shared meals remained a reliable conduit for communicating Jesus' experience of faith precisely because it gave rise to a rich and diverse spectrum of performance.

Paul supplies a fuller example of what we hope to demonstrate more generally. The apostle's relation to Jesus remains a matter of considerable debate[5] and we know that, on occasion, he protests his independence from Jesus' followers, citing Christ himself as his authority (e.g. Gal. 1.11–12, 16). Yet, at a more profound level, the faith of Jesus underpins his life and resources his ministry. Jesus becomes real for him in the *experience of forgiveness* on the Damascus road, an experience precipitated by his persecution of the disciples, when he finds the freedom and the capacity to become a follower of Christ.[6] Although Paul does not mention the *Lord's Prayer* in as many words, the filial orientation towards God communicated therein clearly informs his own spirituality and draws him into a way of relating to God and fellow believers which he traces back to Jesus himself (Rom. 8.12–17; Gal. 4.1–7). With respect to Jesus' *teaching*, things are more complex for, apart from an occasional citation or allusion,[7] the aphorisms and parables of the Gospels are largely absent from his writings. However, there are good grounds for maintaining that the foundations of Paul's theology (e.g. the righteousness of God, the dispensation of grace, life in the Spirit) resonate with Jesus' perception of the Kingdom.[8] In addition, it seems reasonable to assume he must have been familiar with Jesus' message and the practice of his ministry; otherwise, his violent opposition to Jesus and his followers becomes inexplicable.[9] The centrality of the *Lord's Supper* and, more generally, of hospitality and table-fellowship within the apostle's thinking are much easier to demonstrate,[10] as is his dependence upon Jesus' *law of love*.[11] Finally, Paul was convinced of his call to be a *servant and apostle of Jesus Christ*,[12] whom he sought to imitate and make known.[13] Hopefully, this helps to clarify what we mean when claiming that the characteristics of Jesus' faith supplied the matrix for defining his experience of God and the currency through which others came to participate within it. Let us, then, consider whether early Christian sources confirm this hypothesis. We shall focus on each characteristic of Jesus' faith in turn and explore how it contributes to the formation of a Christian identity.

## An Experience of Forgiveness

We noted in the previous chapter how Jesus trained a group of disciples to share his vocation, and presented evidence from the Gospels suggesting they were actively involved in this pursuit during his lifetime, presumably as part of their apprenticeship. The Last Supper signals the completion of their induction as Jesus formally entrusts his faith and commissions them to minister in his name. It is no coincidence, therefore, to find the disciples fulfilling their responsibilities after the crucifixion. From what we can gather they used a similar missionary strategy to Jesus himself, that is, through dynamic and convincing preaching, together with memorable acts of release, they generated opportunities for encounter. Encounters which, when interpreted as the powerful presence of God, mediated liberation, facilitated change and invited response.

Although the Acts of the Apostles presents a rather idealistically homogeneous and coherent picture of the spread of Jesus' faith in the years following the crucifixion, there is little reason to doubt that traditions of historical worth inform much of the author's presentation.[14] It is striking, therefore, how much emphasis is placed upon the apostles' preaching and performance of various kinds of healing and deliverance.[15] What is also interesting is how such initiatives are interpreted as manifestations of power drawing their significance from Jesus – *it is Jesus who continues his ministry through them*.[16] In this way, a continuity of experience of forgiveness, spanning the crucifixion, is established through spirited testimony, convincing exhortation and extraordinary happenings. For example, after the powerful preaching and disturbing occurrences of Pentecost, Peter draws the audience's attention to Jesus of Nazareth, a 'man attested . . . by God with deeds of power, wonders, and signs that God did through him' (Acts 2.22; cf. 10.37–8), as the authority for their actions. Similarly, when the apostle is challenged about his involvement in helping a crippled beggar to walk, he responds thus:

'Rulers of the people and elders, if we are questioned today because of a good deed done to someone who was sick and are asked how this man has been healed, let it be known to all of you, and to all the people of Israel, that this man is standing before you in good health by the name of Jesus Christ of Nazareth, whom you crucified, whom God raised from the dead . . . There is salvation in no one else, for there is no other name under heaven given among mortals by which we must be saved.' (Acts 4.8–10, 12)

This emphasis upon Jesus as the source and guarantor of the apostle's ministry is stressed throughout the Acts of the Apostles as well as in many of the apocryphal Acts, where the pursuits of Peter, Paul, Thomas and others are described in more detail and with greater poetic licence.[17] It is also noteworthy how often the experience of forgiveness occasions faith either in the recipient or amongst bystanders.[18] Equally important for our investigations are those cases where faith is identified as a vital component within the communication of forgiveness. It was Jesus who first drew attention to faith's potential in this respect and he may well have emphasized this dimension within his own ministry.[19] Understandably, therefore, those entrusted with his vocation would be expected to share his faith and so to be resourced to act in his name.[20] A particularly striking incidence of this is recorded in Acts 3, when Peter offers the following explanation for the healing of a crippled beggar outside the Jerusalem Temple: 'And by faith in his name, his name itself has made this man strong, whom you see and know; and the faith that is through Jesus has given him this perfect health in the presence of all of you' (Acts 3.16; cf. 3.1–10). This verse is notoriously difficult to translate,[21] but it does seem to reflect the conviction that Peter ministers forgiveness through the practice of Jesus' faith.

Confirmation for the strategic role of forgiveness within the ministry of Jesus' followers comes from the letters of Paul. From what we can gather, power-filled proclamation and demonstration of the gospel were central to his missionary work and, as with Jesus, provided an effective means of demanding attention and generating response. A number of his letters reflect how the recipient faith communities were established via these means (e.g. 1 Cor. 2.3–5; Gal. 3.5; 1 Thess. 1.5), whilst in Romans we find a more programmatic assessment:

> For I will not venture to speak of anything except what Christ has accomplished through me to win obedience from the Gentiles, by word and deed, by the power of signs and wonders, by the power of the Spirit of God, so that from Jerusalem and as far around as Illyricum I have fully proclaimed the good news of Christ. (Rom. 15.18–19)

In addition, Paul includes preaching, together with the performance of healings and other miraculous acts, among the gifts of Christ to his people, who constitute his bodily presence on earth (1 Cor. 12.9–10, 27–30; cf. 13.2).[22] Evidently, the issue was also critical in establishing his credentials as an apostle, a regular preoccupation for Paul. In one defence, he offers the following evidence: 'The signs of a true apostle were performed among you with utmost patience, signs and wonders and mighty works' (2 Cor. 12.12). Clearly, if Jesus and his first disciples ministered in this way, no less could be expected, or was forthcoming, from Christ's apostle to the Gentiles!

Another dimension to the ministry of forgiveness as we have defined it relates to *the rite of baptism*.[23] We noted earlier how Jesus was a disciple of John the Baptist and may have incorporated baptism within his own ministry. Certainly, it became an integral component within communicating the faith soon after his death – something easier to account for if his followers were simply continuing established practice. Before long, baptism was recognized as the authorized means of initiation into the Christian community, serving as a powerful rite of liberation through which candidates symbolically break free from the past and are given a fresh opportunity to see themselves differently within the love of God and the fellowship of those who share the faith of Jesus.[24] Thus, in Acts we find Jesus' followers not only preaching and performing powerful feats, but also baptizing in his name as part of their missionary initiatives.[25] The symbolic power of the baptismal ritual to effect forgiveness is particularly pronounced in Pauline thought where the apostle describes baptism as a dying to sin and the old self so that new life can emerge within the faith of Christ.[26] Such an understanding clearly imbues the baptismal act of full immersion, especially when experienced by those old enough to appreciate it, with transforming potential.

## A Way of Praying

We know from the *Didache*, an early manual of faith,[27] that the Lord's Prayer (8.2) was an essential component of Christian definition, at least in certain areas, by the end of the first century. As with its Jewish counterpart, the Eighteen Benedictions, the author commends it be recited three times each day (8.3), no doubt to encourage a particular discipline of prayer and theological orientation to life. The presence of the Lord's Prayer in Matthew and Luke (Matt. 6.9–13/ Luke 11.2–4), although strangely not in Mark, reinforces its currency within faith communities from an early stage.[28] The continuing impact of Jesus' contribution to prayer, however, is not simply a measure of the usage of this formulation, but whether the orientation towards God contained therein was translated into the experience of those who sought to follow him. Significantly, there are strong grounds for maintaining this was the case.

The Fourth Gospel does not include the Lord's Prayer in as many words, but there are clear indications that Jesus' way of relating to God and understanding of his place within God's purposes encapsulated therein were appropriated by and integrated within the practice of faith reflected in this document.[29] A number of the monologues peculiar to John expound in great detail the intimate and sympathetic relationship Jesus shared with God, which can be summed up in the declaration, 'The Father and I are one' (10.30).[30] A relationship of mutual indwelling from which Jesus draws his vitality and vocation (cf. 'My Father is still working, and I also am working', 5.17), and through which God becomes present and knowable (cf. 'Whoever has seen me has seen the Father', 14.9).[31] Here we discern a profound interpretation of the Lord's Prayer where the ministry of Jesus becomes the definition of God's will on earth and the exposition of what is realizable through entering into his way of relating to God. Furthermore, given that John portrays Jesus as inviting others to share in this relationship, we can assume it characterized Christian experience:[32]

'If you abide in me, and my words abide in you, ask for whatever you wish, and it will be done for you. My Father is glorified by this, that you bear much fruit and become my disciples. As the Father has loved me, so I have loved you; abide in my love. If you keep my commandments, you will abide in my love, just as I have kept my Father's commandments and abide in his love. I have said these things to you so that my joy may be in you, and that your joy may be complete.' (15.7–11; cf. also 14.12–17; 17.20)

Paul speaks of the same phenomenon from a different perspective. The apostle's orientation towards God was radically transformed by the happenings on the Damascus road, when in some profound sense God apprehended him through Christ. As we have suggested, this overwhelming experience of forgiveness, centring on a call to follow Christ and to share him with the Gentiles, underpins his theological reflections and informs his appreciation of the life of faith. Put simply, Christ becomes the one in whom opposites meet, where the righteous God of grace overwhelms human sinfulness with reconciling effect.[33] The cross constitutes for all time the ultimate expression of this drama of salvation, where Christ's obedience communicates not only God's unconditional love and covenantal faithfulness, but also embodies humanity's response (e.g. Rom. 3.21–6; Gal. 2.15–21). Thus, to encounter God is to encounter God in Christ and to respond to God is to be located within Christ's response to his heavenly Father.

The life of faith, therefore, is about being formed in Christ's image through the inspiration of the Spirit, who communicates his continuing presence (e.g. Rom. 8.1–17). It begins with forgiveness (e.g. 1 Cor. 2.1–5; Gal. 3.1–5). Through baptism, believers are located within the dispensation of grace, mediated by the cross (e.g. Rom. 6.1–14; Gal. 3.23–9), and within the community of faith they discover what it means to call God Father, come to appreciate the extent of his love, and become conversant with their privileges and responsibilities (e.g. Rom. 12.1—15.6; 1 Cor. 13—14). Further, as part of the community of faith, each person becomes an integral part of the re-forming or re-membering of Christ's body on earth through which he continues to minister (Rom. 12.3–8; 1 Cor. 12). In these and other ways, the apostle gives shape to his hope that the promise of God's authentic life realized in Jesus may be fulfilled in all people. As with the Fourth Gospel, we scan the letters of Paul in vain in search of the Lord's Prayer and yet the grammar of that prayer informs much of his own articulation of the faith of Christ:

> But when the fullness of time had come, God sent his Son, born of a woman, born under the law, in order to redeem those who were under the law, so that we might receive adoption as children. And because you are children, God has sent the Spirit of his Son into our hearts, crying, 'Abba! Father!' So you are no longer a slave but a child, and if a child then also an heir, through God. (Gal. 4.4–7; cf. also Rom. 8.9–17)

It appears this insight into faith as a means of living within the climate of Jesus' relationship with God, a relationship celebrated in the Lord's Prayer and finding expression throughout his ministry, was highly influential in the period following the crucifixion. We shall have cause to consider different aspects later; here, we simply observe how belief in Christ entailed far more than affirming convictions about him, but revolved around *embracing his habitus and living out of his legacy*. That is to say, *of being located within a matrix of resources, practices and perceptions embodied by Jesus and giving substance to discipleship*. This is one reason why John and Paul, among others, express such high expectations for Christian community. They recognized what Jesus perceived from an early stage, namely, that without lively and attractive expositions of the difference God makes to life, faith is reduced to abstract proposition or unfulfilled hope. The *Shepherd of Hermas*, a second century Christian work originating in Rome, speaks of faith as the principal foundation of the church and the only means of fulfilling her vocation (e.g. *Vis.* 3.8; *Sim.* 9.15). But such faith clearly extends far beyond a body of beliefs (cf. *Man.* 1.1) to include an orientation towards God and a discipline of life which, as we find in the Letter of James (cf. 2.14–26), translates the potentialities associated with living unto God exemplified by Jesus into the concrete experience of those who seek to share his way:

> 'So despise double-mindedness and overcome it in every case, putting on a faith that is strong and powerful, for faith promises all things, perfects all things. But double-mindedness, which does

not trust itself, fails in all that it does. So you see,' he said, 'that faith is from above, from the Lord, and has great power; but double-mindedness is an earthly spirit from the devil, which has no power. So serve faith, which has power, and refrain from double-mindedness, which has no power, and you will live to God and all who are so disposed will live to God.' (*Man.* 9; cf. also *Sim.* 6.1)

## A Treasury of Wisdom

One area where Jesus evidently made a considerable impact, at least in certain quarters, was in the practice of wisdom. We noted in Chapter 4 how wisdom was highly valued in the ancient world and we alluded to some of the expositions current in first-century Galilee. Scholarly opinion varies enormously over whether Jesus associated himself with a particular movement (e.g. Cynic, Essene, Pharisee) or attempted to conform to a particular stereotype (e.g. rabbi, Jewish charismatic, Hellenistic divine man). He must, however, have been aware that he offered an innovative interpretation of what it means to be a faithful Jew and, presumably, found himself in debate with exponents of alternative positions, both within and beyond Judaism. From what we can gather, Jesus was principally an itinerant preacher who, like the sower scattering seed across variegated terrain, was undiscerning about his audience, although the question of whether he reserved special instruction for his closest followers remains unresolved. Certainly, this proposal supplies one explanation for the origin of Jesus' monologues in the Fourth Gospel, so unlike the style of his public ministry in the Synoptics, and finds support elsewhere.[34]

The Gospels indicate Jesus had little difficulty attracting audiences.[35] Presumably, his reputation preceded him with an appeal to people from various backgrounds and outlooks. No doubt, many of those who listened made no formal commitment to his overall vision, but returned to their previous patterns of life, albeit richer for the insights gleaned. Others, however, may have found Jesus' wisdom to be sufficiently attractive and persuasive to make it a thoroughgoing pursuit. Some will have joined Jesus' entourage and travelled with him, although it is conceivable that his sayings and parables were also collected, remembered and practised by those whose circumstances or inclinations did not translate into this level of personal commitment.[36] Unlike other aspects of his habitus, Jesus' contribution to the search for wisdom is relatively free-standing in that it assumes no particular interpretative framework and is largely self-authenticating. For instance, the following random selection is valuable not because of who said them, but because of the insights they impart and the quality of life they inform for those who make them their own:

'Why do you see the speck in your neighbour's eye, but do not notice the log in your own eye? Or how can you say to your neighbour, "Friend, let me take out the speck in your eye", when you yourself do not see the log in your own eye? You hypocrite, first take the log out of your own eye, and then you will see clearly to take the speck out of your neighbour's eye.

'No good tree bears bad fruit, nor again does a bad tree bear good fruit; for each tree is known by its own fruit. Figs are not gathered from thorns, nor are grapes picked from a bramble bush. The good person out of the good treasure of the heart produces good, and the evil person out of evil treasure produces evil; for it is out of the abundance of the heart that the mouth speaks.' (Luke 6.41–5; cf. Matt. 7.3–5, 16–20; 12.33–5)

'It is impossible for a man to mount two horses, or to draw two bows. A servant cannot serve two masters; he will honour the one and scorn the other. No one drinks vintage wine and immediately wants to drink new wine; and new wine is not put into old wine skins lest they burst, and vintage wine is not poured into new wineskins lest it spoil. No one sews an old patch on to a new garment, because there will be a tear.' (*Gos. Thom.* 47; cf. Matt. 6.24/Luke 16.13; Matt. 9.16–17/Mark 2.21–2/Luke 5.36–9)

A particularly interesting area of New Testament research at present relates to the common material found in the Gospels of Matthew and Luke, but missing from Mark. Many scholars maintain these traditions reflect an earlier source, now referred to as Q,[37] which was used by the authors of the First and Third Gospels in addition to the Second.[38] This is a particularly significant hypothesis for our own investigations because Q consists largely of a collection of Jesus' sayings and parables without narrative framework or reference to most of the major events in his life.[39] If such a source existed then it bears witness to an interest in Jesus' sapiential legacy for its own sake and one which may have originated in his Galilean ministry. Furthermore, given Q did not drop from the sky, it must have emerged from a particular historical context, possibly a community or communities who discovered in Jesus' wisdom a radical embodiment of faith and one they found insightful and enriching.[40]

The discovery of the *Gospel of Thomas* in 1945 provided further evidence for the existence of faith communities drawing their inspiration principally from Jesus' wisdom.[41] A manuscript written in Coptic containing the full text was found within the so-called Gnostic Library at Nag Hammadi, Egypt. The *Gospel of Thomas* consists of 114 sayings or parables, many paralleled in the canonical Gospels or other New Testament documents, although others communicate a rather more esoteric form of wisdom. For example:[42]

> 'Blessed is he who existed before he was created. If you become my disciples and you hear my words, these stones shall serve you. For you have five trees in paradise which do not move in summer or winter and their leaves do not fall. Whoever knows them shall not taste death.' (19)

> 'When you make the two one, and when you make the inner as the outer and the outer as the inner and the upper as the lower, and when you make the male and the female into a single one, so that the male is not male and the female not female, when you make eyes in place of an eye, and a hand in place of a hand, and a foot in place of a foot, an image in place of an image, then you shall enter the kingdom.' (22b)

> 'I tell my mysteries to those who are worthy of my mysteries.' (62a)

Opinions vary over the value of the *Gospel of Thomas* as an independent source of information about Jesus.[43] The original is usually dated to the second century, but the author clearly draws on older sources. Whether the sayings paralleled elsewhere are more primitive in *Thomas* or whether those unique to the *Gospel* can be traced back to Jesus cannot be determined with any confidence, nor are these issues critical for our inquiries. What is relevant, however, is that at a time when the canonical Gospels were in circulation, emphasizing the importance of the crucifixion and expressing belief in his resurrection, at least some people continued to find in Jesus' wisdom a source of faith.

If the Q document and the *Gospel of Thomas* throw light on how Jesus' wisdom became a singular pursuit, then the canonical Gospels and the *Didache* indicate how this dimension of his faith was integrated with other vital components. We shall return to the former at the end of the chapter, but here we note how Jesus' teaching is represented in the latter. The *Didache* is probably our earliest extant Christian manual. Significantly, all the characteristics of Jesus' faith outlined in the previous chapter are represented in one form or another: forgiveness (baptism, 7), prayer (Lord's Prayer, 8), wisdom (ethical teaching, 1—6), joyous living (celebrating the eucharist, 9—10), love commandment (2), vocation (responsible/committed membership of God's people, 11—16). As far as wisdom is concerned, it is Jesus' ethical injunctions which are drawn upon to supply pre-baptismal instruction for those wishing to embrace Christian faith (1—6): 'There are two ways – one of life, and one of death. And there is a great difference between the two ways' (1.1; cf. Matt. 7.12–13; 1QS 3.18—4.25). Although pride of place is given to Jesus,[44] we also find teaching drawn from the Decalogue (Exod. 20.13–17) as well as from other biblical and intertestamental works. One of the striking characteristics about the *Didache* is the way in which Christian faith is presented as an 'orthopraxy' rather than an 'orthodoxy'. That is to say, faith is conceived fundamentally as a habitus of life finding its definition and inspiration in Jesus.

Before drawing this section to a close, a word needs to be said about Jesus' teaching and exhortations relating to imminent crisis precipitated by God's sovereign intervention. A number of the parables include this dimension of judgement,[45] although it seems likely that one reason why Jesus used this feature was to concentrate attention on the present as a time of choice and to encourage reorientation in life.[46] For instance, the parable of the sheep and the goats (Matt. 25.31–46) may not be a blueprint for what is to come, but a challenge to translate faith in God into practical service.[47] Yet elsewhere we do find apocalyptic sayings and timetables attributed to Jesus, including his expectation of forthcoming judgement at the hand of a Son of Man figure:[48]

> 'Those who are ashamed of me and of my words in this adulterous and sinful generation, of them the Son of Man will also be ashamed when he comes in the glory of his Father with the holy angels.' And he [Jesus] said to them, 'Truly I tell you, there are some standing here who will not taste death until they see that the kingdom of God has come with power.' (Mark 8.38—9.1)

Jesus may well have understood his death as strategic within the fulfilment of God's Kingdom in some way.[49] Further, we know that after the crucifixion his eschatological perspective was appropriated by his followers, who equated Jesus with the expected harbinger of the messianic age.[50] What is significant for us, however, is that although the delay of Christ's return and the realization of his vision must have been a source of disillusionment, they did not spell the end of the Jesus movement. Why? No doubt there are many reasons, but it must have something to do with *Jesus' habitus identified in the previous chapter which was capable of sustaining his disciples and enabling them to communicate his vision to others*. And although we find many theological interpretations of Jesus in the early church, what actually maintained his accessibility and enabled others to enter into his experience of God was the practice of his faith. This is surely the golden thread which cannot afford to be broken if faith is authentically to be rooted in the person of Jesus of Nazareth.

## An Exposition of Joyous Living

They devoted themselves to the apostles' teaching and fellowship, to the breaking of bread and the prayers. Awe came upon everyone, because many wonders and signs were being done by the apostles. All who believed were together and had all things in common; they would sell their possessions and goods and distribute the proceeds to all, as any had need. Day by day, as they spent much time together in the temple, they broke bread at home and ate their food with glad and generous hearts, praising God and having the goodwill of all the people. And day by day the Lord added to their number those who were being saved. (Acts 2.42–7)

The author of Acts supplies us with a profound cameo of life for Jesus' followers after the crucifixion. In certain respects, it seems rather artificial and unrealistic, although we know that many of these characteristics were practised or at least pursued within the early church.[51] The overall impression is one of joyous living where the faith of Jesus is communicated through the experience of forgiveness followed by participation in his common life – attending to wisdom, learning to pray, sharing in table-fellowship, embracing the discipline of love. Throughout the Hebrew Scriptures and beyond, joy is the disposition of blessedness associated with living in right relation to God and being in receipt of his bountiful goodness.[52] If mourning is the resultant condition of being cut off from God, then joy signals his presence and favour. As we have seen, Isaiah in particular draws on this association when portraying the end of the Babylonian exile as a return of joy:

> And the ransomed of the Lord shall return,
> and come to Zion with singing;
> everlasting joy shall be upon their heads;
> they shall obtain joy and gladness,
> and sorrow and sighing shall flee away.
> (Isa. 35.10/51.11)

> For you shall go out in joy,
> and be led back in peace;
> the mountains and the hills before you
> shall burst into song,
> and all the trees of the field shall clap their hands.
> (Isa. 55.12)

It is significant, therefore, how joy remains a defining characteristic within the Jesus movement after the crucifixion,[53] suggesting that the sense of being blessed by God associated with Jesus was not only sustained within those who knew him personally, but also capable of being mediated to those who subsequently came to share his faith. This *transference of joy* through adopting a particular habitus is captured succinctly in the farewell discourses of John's Gospel: 'If you keep my commandments, you will abide in my love, just as I have kept my Father's commandments and abide in his love. I have said these things to you so that my joy may be in you, and that your joy may be complete'(15.10–11; cf. 16.20–4; 17.13).

From what we can gather, hospitality remained a vital co-ordinate within joyous living as a tangible demonstration of God's acceptance and generosity.[54] As with Jesus, meals provided a suitable context for participation in God's blessings and surviving sources indicate a rich variety of performance.[55] Following Jesus' initiative, early celebrations included full meals, although this clearly caused problems in some quarters. Paul's Corinthian correspondence alerts us to at least two areas of concern.[56] First, excessive consumption could become a preoccupation at the expense of mutual support and fellowship. It appears that wealthy participants were looking after themselves without giving due consideration to their less fortunate brothers and sisters. In such cases, Paul maintains, the integrity of the celebration is compromised and the continuity with Christ's practice broken. As a result, the meal fails to embody the blessings associated with his presence: 'When you come together, it is not really to eat the Lord's supper. For when the time comes to eat, each of you goes ahead with your own supper, and one goes hungry and another becomes drunk' (1 Cor. 11.20–1; cf. 1 Cor. 11.33–4; 2 Pet. 2.13; Jude 12–13). A similar abuse may be reflected in the following passage from the *Shepherd of Hermas*, reflecting the situation in Rome during the middle of the second century:

> 'Now then listen to me and be at peace among yourselves, and be concerned for one another and help one another, and do not take the creation of God for yourselves alone, but share the gravy of life with those also who are in need. For by eating too much some are bringing on themselves illness in the flesh and are injuring their flesh; and the flesh of those who do not have food to eat is injured because there is not sufficient food and their body is wasting away. So this lack of community spirit is harmful to you who have and do not share with the needy.' (*Vis.* 3.9)

The second issue revolved around the provenance of the food consumed. As in Judaism prior to the fall of the Jerusalem Temple, sacrifice was a major part of religious observance for many Graeco-Roman cults.[57] In cases where the entire sacrifice was not consumed, the worshipper could opt to eat the remainder in the temple precincts or at home or, indeed, to sell it. The problem arose in Corinth over whether such food, presumably purchased from non-Christian sources, could be used in eucharistic celebrations. Paul maintains that, in principle, there is no difficulty, given the gods in whose honour the sacrifices were offered do not exist, but, in practice, personal freedom should be moderated by the sensibilities of others (1 Cor. 8.1–13; cf. also 10.23–33; Rom. 14.1–4). Later on in the letter, however, he returns to the subject and appears to reach the opposite conclusion, although the participation of Christians in sacrificial meals to other deities may be specifically in mind: 'No, I imply that what pagans sacrifice, they sacrifice to demons and not to God. I do not want you to be partners with demons. You cannot drink the cup of the Lord and the cup of demons. You cannot partake of the table of the Lord and the table of demons' (1 Cor. 10.20–1).[58] As we shall see shortly, Paul's attitude here reflects an important transition in the performance of Jesus' table-fellowship with the emphasis shifting from feasting together in reconciled communion to partaking of sacred food.

Paul's letter to the Galatians draws attention to another area of conflict which emerged when the faith of Jesus was embraced by Gentiles. We noted previously how one of the innovative features of Jesus' practice of table-fellowship was his willingness to eat with all Jews irrespective of their background or spiritual disposition. It is unclear whether he did or would have been willing to extend eucharistic hospitality to those outside the covenant. This issue soon became a source of division with recognition that Jesus' faith was accessible to all people whatever their nationality or culture. We know Paul established communities in Galatia where Gentiles embraced the habitus without becoming Jewish proselytes. However, other Jewish Christians, possibly under the direction of Jesus' brother James, took a different view, maintaining Jewishness was an integral component of Jesus' faith and not an optional extra. The controversy came to a head when Peter, who was visiting the area, withdrew from table-fellowship with Gentile Christians when a delegation of Jewish Christians arrived from Jerusalem (Gal. 2.11–14).[59] From what we can gather, this became a major dilemma for those responsible for Jesus' legacy of faith and one which caused division, although some sort of compromise appears to have been reached (Gal. 2.1–10; Acts 15.1–35).[60] Whether this enabled Gentile and Jewish Christians to eat together or whether it, in effect, established two integrities is unclear; what is sure is that practice will have continued to vary from area to area with communities appropriating this component of Jesus' habitus in different ways.

Paul alerts our attention to another major shift in eucharistic performance when in 1 Corinthians 11 he focuses on bread and wine as the principal communicators of Jesus' presence. Although the transition is not complete, we can discern here a movement away from the experience of blessing associated with continuing Jesus' practice of sharing meals together to a concentrating of Jesus' presence within foodstuffs, bread and wine, characteristic of his practice and, especially, of his last meal(s) of entrusting. This is evident both from his inclusion of the institution narrative (11.23–6) and from the following verses where he speaks of the effects of participation. Where the bread and wine are received worthily, Christ's presence is a source of blessing; where they are consumed unworthily, he brings judgement. But, either way, Christ is present (1 Cor. 11.27–34)!

A stronger sacramental understanding is attested in the Fourth Gospel.[61] Although the author draws out the meaning of the Last

Supper by replacing the narrative of institution with an exposition of service and commissioning of his disciples (13.1–35), he also uses Jesus' feeding of the multitude (6.1–15) as an occasion to present his or his community's appreciation of the eucharist (6.22–59). The identification of Jesus' presence with the bread and wine is unmistakable and conceived in essentially substantial and materialist terms, as participants find themselves feeding on Christ's flesh and blood:

> 'Very truly, I tell you, unless you eat the flesh of the Son of Man and drink his blood, you have no life in you. Those who eat my flesh and drink my blood have eternal life, and I will raise them up on the last day; for my flesh is true food and my blood is true drink. Those who eat my flesh and drink my blood abide in me, and I in them.' (John 6.53–6)

Bishop Ignatius of Antioch,[62] writing at the beginning of the second century, reflects a similar appropriation of Jesus' table-fellowship with the eucharistic bread and wine, presumably consumed outside of a conventional meal, becoming 'medicine of immortality, the antidote which results not in dying but in living forever in Jesus Christ' (*Eph.* 20.2). Elsewhere, he is even more explicit about the identification between Jesus' presence and the elements: 'I take no pleasure in the food of corruption or in the pleasures of this life. I desire the bread of God, which is the flesh of Jesus Christ (who was of the seed of David), and for drink I desire his blood, which is imperishable love.' (*Rom.* 7.3)[63]

The *Didache* reflects either two stages in development or two types of performance.[64] In one, emphasis is upon thanksgiving for a meal celebrated in Jesus' name and praying for the eucharistic communion to be a source of reconciliation (9). A number of the Gospel resurrection narratives resonate with this understanding (e.g. Luke 24.13–35; John 21.1–14). In the other, the focus shifts to the elements consumed with a corresponding concentrating of Jesus' presence: 'You, Almighty Master, created everything for your Name's sake; you have given food and drink to men for their pleasure, so that they might give you thanks. And to us you have graciously given spiritual food and drink, and life eternal through Jesus your Servant' (10.3).

One of the unfortunate implications of more sacramental performances of Jesus' exposition of joyous living embodied in table-fellowship was the tendency for the eucharist to be divorced from regular mealtimes and to be ritualized into a sacred feast. We see this particularly in the way baptism becomes a prerequisite for participation: 'But let no one eat or drink from your Eucharist except those who are baptized in the Lord's Name. For the Lord also has spoken concerning this: "Do not give what is holy to dogs"' (*Did.* 9.5).[65] With both Jews and Gentiles embracing the faith of Jesus, perhaps baptism was the only meaningful way of defining the people of God. However, it inevitably had the effect of transforming what in Jesus' hands was a celebration of divine generosity and forgiveness for all into a membership meal for the initiated – the very practice Jesus appeared to shun!

## A Discipline of Love

Love as an expression of faith did not originate with Jesus. It has a long pedigree, especially within Jewish tradition, originating in the conviction of being loved by God which, in turn, grew out of the perception of being blessed. God loves Abraham because he enjoys a long life, prosperity and a large family. God loves the descendants of Abraham enslaved in Egypt because of their deliverance from captivity and procurement of a homeland. Evidence of God's love can be discerned in the provision of food, in deliverance from enemies and premature death, in the birth of children, as well as in many other ways. Further, God's love was not conceived as random or indiscriminate, but reflecting a predilection towards a particular group who were the beneficiaries of divine favour. This special relationship is conceived in terms of a covenant between God and a chosen people, where love prescribes the contribution of both parties. Within Jewish faith, therefore, love of God and love of humanity become expressions of covenantal fidelity. For this reason, love is often equated with obedience to God's will, where God's will is defined in Torah, discerned through the pursuit of wisdom or declared by the prophets.

We noted in the previous chapter that Jesus' legacy in relation to love resides principally in the area of *motivation*. This is not to underestimate the importance of obedience within his faith or of innovative interpretations of existing canons of covenantal fidelity, but to recognize that his personal experience of being blessed by God was itself an authority for informing behaviour and formulating response. Put simply, although Jesus was trained in the discipline of loving God through studying Torah, wisdom and prophetic traditions, participation in family and community life, and so forth, his own sense of God's presence and purposes constituted an alternative source of inspiration. Jesus is remembered as one who did not need to be told what it means to love God.

From an early stage, therefore, not only is the centrality of love confirmed within the Christian way,[66] but, more significantly, *Jesus is established as an authority for mediating relationship between God and humanity, defining what it means both to be loved by God and to respond to that love.* We see this especially in the Johannine literature where Jesus embodies the effects and potential of this way of being:

> 'As the Father has loved me, so I have loved you; abide in my love. If you keep my commandments, you will abide in my love, just as I have kept my Father's commandments and abide in his love . . . This is my commandment, that you love one another as I have loved you.' (John 15.9–10, 12)

> Beloved, let us love one another, because love is from God; everyone who loves is born of God and knows God. Whoever does not love does not know God, for God is love. God's love was revealed among us in this way: God sent his only Son into the world so that we might live through him. In this is love, not that we loved God but that he loved us and sent his Son to be the atoning sacrifice for our sins. Beloved, since God loved us so much, we also ought to love one another. No one has ever seen God; if we love one another, God lives in us, and his love is perfected in us.

> By this we know that we abide in him and he in us, because he has given us of his Spirit. (1 John 4.7–13)

What is remarkable here is the *christologizing of love* in which a fundamental religious currency is revalued in terms of Jesus' faith. This is surely the innovative contribution within the 'new' commandment (John 13.34; cf. 1 John 2.7; 2 John 5) emerging from his ministry, namely, that love finds its fullest exposition in a particular dynamic of human being in relation to God, rather than in a set of prescriptions of what God requires.[67] Further, and in certain respects more noteworthy, is the recognition that this dynamic was itself communicable – defining faith and informing discipleship. We find this again in the letter to the Ephesians when the author prays for those in his care, saying: 'I pray that . . . Christ may dwell in your hearts through faith, as you are being rooted and grounded in love. I pray that you may have the power . . . to know the love of Christ that surpasses knowledge, so that you may be filled with all the fullness of God' (Eph. 3.16–19). If the legacy of Moses' relationship with God was encapsulated in the Ten Commandments, then Jesus' was understood as an *opportunity to experience God in a particular way*. A way soon found to be independent of Jewish structures delimiting divine-human encounter (e.g. Torah, Temple, etc.)[68] and, as a result, transferable across religious and cultural boundaries.

Another implication of this development was a growing *hypostasization* of love as this quality, embodied in Jesus and shared by others, is perceived as a discrete entity. Rather than being equated principally with the fulfilment of covenantal obligations or codified in some other way, love is considered to possess her own anatomy and autonomy, giving access to Jesus' experience of God.[69] The clearest example of this is the great hymn to love in 1 Corinthians 13. In the previous chapter, Paul explains how the faith of Jesus continues to be embodied through the exercise of those giftings finding their correlate and significance in his ministry (1 Cor. 12.1–11). He goes on to claim that by this means Jesus' presence is re-membered within the Christian community: 'Now you are the body of Christ and individually members of it. And God has appointed in the church first apostles, second prophets, third teachers; then deeds of power, then gifts of healing, forms of assistance, forms of leadership, various kinds of tongues' (1 Cor. 12.27–8). We shall consider the role of the Spirit in this process later, but what is equally striking is the way Paul describes love as the source of inspiration indwelling the practice of faith with transforming effect (cf. 1 Cor. 13.1–3):

> Love is patient; love is kind; love is not envious or boastful or arrogant or rude. It does not insist on its own way; it is not irritable or resentful; it does not rejoice in wrongdoing, but rejoices in the truth. It bears all things, believes all things, hopes all things, endures all things. (13.4–7)

It appears love, no less than spiritual gifts, is capable of pursuit (1 Cor. 14.1) and an essential requisite for full participation within an experience of God defined by Jesus Christ. Unlike other passages where the apostle offers the cross as the ultimate expression of Christ's love (e.g. Rom. 5.1–11; 8.31–9; 2 Cor. 5.14–15; Gal. 2.20), here it is the dynamics and capacities of love that find their definitive exposition in Jesus. Paul alludes to the dispositional effects of sharing in Christ's love elsewhere (e.g. Gal. 5.22; 1 Thess. 5.8; Col. 3.14) and, in the Pastoral Epistles, the apostle's own life-changing encounter with Christ on the Damascus road is explained in terms of being overwhelmed by his faith and love:

> I am grateful to Christ Jesus our Lord, who has strengthened me, because he judged me faithful and appointed me to his service, even though I was formerly a blasphemer, a persecutor, and a man of violence. But I received mercy because I had acted ignorantly in unbelief, and the grace of our Lord overflowed for me with the faith and love that are in Christ Jesus. (1 Tim. 1.12–14)[70]

Ignatius of Antioch similarly understands love, often in association with faith, as the medium linking believers with Jesus and facilitating participation in his relationship with God. We noted in the previous section how the bishop's sacramental understanding of the eucharist enabled him to speak of sharing in the bread and wine as sharing not only in Jesus' flesh and blood, but also in his love (and faith).[71] Consider also his purpose for writing to the Christians in Magnesia, near Ephesus, where union with God comes through being drawn into the lively communion between Jesus and the Father, characterized by faith and love:

> For being judged worthy of a most godly name, in the bonds which I bear I sing of the churches and I pray that in them there may be a union of the flesh and spirit of Jesus Christ, our life forever; of faith and love, to which nothing is preferable; and most important – of Jesus and the Father. If in him we endure the whole evil treatment of the prince of this age, and escape, we shall attain to God. (*Mag.* 1.2–3)[72]

Predictably, and somewhat in contrast to his practice, we also find Jesus providing the basis for a Christian morality where the discipline of love is prescribed in terms of particular attitudes or patterns of behaviour:[73]

> Husbands, love your wives, just as Christ loved the church and gave himself up for her, in order to make her holy by cleansing her with the washing of water by the word, so as to present the church to himself in splendour, without a spot or wrinkle or anything of the kind – yes, so that she may be holy and without blemish. (Eph. 5:25–7; cf. 5.21—6.9)

It was, perhaps, inevitable that Jesus' contribution to what it means to love God and humanity would come to be understood in these terms, as the foundations for a new Torah for all God's people.[74]

However, there is ample evidence to suggest that love was also experienced as a dynamic phenomenon informing a spirituality characteristic of Jesus' own practice of faith and resourcing fresh embodiments.

## A Vocation to Pursue

One of the observations made in the previous chapter is that Jesus inducted his closest disciples in the habitus of faith until a point, now associated with his death, when he entrusted that faith, embodying his vocation and encapsulating his vision of the Kingdom, into their hands. We noted how this entrusting, while bringing form and direction to their grief, will have placed a burden of responsibility, even of obligation, upon his followers to continue in his pattern of life and ministry. It is no surprise, therefore, to find evidence in early Christian sources of Jesus being portrayed as an exemplar, worthy of imitation.[75] What is more, it is not simply Jesus who performs this paradigmatic function – a measure of the transferability of his faith:

I [i.e. Paul] appeal to you, then, be imitators of me. (1 Cor. 4.16)

Be imitators of me, as I am of Christ. (1 Cor. 11.1)

Brothers and sisters, join in imitating me, and observe those who live according to the example you have in us. (Phil. 3.17)

And you became imitators of us and of the Lord, for in spite of persecution you received the word with joy inspired by the Holy Spirit, so that you became an example to all the believers in Macedonia and in Achaia. (1 Thess. 1.6–7; cf. 2.14)

For you yourselves know how you ought to imitate us . . . but in order to give you an example to imitate. (2 Thess. 3.7, 9)[76]

These passages alert us to an important insight concerning the way faith continued to be conceived and communicated in the early years after the crucifixion: *It was embodied in lives rather than defined in creeds, with continuity flowing from assimilation through imitation as the habitus was performed, appropriated and indwelt.* The source of this faith could even be traced back beyond Jesus to God, suggesting the divine origin of its form and practice – 'Be imitators of Jesus Christ, as he himself is of his Father' (Ignatius, *Phil.* 7.2; also Eph. 5.1–2; Ignatius, *Eph.* 1.1; 10.1–3; *Trall.* 1.2)[77]

Consider also this profound passage from the *Epistle of Barnabas*, written towards the beginning of the second century, in which the author likens the life of the believer to a temple needing to be inhabited by the lively presence of God:

> The word of his faith, the invitation of his promise, the wisdom of his righteous ordinances, the commandments of his teaching; himself prophesying in us, himself dwelling in us – by opening for us the door of the Temple, which is the mouth, and giving us repentance, he leads those who had been in bondage to death into the incorruptible Temple. For he who longs to be saved looks not to the (external) man, but to him who dwells in him and speaks in him, and he is amazed at the fact that he never either had heard him speak such words from his mouth nor had himself ever desired to hear (them)! This is a pneumatic Temple built for the Lord! (16.9–10)

Without question, however, it is the onset or prospect of oppression that generates most interest in Jesus as exemplar.[78] Clearly, the stakes are raised when faith requires not only a change in lifestyle but also a readiness to suffer for the name of Christ. In such circumstances, as we recognized in relation to Jesus' death, there is an urgent need to invest adverse conditions with meaning and significance. One of the most effective means of responding to this challenge was *to interpret suffering sustained on account of faith as in some sense a fulfilment of Jesus' vocation.* Paul, for instance, speaks of sharing in the sufferings of Christ both as a prerequisite for his own salvation (e.g. Rom. 8.17–18; Phil. 3.10; cf. Acts 9.16) and as a consequence of fulfilling his apostolic commission (e.g. 2 Cor. 1.5–7; cf. Col.1.24).[79]

A number of New Testament documents addressing oppressed communities develop the paradigmatic quality of Jesus' faith in a more explicit way. The Epistle to the Hebrews presents Jesus as the great exemplar,[80] standing at the head of faith's roll of honour:

> Therefore, since we are surrounded by so great a cloud of witnesses, let us also lay aside every weight and the sin that clings so closely, and let us run with perseverance the race that is set before us, looking to Jesus the pioneer and perfecter of [our] faith, who for the sake of the joy that was set before him endured the cross, disregarding its shame, and has taken his seat at the right hand of the throne of God. Consider him who endured such hostility

against himself from sinners, so that you may not grow weary or lose heart. (12.1–3)[81]

Earlier in the letter, the author establishes Jesus' credentials as one who was every bit as vulnerable to temptation and persecution as his readers (2.5–18; 5.7–10), but who remained faithful to God's way and was crowned with the prize of eternal life (4.14—5.10). Although Jesus performs a unique function within salvation, having become God's archetypal intercessor (i.e. high-priest: 7.26—10.18), his life remains both the benchmark for faith and the inspiration for those who seek to follow in his footsteps, especially when passing through testing times (3.14; 4.15–16; 10.19–39; 12.3–13). Interestingly, the author also offers the leaders of the community as worthy of emulation: 'Remember your leaders, those who spoke the word of God to you; consider the outcome of their way of life, and imitate their faith' (13.7; cf. 6.12).[82]

Likewise, the First Letter of Peter draws attention to Jesus as one whose own experience establishes suffering as an essential component within the fulfilment of his vocation and constitutes the definitive example for those seeking to share his faith.[83] In a similar fashion to Hebrews, the motivation for forbearance is not simply fidelity to Jesus' own ministry (4.1–2), but also the prospect of participating in his salvation (1.6–9; 4.13). These insights evidently inform much of the author's exhortation to the community as a whole, although they find clearest expression in relation to slavery, where their application now seems morally questionable:

> Slaves, accept the authority of your masters with all deference, not only those who are kind and gentle but also those who are harsh. For it is a credit to you if, being aware of God, you endure pain while suffering unjustly. If you endure when you are beaten for doing wrong, what credit is that? But if you endure when you do right and suffer for it, you have God's approval. For to this you have been called, because Christ also suffered for you, leaving you an example, so that you should follow in his steps. (1 Peter 2.18–21)

It may well be the case that the faith of Jesus demonstrated in the face of suffering and persecution also supplies a source of encouragement and challenge for the Christians addressed in the Revelation to John.[84] The author claims the authority of 'Jesus Christ, the faithful witness' (1.5) for his work, where 'faithful witness' would have been understood as 'martyr of the faith'. In Revelation 2, the Christians in Pergamum, of the Roman province of Asia, are praised for their faithfulness in the face of opposition, presumably, emanating from the practice of the cult of the emperor or some Greek deity (e.g. Zeus): 'I know where you are living, where Satan's throne is. Yet you are holding fast to my name, and you did not deny my faith even in the days of Antipas my witness, my faithful one, who was killed among you, where Satan lives' (2.13).[85] Later on, we find 'a call for the endurance of the saints, those who keep the commandments of God and hold fast to the faith of Jesus' (14.12). Given the centrality of Jesus' sacrificial death, symbolically referred to as the slaughter of the Lamb (e.g. 5.6–14; 7.9–17), there can be little doubt that his faith, tested and found secure on the cross, was held up as worthy of emulation.[86] Consider the following descriptions of Christian martyrs: 'These are they who have come out of the great ordeal; they have washed their robes and made them white in the blood of the Lamb' (7.14); and, 'But they have conquered him by the blood of the Lamb and by the word of their testimony, for they did not cling to life even in the face of death' (12.11).

Finally, bishop Polycarp of Smyrna in Asia, writing at the beginning of the second century to the Christians in Philippi, once again places great emphasis upon sharing in Christ's vocation and following his example when the practice of faith occasions adversity:

> Let us persevere, then, constantly in our hope and the pledge of our righteousness, which is Christ Jesus, who 'bore our sins in his own body on the cross', 'who did no sin, nor was any deceit found in his mouth'; but he endured all things for us that we might live in him. Let us be imitators, then, of his endurance, and if we suffer for his name, let us glorify him. For this is the 'example' which he set in himself; and this we learned to believe . . . Stand firm, then, in these things and follow the example of the Lord, strong in the faith and immoveable, affectionate to the brotherhood, devoted to one another, united in the truth, serving one another with the gentleness of the Lord, despising no man. (Polycarp, *Phil.* 8, 10)

Significantly, Polycarp's own martyrdom became a source of inspiration: 'For him we worship as the Son of God; but the martyrs we love as disciples and imitators of the Lord, as they deserve because of their incomparable loyalty to their own King and Teacher. May it also be granted us to become their partners and fellow disciples'

(*Mart. Pol.* 17.3; also 19; 22). In this way, the faith entrusted by Jesus to his first disciples is made more generally accessible through a process of 'imitation – embodiment – imitation', giving rise to communities rooted in the vocation of Jesus, committed to his vision, and hopeful of sharing his future when the wine of the Kingdom would be enjoyed in communion once more.

## Gospel and Spirit

So far in this chapter we have attempted to offer a brief overview of how the principal characteristics of Jesus' faith continued to sustain his followers and provide a means of maintaining his significance and accessibility. As we would expect, not all components of this generative core are equally significant for fresh embodiments. There is also evidence of considerable re-articulation and embellishment, together with the forming of trajectories,[87] as existing performances give rise to new ones. The challenge of communicating forgiveness, the potential of relating to God as Father, the vitality of wisdom, the contours of joyous living, the dynamics of loving, the meaning of vocation. The creative possibilities of each of these dimensions is considerable, but together they constitute a nucleus possessing significant capacity for communicating the faith of Jesus across delimitations of culture, class, gender and creed.

One of the most effective means of doing this proved to be the *gospel genre*. As we noted earlier, one impetus leading to their formation can be traced back to the grief of Jesus' earliest followers and their need to continue the ministry he entrusted to them. Our concern here is not to give an account of how they came into being, but simply to reflect a little more upon their purpose. Two presuppositions relevant to our investigations have been influential in the study of the Gospels during the second half of this century. The first concerns Jesus' relation to faith and the conviction that it was the resurrection or, if distinguishable, the birth of the Christian proclamation (*kerygma*) which established his theological credentials.[88] Before then, he was a Galilean Jew – afterwards he becomes God's unique mediator who is worthy of belief and veneration. Within this scenario, traditions about Jesus only become significant for faith in as much as they reflect his elevated status and, for this reason, the Gospels need to be interpreted as Easter creations telling us much more about how Jesus came to be understood than about his earthly life and ministry. Although not without its advocates, the foundations of this approach have been gradually undermined in recent decades by developments in our appreciation of Jesus as a first-century Palestinian Jew and our recognition of the biographical character of the Gospels.[89] We simply need to note here that our own findings lend support to this revisioning process, for if Jesus was remembered primarily because he embodied a particular expression of faith, and one others came to share through personal encounters with him, then the Gospels represent an attempt to maintain accessibility, both to Jesus and to his faith. Indeed, perhaps we can venture further and claim that the Gospels, rather than being products of resurrection faith, *reflect a faith that 'resurrects' Jesus as an expression of his continuing influence.*

The second presupposition relates to readership. The rise of redaction criticism in the 1950s shifted attention on to the contribution of the Evangelists in the process of Gospel production with the recognition that their choice and presentation of material, together with editorial comments, reflect the circumstances of particular Christian communities and the issues they were facing.[90] One implication of this development was that the Gospels came to be seen as occasional literature, comparable to the letters of the New Testament, written for specific church situations. Recently, however, this conclusion has been challenged on the basis of comparisons of the Gospels with distribution and readership patterns of similar contemporary literature, a growing appreciation of the means and extent of communication in the world of early Christianity, and recognition that the Evangelists themselves were probably itinerant ministers and not leaders of Christian communities.[91] All this suggests the Gospels, while reflecting the dynamics of particular church situations, were written for a broader circulation in order to communicate the story of Jesus as extensively as possible. Our own assessments of the Gospels as attempts to draw together the different strands of Jesus' faith in such a way as to ensure accessibility and commend consideration add further support to this re-evaluation.

There is one final matter we must consider before drawing this part of our study to a close. To date, almost nothing has been said about the *contribution of the Spirit* within the habitus of faith practised by Jesus and his successors. It is, of course, remarkably difficult to evaluate the contribution of such a phenomenon, but some attempt must be made to account for what is identified by many early Christian writers as the essential medium for God's powerful presence and principal resource for faith-filled living.[92] For instance, the Spirit of God empowers Jesus' ministry (e.g. Matt. 3.16/Mark 1.10/Luke 3.21–2; John 1.32–3; Matt. 12.28; Luke 4.14, 18; 10.21; Acts 10.38), raises him from the dead (e.g. Rom. 1.4; 8.11), is outpoured upon his followers at Pentecost (Acts 2.1–4), equips believers for discipleship (e.g. 1 Cor. 12.1–11) and draws them into the experience of Christian community and worship (e.g. Rom. 8.9; 1 Cor. 12.3, 12–13; 1 John 4.2). The key issue for our investigations is how the Spirit relates to the habitus of faith outlined above. Put simply, does the Spirit give rise to the practice of faith, or does the practice of faith nurture an empathy towards the Spirit, if not engender spiritual presence?

I am aware that the theological implications raised by this dichotomy reverberate through many of the great debates of the first Christian centuries, not least the question of whether faith is a gift from God or an expression of human volition.[93] However, if we take our lead from the earliest sources then priority does appear to rest with the habitus of faith. For instance, it is as Jesus participates in John's repentance movement by undergoing baptism that he is empowered by the Spirit. The Spirit comes upon Jesus' disciples sometime after they have adopted and been inducted in his pattern of faith. Further, it is as the accessibility of Jesus is maintained through the practice of the different components of his faith that the Spirit becomes manifest. We see this as the experience of forgiveness is communicated through preaching, acts of release and baptism (e.g. Acts 2.14–42; 9.1–19; Gal. 3.1–5; Eph: 1.13–14; 1 Thess. 1.4–5; Heb. 2.3–4). Similarly, the presence of the Spirit becomes real through participating in Jesus' practice of prayer (e.g. Rom. 8.14–17, 26–7), reflecting on his wisdom (e.g. John 14.25–6; 16.12–13; 1 Cor. 2.11–16), enjoying the fellowship of his people (e.g. Acts 2.37–47; 13.48–52; Rom. 15.7–13; 1 Thess. 1.6–7), adopting his discipline of love (e.g. John 14.15—16.24; 1 John 3.24) and embracing his vocation (e.g. John 20.19–23; Acts 2.1–4; 1 Cor.12.1–30; Eph. 4.1–16; 6.10–20). It seems, therefore, that *the Spirit inhabits the habitus of faith within a dynamic and dialectical relation in which practice feeds presence and presence inspires practice.*

This helps to explain why the Spirit comes to be intimately related to Jesus. If the Spirit communicates divine presence and if Jesus' faith gives access to a particular experience of God, then the defining of the former in terms of the latter suggests Jesus' experience of God continued to characterize those who shared his faith. This is surely what the author of the Fourth Gospel wishes to convey when he speaks of the Spirit as the one who keeps Jesus alive and accessible.

'I have said these things to you while I am still with you. But the Advocate, the Holy Spirit, whom the Father will send in my name, will teach you everything, and remind you of all that I have said to you . . . I still have many things to say to you, but you cannot bear them now. When the Spirit of truth comes, he will guide you into all the truth; for he will not speak on his own, but will speak whatever he hears, and he will declare to you the things that are to come. He will glorify me, because he will take what is mine and declare it to you. All that the Father has is mine. For this reason I said that he will take what is mine and declare it to you. (John 14.25–6; 16.12–15)[94]

Paul can also speak of Jesus Christ as the one who interprets and mediates the Spirit.[95] He refers to him as the 'last Adam . . . a life-giving spirit' (1 Cor.15.45), who is the template for the Spirit's transforming work in the life of the believer (2 Cor. 3.18; 4.4). Elsewhere, the Spirit of God is equated with the Spirit of Christ (Rom. 8.9) with the latter communicating Jesus' filial consciousness of God (Gal. 4.6) and strengthening the life of faith (Phil. 1.19).

In conclusion, perhaps we can speak of the Spirit as *the interior life of the habitus, the enlivening presence permeating the performance of the various expressions of faith and imbuing them with an intensity, quality and power that find their correlate in Jesus.*

## NOTES

1 The term 'habitus' has been borrowed from Pierre Bourdieu (1977), esp. pp. 72–95; and has been used to good effect by David Ford, especially in his treatment of the eucharist: see Ford (1995), pp. 359–81, and now (1999), pp. 137–65.
2 Daly (1978); Hengel (1981a); and S. K. Williams (1975); see also the major survey in Grayston (1990).
3 On how Jesus' mediating role of communicating the blessings of God led to his veneration and to his being intimately associated with God, see Bauckham (1992b), pp. 812–19; Hurtado (1988), and (1998), pp. 3–26; also Casey (1991).
4 On the development and significance of the different titles attributed to Jesus, see Hahn (1969); also Cullmann (1963); and Dunn (1980).
5 See Dunn (1998), pp. 182–206, 649–58, and the literature cited there.

Wenham (1995) presents a comprehensive case for Paul's dependence upon Jesus.

6 1 Cor.15.9; Gal. 1.13; Phil. 3.6; cf. Acts 9.1–5; 22.3–9; 26.9–16; see Gaventa (1986), pp. 52–95. On the centrality of Paul's 'Damascus road experience' for his ministry, see Dunn (1990), pp. 89–107; Dupont (1970), pp. 176–94; Kim (1981), pp. 269–311; and E. P. Sanders (1977), pp. 447–523.

7 E.g. Rom. 12.14 (Matt. 5.44; Luke 6.27–8); Rom.12.17 and 1 Thess. 5.15 (Matt. 5.38–48; Luke 6.27–36); Rom.13.7 (Mark 12.17); Rom.14.13 (Mark 9.42); Rom. 14.14 (Mark 7.15); 1 Cor.11.23–6 (Matt. 26.26–9; Mark 14.22–5: Luke 22.15–20); 1 Cor.13.2 (Matt.17.20); 1 Thess. 5.2, 4 (Matt. 24.43); 1 Thess. 5.13 (Mark 9.50); cf. 1 Cor. 7.10; 9.14. In addition to the works of Dunn and Wenham cited above, see Dungan (1971).

8 Especially, Wenham (1995), pp. 34–103.

9 Hengel with Deines (1991), pp. 63–86.

10 Rom.12.13; 1 Cor. 10.14–33; 11.17–34; 12.1–31; Gal. 2.9–14.

11 Rom. 12.9–10; 13.8–10; 1 Cor. 13.1–13; Gal. 5.6, 13–15; Phil. 1.9; 1 Thess. 4.9–10; cf. Eph. 4.15–16; Col. 3.14.

12 Rom. 1.1; 1 Cor. 1.1; 4.1; 2 Cor. 1.1; Gal. 1.1, 10; Phil. 1.1; Tit. 1.1; cf. Eph. 1.1; Col. 1.1 .

13 1 Cor. 11.1; Phil. 3.10; 1 Thess. 1.6.

14 Assessments of the historical value of Acts vary considerably. Hengel (1979) offers a judicious assessment; see also the more sceptical evaluation of Lüdemann (1989). The genre analysis of Palmer (1993), pp. 1–29, adds credibility to the work as a source for earliest Christianity.

15 On the content of apostolic preaching and teaching, see Dodd (1936); Dunn (1977), pp. 11–32; and McDonald (1980). A convenient summary of the miracle traditions in Acts is provided by Neirynck (1979), pp. 169–213; more detailed assessments are supplied by Kanda (1973); and M. H. Miller (1971).

16 Dunn (1975), esp. pp. 157–96.

17 Preaching and acts of forgiveness are often performed 'in the name of Jesus' (e.g. Acts 3.6, 16; 4.30; 9.27–8; 16.18; also *Acts John* 83; *Acts Pet.* 11: *Acts Thom.* 33; 41; 53; 75; cf. Irenaeus, *Haer.* II.32; Justin Martyr, *Dial.* 33; *Apol II* 6; Origen, *Contra Celsum* I.67; II.33; III.24, 28; Tertullian, *Apol.* 23) or draw their authority from him in some other way (e.g. Mark 16.17–20; John 14.12–13; Acts 4.9–12; 16.18; *Acts John* 22; *Acts Pet.*15; 16; 26; *Acts Thom.* 59; 141; Eusebius, *Hist. Eccl.* 2.3). See Achtemeier (1976), pp. 149–86; and Dunn (1975), pp. 163–7.

18 Acts 9.36–43; 13.12; 16.25–34; 19.11–20; also *Acts John* 33; 39; 93; *Acts Pet.* 2; 4; 11; 17; 23–4; *Acts Paul* 37–43; *Acts Thom.* 36–8; 59; cf. Mark 16.15–18; John 2.11, 23; 4.35; 7.31; 20.30–1.

19 Matt. 21.21–2; Mark 11.22–4; Luke 17.6; cf.1 Cor 13.2; also the saying of Jesus most repeated in the Gospels, 'Your faith has made you well/ saved you' (Matt. 9.22/Mark 5.34/Luke 8.48; Mark 10.52/Luke 18.42;

Luke 7.50; 17.19). The tradition about the healing of the paralysed boy is particularly insightful here, both for what it tells us about the disciples' apprenticeship and also for what it reveals about the role of faith (Matt. 17.14–20/Mark 9.14–29/Luke 9.37–43). I have discussed these and other relevant texts in Wallis (1995a), pp. 24–64, 181–90.

20 Mark 16.17–18; John 14.12–14; Acts 3.16; 6.5–8; 1 Cor. 13.2; Jas. 5.15; *Acts Pet.* 10; *Acts Thom.* 20; Hermas, *Man.* 9.6–12.

21 Neirynck (1979), pp. 205–13.

22 Schatzmann (1989) offers a helpful analysis of the place of spiritual gifts within the community of faith.

23 Good surveys of the place of baptism in early Christian literature are provided by Beasley-Murray (1972); Dunn (1970); and Lampe (1976). Whitaker (1970) provides a convenient collection of extra-biblical texts.

24 On the power of ritual in this respect, see Turner (1995), esp. pp. 94–130; in relation to baptism, Gelpi (1977), pp. 113–56; and L. T. Johnson (1998), pp. 69–103.

25 E.g. Acts 2.38; 8.16; 10.48; 19.5; cf. 2.41; 8.12–13, 36, 38; 9.18; 10.37, 47; 16.15, 33; 18.8.

26 Rom. 6.1–11; Gal. 3.23–9; Col. 2.8–15.

27 Also known as the *Teaching of the Apostles*; a helpful introduction and review of scholarly research is supplied by Draper (1996), pp. 1–42.

28 Usage of the Lord's Prayer in the early church is conveniently surveyed by Bahr (1965), pp. 153–9; Froehlich (1992), pp. 71–87; and Vokes (1970), pp. 253–60.

29 A not dissimilar approach is adopted by Brooke (1980), pp. 298–311. For literature on prayer in the Fourth Gospel, see Mark Harding's bibliography in Charlesworth (1994), pp. 207–13.

30 E.g. John 5.19–47; 6.25–59; 10.22–42; 14.1–31.

31 I have developed this aspect of Jesus' approach to prayer in Wallis (1995b), pp. 225–50.

32 See the useful study of George (1953), pp. 196–220.

33 This is not the place to offer a thoroughgoing evaluation of Pauline soteriology. I have presented the basis for the following summary in Wallis (1995a), Chapter 3.

34 E.g. Matt. 13.10–13/Mark 4.10–12/Luke 8.9–10; Mark 4.10. See also the infamous 'Secret' Gospel of Mark discovered by Morton Smith in 1958, although its authenticity is questioned by many. This passage follows on from Mark 10.32–4: 'And they came to Bethany, and there was a woman there whose brother had died. She came and prostrated herself before Jesus and said to him: "Son of David, pity me." The disciples rebuked her, and Jesus in anger set out with her for the garden where the tomb was. Immediately a loud voice was heard from the tomb, and Jesus approached and rolled the stone away from the entrance to the tomb. And going in immediately where the young man was he stretched out his hand and raised him up, taking him by the hand. The young man looked on him and loved him, and began to

beseech him that he might be with him. They came out of the tomb and went into the young man's house, for he was rich. After six days Jesus laid a charge upon him, and when evening came the young man comes to him, with a linen robe thrown over his naked body; and he stayed with him that night, *for Jesus was teaching him the mystery of the kingdom of God*. When he departed thence, he returned to the other side of the Jordan' (tr. J. K. Elliott, *Apocryphal New Testament*, p. 149; our emphasis).

35 See the exhaustive analysis of Baird (1969); also Derrett (1973).

36 See the suggestive reconstruction of Horsley and Silberman (1997), esp. pp. 88–113; also Kloppenborg (1990), pp. 71–99.

37 Burton Mack (1993), pp. 29–39, offers a convenient survey of Q research.

38 The case for Q is intimately bound up with Marcan priority, namely, the hypothesis that Mark coined the gospel form and was the principal source for Matthew and Luke. If, however, Matthew wrote first with Mark and Luke using this Gospel as a source, then alternative explanations for the common material in Matthew and Luke absent from Mark suggest themselves. A good introduction to the 'Synoptic Problem', as it is called, can be found in Sanders and Davies (1989), pp. 51–119.

39 There is, however, reference to John the Baptist (Matt. 3.7–12/Luke 3.7–9, 15–18; cf. Matt. 11.2–19/Luke 7.18–35; Matt. 7.12; 21.31–2; Luke 16.16), the temptations of Jesus (Matt 4.1–11/Luke 4.1–13), the commissioning of the disciples (Matt. 9.37–8; 10.1, 7–16/Luke 9.1–6; 10.1–12), the healing of the centurion's daughter/servant (Matt. 8.5–10/Luke 7.1–10) and the Beelzebub controversy (Matt. 9.32–4; 12.22–30/Luke 11.14–23).

40 Sophisticated reconstructions of the Q community's beliefs have been attempted, some identifying multiple layers of redaction within the document, reflecting different stages of development (e.g. Kloppenborg, 1987). A review of alternative positions, together with a less ambitious assessment, is offered by Tuckett (1997), pp. 65–77.

41 The literature on the *Gospel of Thomas* is vast; a helpful introduction can be found in Cameron (1992), pp. 535–40.

42 James Elliott offers an English translation, together with a list of parallels between *Thomas* and New Testament documents, in *Apocryphal New Testament*, pp. 123–47.

43 Cf. Meier (1991), pp. 123–66.

44 See Tuckett (1996), pp. 110–28.

45 E.g. Matt. 21.33–44/Mark 12.1–11/Luke 20.9–18;   Matt. 24.43–4/Luke 12.39–40;   Matt. 24.45–51/Luke 12.42–6;   Matt. 25.14–30/Luke 19.12–27; Mark 13.33–7/Luke 12.35–8; Matt. 13.24–30; 22.11–14; 25.1–13, 31–46; Luke 13.6–9, 24–30; 16.19–31.

46 See Jeremias (1972), pp. 198–219.

47 See J. A. T. Robinson (1956), pp. 225–37.

48 A thorough discussion of the relevant passages and review of scholarly

opinion can be found in Beasley-Murray (1986), Part 3; and Meier (1994), Part 2. Jesus' use of the designation 'Son of Man' presents another complex problem; a helpful summary of the background, texts and issues is provided by George Nickelsburg (1992b), pp. 137–50.

49 The classic statement of this view is that of Schweitzer (1954), pp. 328–95; but see also the important reappraisal of N. T. Wright (1996), Part 3.

50 E.g. 1 Cor. 15.23–8; 1 Thess. 4.13—5.11; Jas. 5.7–8; 2 Pet. 3.11–13; 1 John 2.28; see Rowland (1992), pp. 166–70.

51 On the existence of house churches in the early centuries see Blue (1994), pp. 119–222; Branick (1989); and Theissen (1982). The question of whether Jesus' followers practised a community of good remains a matter of debate, see Mealand (1977), pp. 96–9; and now the important articles of Robert Jewett (1993), pp. 23–43, (1994), pp. 43–58.

52 See, especially, G. A. Anderson (1991); and, more generally, Arnold (1992), pp. 1022–3.

53 E.g. Matt. 28.8; Luke 24.41, 52; Acts 8.8; 13.52; 15.3; Rom. 14.17; 15.13; 2 Cor. 1.24; 2.3; 8.2; Gal, 2.22; Phil. 1.4; 2.29; Col. 1.11; 1 Thess. 1.6; Heb. 12.2; Jas. 1.2; 1 Pet. 1.8; 4.13; cf. Matt. 13.20/Mark 4.16/Luke 8.13; Matt. 13.44; 25.21, 23; Luke 6.23; 10.17. See Morrice (1984).

54 'Contribute to the needs of the saints; extend hospitality to strangers' (Rom.12.13). 'Do not neglect to show hospitality to strangers, for by doing that some have entertained angels without knowing it' (Heb. 13.2). 'What good is it, my brothers and sisters, if you say you have faith but do not have works? Can faith save you? If a brother or sister is naked and lacks daily food, and one of you says to them, "Go in peace; keep warm and eat your fill", and yet you do not supply their bodily needs, what is the good of that? So faith by itself, if it has no works, is dead' (Jas. 2.15–17). Also Acts 15.4; 28.30; Rom. 12.8; 15.7; 2 Cor. 8.1–15; 9.11–13; Gal. 4.13–14; 5.22; Phil. 2.29; 1 Thess. 1.9; 1 Tim. 5.9–10; Jas. 1.17; 2.1–13. See Koenig (1985).

55 Useful surveys of the New Testament and, in some cases, beyond are provided by Dix (1945); LaVerdiere (1996); Lietzmann (1979); I. H. Marshall (1980); and Moloney (1997). See also the collection of eucharistic prayers in Jasper and Cuming (1987).

56 On Paul's understanding, see, especially the essays in Meyer (1993); also Dunn (1998), pp. 599–623, for a good introduction and bibliography. See also Robert Jewett's analysis of the church situation reflected in 2 Thessalonians 3.10 where, he suggests; a form of 'love communalism' was practised (1993), pp. 23–43, (1994), pp. 43–58.

57 For further information and references, see Smith (1992), pp. 653–5.

58 Cf. Col 2.16; Rev. 2.14; also the following extract from one of the Ignatian Epistles (*c.* 110): 'I exhort you therefore – not I but the love of Jesus Christ – use only Christian food and abstain from every strange plant, which is heresy. For they mingle Jesus Christ with them-

selves, feigning faith, providing something like a deadly drug with hon-eyed wine, which the ignorant man gladly takes with pleasure; and therein is death' (*Trall.* 6–7).

59 Dunn (1990), pp. 129–82, offers a detailed analysis of this event and its broader implications.

60 One of the difficulties with establishing what happened at the so-called Jerusalem Council is knowing which of Paul's visits to Jerusalem cor-responds to the one described in Gal. 2.1–10 (cf. Acts 11.27–30; 12.25; 15.1–30; 18.22). See the review of Cousar (1992), pp. 766–8; and the thorough discussions of Jewett (1979); and Lüdemann (1984), esp. Chapter 3.

61 Higgins (1952), pp. 74–88; and Moloney (1997), pp. 113–50.

62 Schoedel (1985) offers a good introduction to Ignatius' eucharistic thought; see also Gibbard (1966), pp. 21–18; and LaVerdiere (1996), pp. 148–66.

63 Also Ign., *Phil.* 4.1; *Smyrn.* 7.1; cf. 'For we do not receive these things as common bread or common drink; but just as our Saviour Jesus Christ, being incarnate through the word of God, took flesh and blood for our salvation, so too we have been taught that the food over which thanks have been given by a word of prayer which is from him, (the food) from which our flesh and blood are fed by transformation, is both the flesh and blood of that incarnate Jesus' (Justin, *Apol. I* 66.1; tr. Jasper and Cuming (1987), p. 29).

64 See, especially, the excellent articles of Riggs (1995), pp. 256–83, (1984), pp. 83–101; also Betz (1996), pp. 244–75; and Mazza (1996), pp. 76–99.

65 Also *Acts Pet.* 5; *Acts John* 85–6; 109–10; *Ap. Trad.* 32.2; Justin, *Apol. I* 66.1. It appears that eucharistic celebrations became even more divi-sive – Christians refusing to participate with those who did not share their understanding (e.g. Ign., *Smyrn.* 6–8).

66 'There are two ways – one of life, and one of death. And there is a great difference between the two ways. On the one hand, then, the Way of Life is this: First, you shall love the God who made you. Second, your neighbour as yourself. And whatever you do not want done to you, do not do to anyone else' (*Did.* 1.1–2). 'There are three doctrines of the Lord of life: Hope, the beginning and end of our faith; and Righteousness, the beginning and end of judgement; (and) Love, a witness of joy and gladness of works done in righteousness' (*Barn.* 1.6; also Rom. 12.9–10; 13.8–10; Gal. 5.14; Heb. 13.1; Jas. 2.8; 1 Pet. 4.8; 1 John 4.1–21; Hermas, *Sim.* 9.15; *Vis.* 3.8). See the reviews of Klassen (1992b), pp. 381–96; Osborn (1981), pp. 223–43; and Stauffer (1964), pp. 49–55.

67 See, especially, Bultmann (1971), pp. 524–7; also Barrett (1978), p. 452.

68 It may well be that the notion of love, realized in Jesus and constitut-ing the fulfilment of the law, communicates a similar idea (cf. Rom. 13.8–10; Gal. 5.14; Jas. 2.8).

69 On the christologizing of love, see especially Klassen (1992b), p. 393, and the literature cited there.

70  Cf. 2 Tim. 1.13. I have drawn attention to how faith and love relate the practitioner to Jesus Christ in Wallis (1995a), pp. 134–44.

71  Ign., *Rom.* 7.3; also, 'Therefore, you must take on gentleness and renew yourself in faith, the Lord's flesh, and in love, the blood of Jesus Christ' (*Trall.* 8.1; cf. *Smyrn.* 12.2).

72  Cf. 'I became acquainted through God with your well-beloved name which you acquired because of your righteous nature in relation to faith and love in Christ Jesus our Saviour. You are imitators of God, and after rekindling, by the blood of God, the task natural to you, you have completed it perfectly' (Ign., *Eph.* 1.1; cf. also *Eph.* 13.1; 20.1–2; *Mag.* 13.1; *Rom.* Inscr.; *Smyrn.* Inscr.; 1.1).

73  On the emergence of a distinctively Christian morality see the brilliant evaluations of Hays (1996); and Meeks (1993).

74  Consider, for instance, the portrayal of Jesus as the new Moses in Matthew's Gospel; see Allison (1993); and W. D. Davies (1966).

75  On the role of imitation in early Christianity in relation to both Jewish and Graeco-Roman understandings, see Wilkins (1992), p. 393, and the literature cited there.

76  On imitation in Paul, see Belleville (1996), pp. 120–42; Hawthorne (1996), pp. 163–79; Kurz (1985), pp. 103–26; and Thompson (1991).

77  Cf. the useful comparative study of Wild (1985), pp. 127–43.

78  As we noted earlier, the idea of the suffering and martyrdom of God's righteous ones providing an example for those who inherit their faith flourished during the intertestamental period, especially in relation to the Maccabean uprisings: 'Therefore, by bravely giving up my life now, I will show myself worthy of my old age and leave to the young a noble example of how to die a good death willingly and nobly for the revered and holy laws' (2 Macc. 6.27–8; also 6.31). 'Brothers, let us die like brothers for the sake of the law; let us imitate the three youths in Assyria who despised the same ordeal of the furnace' (4 Macc. 13.9; cf. also 9.23; 12.16; 17.23).

79  The verse from Colossians is remarkable in that it invests not only Jesus' sufferings with redemptive capacity, but also those of his followers: 'I am now rejoicing in my sufferings for your sake, and in my flesh I am completing what is lacking in Christ's afflictions for the sake of his body, that is, the church' (Col. 1.24); cf. 'Perhaps also just as we have been redeemed by the precious blood of Jesus, Jesus who has received the name that is above every name, so also some are redeemed by the precious blood of the martyrs' (Origen, *Exhortation to Martyrdom* 50; tr. Oulton and Chadwick (1954), p. 429).

80  See Wallis (1995a), pp. 145–61.

81  It is noteworthy how attempts have been made to distance Jesus from the body of believers celebrated in Chapter 11. We need to remember that the earliest New Testament manuscripts do not divide the text into chapters and verses; originally, therefore, Heb. 12.1–3 simply followed on from 11.40. Further, most translations qualify 'faith' in 12.2 with

the personal pronoun 'our'; there is, however, no basis for this addition. On the contrary, the clear meaning of the Greek is that Jesus is the ultimate embodiment of faith, a faith he shared with all God's people back, it appears, to Abel. See Wallis (1995a), pp. 145–61.

82 Lane (1996), pp. 203–24.

83 J. H. Elliott (1985), pp. 184–208; and Michaels (1996), pp. 248–68. Elders could also act as exemplars of faith (1 Pet. 5.3).

84 See Wallis (1995a), pp. 161–72.

85 The NRSV gives 'my faith' as a variant reading in place of 'faith in me'. The Greek construction (*ten pistin mou*) is comparable to the one translated as 'my name' (*to onoma mou*) earlier in the verse and should be understood as a subjective genitive.

86 Aune (1996), pp. 269–84.

87 See, for example, James Robinson's reconstruction of a wisdom trajectory (1971), pp. 71–113; also Helmut Koester's suggestive article (1971), pp. 114–57.

88 See Käsemann (1969) pp. 23–65; Marxsen (1992), pp. 76–95; and the reviews of Meyer (1979), pp. 25–59; and N. T. Wright (1996), pp. 3–27.

89 See, for example, the studies of Aune, Burridge, Chilton, Evans, Meier, Riches, Sanders, Vermes and Wright cited in the bibliography.

90 The founding redactional studies for the Gospels are Bornkamm, Barth and Held (1963); Marxsen (1969); Conzelmann (1961); and Martyn (1979).

91 See, for example, the stimulating collection of essays in Bauckham (1998).

92 Extensive reviews of the role of the Holy Spirit in the New Testament can be found in Horn (1992), pp. 260–80; and Schweizer (1968), pp. 396–455. See also the important studies of Dunn (1975); and L. T. Johnson (1998).

93 Cf. 'For by grace you have been saved through faith, and this is not your own doing; it is the gift of God – not the result of works, so that no one may boast' (Eph. 2.8–9). See McGrath (1986).

94 Burge (1987), pp. 198–221.

95 Dunn (1975), pp. 318–26, and (1998), pp. 260–4.

# — 6 —

# Living the Legacy:
# Contemporary Reflections

In the previous chapters, we attempted to offer an alternative approach to the beginnings of Christian faith – one which reaches beyond the crucifixion to the ministry of Jesus. We identified the principal characteristics of Jesus' faith, embedded within what we described as his habitus: the experience of forgiveness, a way of praying, a treasury of wisdom, an exposition of joyous living, a discipline of love and a vocation to pursue. We suggested that, in addition to deposits formed within the lives of those to whom he ministered, Jesus specifically inducted a small group of disciples within this habitus and, prior to death, entrusted it to them. This was Jesus' legacy and one which his followers embraced as they mourned the loss of their beloved leader, drew on the resources of their Jewish tradition to give meaning to his execution, and honoured his memory by fulfilling their commitment to him. In the course of this, they realized his practice of faith continued to give access to his experience of God and exposition of human being. Furthermore, as Jesus enabled them to share in this habitus, so they in turn discovered a capacity to do likewise. As a consequence, Jesus' enduring significance for faith began to emerge and with this a need to account theologically for his impact, to commend his habitus to a broader audience and to defend his approach in the face of opposition.

We need to remember that Jesus and his disciples may never consciously have analysed faith in terms of the categories and characteristics noted above. Faith was a habitus, a way of life embodied by Jesus and communicated through personal encounter. As such, Jesus was the definitive exposition, requiring no further clarity so long as he was alive and his faith could be practised in relation to existing Jewish structures and canons of authority (e.g. Scripture, synagogue, Sabbath and feasts). However, mounting antagonism within Judaism precipitated a process of distillation through which Jesus' particular contribution to faith began to emerge. This probably began prior to the crucifixion, but soon picked up momentum afterwards and, predictably, generated considerable differences of opinion. A major watershed came with the recognition that Jesus' faith was being practised outside of Jewish identity and observance. This, in turn, raised questions over whether alternative structures, rituals and beliefs to those of Judaism would be required to sustain this new phenomenon.[1]

We also need to remember that Jesus' faith was principally *a resource for living*, a set of insights, practices and disciplines, and not a body of beliefs, although convictions about the nature of God, creation and humanity were implicit. It is no surprise, therefore, to find Jesus' faith very quickly giving rise to a broad spectrum of performance, embodied within the lives of those whom he encountered either personally or, indirectly, through a continuity of testimony reaching back to himself.[2] Throughout his life, however, Jesus remained to all intents and purposes a practising Jew whose approach to God was shaped by his Jewish heritage. There is little evidence that he wished to distance himself from this or to undermine Jewish identity. On the contrary, his concern was to rediscover the heart of the faith entrusted to his forebears and, through it, to bring blessing to all God's people. In this respect, he performed a dual function: first, of focusing attention on the essential dynamics of faith; and, second, of translating them into human experience. Put simply, *he embodied the difference God can make to life and, as such, came to be venerated as a living canon of faith.*

After his death, the necessity for an adequate definition soon became apparent, especially with increasing numbers of non-Jews embracing his habitus. Gentiles could not draw on the theological insights, moral disciplines and religious practices from which Jesus' faith emerged and which to a measure provided the matrix for interpretation and participation. This, in turn, complicated the task of maintaining Jesus' accessibility and spawned rich seams of christological reflection which attempted to communicate his universal significance. There was also a need to develop a morality congruent with Jesus' faith, as well as resources for worship of God and for maintaining a common life. Issues of authority and control soon emerged: Who are the custodians of Jesus' faith? How do you decide whether a particular embodiment is authentic? Should followers of Jesus be able to worship together? What is the potential of Jesus' faith for transcending cultural, ideological and political boundaries? These and other questions quickly became pressing and gave rise to a normalizing tendency which attempted to regulate Jesus' faith through establishing structures of authority responsible for belief and practice. Before long, Jesus' faith became an *orthodoxy*, defined by apostolic witness, credal definition and liturgical form, with so-called 'heretics' required to fall in line or face the consequences.[3]

In certain respects, all this was inevitable if access to Jesus' faith was to be increased and maintained, although the stakes were raised considerably with the realization of Christianity's potential for empire-building or consolidation. However, the dangers of institutionalizing a phenomenon which itself began as a reaction to institutionalized faith are obvious. There is, then, a constant need for those entrusted with Jesus' faith, the church of many denominations and complexions, to rediscover it by nurturing a critical dialogue with its own past and, especially, with its origins. With this in mind, I wish to conclude by reflecting a little on what this might mean for being the church today. The following comments are far from exhaustive and are offered to encourage debate and further exploration. I write as a minister within the Anglican tradition working in the north of England, although I hope what is said is of broader interest and relevance.

## Embodying Forgiveness

We concluded earlier that Jesus' ministry of forgiveness should be understood *as the mediation of divine generosity with transforming effect*. From what we can gather, there was a creative resourcefulness associated with encountering Jesus which enabled people to see themselves differently, through gaining distance from debilitating constraints and diminishing habits, so that fresh opportunities for joyful living could be embraced. In most cases, the point of contact was the presenting need of the individual or the sense of incompleteness emerging from sharing Jesus' company – people came to him in search of something or, when in his presence, recognized what they lacked. As a result, the ensuing experience of forgiveness was, more often than not, existentially prepossessing and personally satisfying because it corresponded to the recipient's condition and could be appreciated as such. Jesus performed forgiveness, but beneficiaries knew themselves to be forgiven because of a revisioned perception of self.

This, I think, brings into focus one of the ongoing challenges facing the church, namely *of nurturing a distinctively Christian ministry of forgiveness rooted in the practice of Jesus' habitus of faith, relating directly to human need and capable of mediating divine generosity.*[4] Over the centuries, it is questionable whether forgiveness has become so absorbed into theological discourse and ritual performance as to have lost its co-ordinates within human experience.[5] The language of sin and redemption, the rituals of penitence and other liturgical expressions, struggle to communicate the vitality of forgiveness associated with Jesus. Instead, they foster the impression of forgiveness as an impersonal transaction conducted within the councils of heaven and drawing on the currencies of atonement not readily translatable into everyday life. As a result, forgiveness comes to be seen as a maintenance operation, moderating the status quo in relationship with God, rather than as a vehicle for mission in which divine generosity reaches into human need and aspiration.

The importance of identifying what people lack or long for is clearly integral to formulating a more adequate exposition of forgiveness, but if this is to be conducted with integrity it must be undertaken through the lens of an appropriate interpretative paradigm. In this respect, it is worth remembering that Jesus was prepared to disappoint and disillusion those whose desires lay outside his vision and vocation. Those seeking signs were confounded and, presumably, challenged to revise their outlooks (cf. Matt. 12.38–9/Luke 11.29; Matt. 16.1–4/Mark 8.11–13; John 6.30). This should sound a note of caution when evaluating how relevant or attractive the church should seek to make itself in this or any respect. If part of our vocation is to maintain accessibility to Jesus' faith, then we must discover contemporary embodiments capable of communicating a more authentic perception of self in relation to Jesus and his God. That is to say, the church's relevance and attractiveness should emerge naturally from practising Jesus' faith.[6] For instance, the church becomes relevant when demonstrating that faith is about *being human and giving access to more satisfying patterns of life capable of building communities of reconciliation and common worth.* Similarly, it becomes attractive when exhibiting *a quality of human being that is profound, engaging and enriching in the face of the challenges, opportunities and responsibilities of existence.*[7]

One key requirement, I think, within this re-sourcing of forgiveness is for the church *to allow Jesus to be a human being once more.* I have explored elsewhere the dangers of maintaining there is something more fundamental about Jesus than his humanity.[8] Once we allow what Jesus communicates about being human in relation to

God to be interpreted within the context of his divinity then, paradoxically, his ability to mediate forgiveness diminishes as he becomes distanced from those who need his help. Jesus' humanity becomes secondary – a temporary chapter within the life of the eternal Word or Son of God. In effect, this greatly reduces his authority to practise faith and to embody the difference it can make to life because the common ground he shares with the rest of humanity is eroded and replaced by the suspicion that he was a special case, able to draw on exclusive divine resources. As we have seen, Jesus' power to forgive resides in his ability to draw others into a quality of being-in-relation-to-God that he himself expounded and which he claimed was the inheritance of all God's people.

By restoring Jesus' body, mind and spirit, so to speak, and, by implication, his faith, we do not diminish his importance, but refocus it. *He evokes our worship as God's icon of humanity, expounding the opportunities, responsibilities and challenges inherent in human being while demonstrating how living in God's presence brings an integrity to life's variegated experiences, capable of causing cadences of joy to resonate through the pursuit of an authentic self in relation to God's commonwealth of blessing.*[9] In Jesus, we encounter a lively paradigm and canon of faith, demanding our attention and drawing us into a common pursuit in which we are free to celebrate expressions of God's generosity and forgiveness, wherever and in whomever they may be manifested (cf. Mark 9.38–41).

In one sense, the rest of this chapter is concerned with the implications of the previous paragraphs, because the dynamics of forgiveness inform Jesus' habitus of faith in a thoroughgoing manner. For this reason, we shall limit our comments here to one particular concern, namely, the importance of rediscovering the *disturbing quality of forgiveness*.[10] Whatever else can be learned from Jesus' ministry, we cannot fail to be impressed by the transforming effects of generosity when practised in apparently 'godless' situations or among those living in God's perceived absence. In many cases, generosity finds expression in Jesus' readiness to acknowledge or accommodate people without placing prior demands upon them. He is even remembered as greeting Judas with a kiss (Matt. 26.48–9/ Mark 14.44–5/Luke 22.47–8) and extending generous words to those with whom he found solidarity in suffering (Luke 23.39–43). Such a practice of generosity can be understood as *an offering of time* (perhaps the only commodity genuinely ours to offer), which of itself conveys value and worth. Jesus' personal investment communicated acceptance, openness and a willingness to be a source of blessing. And it appears that through such encounters blessing was often experienced in the form of restored or revisioned perceptions of self in relation to God's economy of grace.

All this should encourage communities of faith seeking fresh embodiments of his *habitus* today to explore what it means to reflect this disturbing generosity at the heart of forgiveness.[11] To extend in God's name a sincere welcome not only to those whose lives appear to conform to God's expectations of them, but especially to those who fall short, at least in our perception, or who would never consider themselves as friends of God. What is at stake here is much more than becoming aware of those different from ourselves and being prepared to make newcomers feel at home. It entails nurturing a *spirituality of munificence* informed by patterns of worship and common life capable of communicating grace indiscriminately, whilst sustaining people of very different outlooks, experience and expectation. A more authentic humanity may then emerge through encountering the God of Jesus Christ and finding a measure of reconciliation with one another. It involves, I suspect, a greater readiness to give God away through attending to his causes wherever they appear and to honour those who share this commitment, even when they know God by another name or no name at all.[12]

## Living (the) Prayer

In Chapter 4, we noted that the Lord's Prayer gives access to Jesus' faith in terms of how he related to God and conceived of his role within God's world. What is equally remarkable is that Jesus invited his followers to pray this prayer with him – a discipline believers adopted from an early stage. Although the Lord's Prayer has earned a place in most acts of Christian worship through the centuries, more often than not it is required to keep company with formulations favouring a rather different attitude towards Jesus and his God. This is because prayer soon came to be reformulated in trinitarian terms, with access to God the Father mediated through God the Son and facilitated by God the Holy Spirit.[13] This is not the place to assess the fruitfulness of interpreting prayer through the prism of the Trinity;[14] however, there is reason to doubt whether it adequately reflects Jesus' practice and legacy to his disciples.

The key issue hinges on *orientation*. In the Lord's Prayer, we become members of God's family, called to share with Jesus the privileges and responsibilities of relating to God as Father and of living as God's children in God's world. By contrast, through trinitarian prayer we are encouraged to see ourselves as redeemed sinners and naturalized aliens, with little if anything to contribute towards our place within God's pleasure apart from a stake in the incarnation, the merits of Jesus' atoning death and the regenerative power of the Spirit. The former conceives of prayer as an instinctive and heuristic pursuit – a way of being in which we learn with Jesus to be true to ourselves within the climate of God's all-encompassing presence. It is like becoming fluent in our native tongue where we are inspired by our mentor to emulate his example in order to communicate meaningfully and flourish as persons. In the case of the latter, however, prayer is a cry for help uttered in a spirit of unworthiness and self-doubt as we trust Jesus for salvation, hoping God will purge us of our sins and make us acceptable in his eyes. Trinitarian prayer is comparable to learning a foreign language whilst being ever mindful of the difficulties of the task, never expecting to be successful and always relying on the good offices of a competent interpreter.

There is, no doubt, value in both these approaches; but only one of them originates in Jesus' habitus of faith, whilst the other is a later attempt to account for his enduring significance.[15] This, in turn, causes us to question whether the pattern of prayer we nurture today through our liturgies, hymns, creeds and theology adequately accommodates this intense being-in-relation to God communicated through the Lord's Prayer and embodied by Jesus. The issue here is neither the priority of grace nor the centrality of Jesus for salvation; it is, rather, *a readiness to inhabit instinctively the dignity of God's children and to work out what that means within a climate of acceptance, affirmation and responsibility*. According to our earliest sources, Jesus demonstrated little interest in how God's abundant resourcefulness and forgiving generosity became intimately associated with human being and the liveliness of creation. And yet this soon preoccupied church leaders as they sought to communicate Jesus' lively faith within an intellectual milieu informed by Platonism and other philosophies which opened up a chasm between the created order and the Creator, only breachable through divine initiative.[16] Philosophical trends change, but one of the consequences of this world-view within the church is, I fear, a culture of learned helplessness and unproductive dependence upon the uniqueness of Christ. All too often, liturgical worship encourages us to pray as though God were far off, to be suspicious of our motivations and capabilities, and to throw ourselves at the foot of the cross in the hope that we may be saved at the consummation of time. Quite simply, this is not the climate of the Lord's Prayer!

We noted earlier how Jesus' faith found expression in relating to God as Father, an existentially intense and all-pervading relationship from which his identity and value flowed, as he lived out of the blessings of God and responded by celebrating God's presence and championing God's causes. Jesus manifestly conceived of himself as one of God's beloved sons and intercessors – an ambassador for the King and a harbinger of God's powerful reign. In his eyes, this was an exemplary, even definitive, role, but it was not an exclusive one. It was an embodiment of faith he invited others to aspire to. In the light of this, perhaps another of the challenges facing the church at this time is to find ways of communicating this invitation through *allowing Jesus' prayerfulness to permeate its worship and mission in a thoroughgoing manner.*[17] We often forget how Jesus' first disciples must have struggled to take themselves as seriously as he palpably did and, as he claimed, God did. There must have been an initial strangeness about praying with Jesus and seeking to interpret and expound that prayer throughout life. But they managed to live with the incongruity, to practise the faith of Jesus, until it started to become second nature. In a similar manner, we may struggle with the theological imprecision and incompleteness of the Lord's Prayer, we may balk at the optimistic perception of humanity it implies; but it is the only prayer Jesus bequeathed to his followers and, as such, should be allowed to shape all worship and service performed in his name.

## Purveying Wisdom

Theological discourse has always been a form of 'techno-speak' – a language with nomenclature and concepts not readily accessible to the vernacular.[18] Recent decades have witnessed a further sinking of theology into the private sphere with proportionally fewer people being exposed to its parlance. And for at least some of those who are, members of church communities included, it remains a closed book with, at best, tangential relevance for the practice of faith. Some might argue this is inevitable and should not unduly cause concern; after all, millions of us enjoy the benefits of medical science and the digital revolution in blissful ignorance of how these 'mysteries' are made possible. However, if one of the principal functions of theology, and, indeed, liturgy for that matter, is to make God accessible linguistically then this must be an unsatisfactory state of affairs.

This, of course, is not a new problem, but it is salutary to reflect on Jesus' approach. He composed parables drawing on the stock of common experience to create opportunities for reflection on God and exploration of what it means to live in God's world among God's people. He formulated sayings capable of gathering up the fragments of life or concentrating attention on the particular in such a way as to provide co-ordinates for living, with the potential for guiding his audience into a more wholesome pattern of being. In many cases, Jesus' parables and sayings were theologically opaque in the sense that God is not named. And yet they give access *to the giftedness of life and to a world of meaning, choice and possibility where we are encouraged to discover our significance and to work out what it means to go with or against the grain of the Giver.* They engender a particular kind of worship where their poignancy or self-authenticating rightness demands our allegiance and respect, and inclines us towards the Source of wisdom from which they flow. Without question, Jesus was wise and put his wisdom to work within the furtherance of his vocation. Evidently, he believed that the language of story and simile, of observation and insight, supplied a lingua franca through which to communicate faith. And, by so doing, he knowingly placed himself within a sapiential heritage boasting a long pedigree not only in Judaism, but also in other faith traditions. Significantly, Jesus does not appear to have considered the ubiquity of wisdom incompatible with his vision of God's lively presence and, presumably, as an accomplished teacher, he recognized its suitability not only as an effective medium, but also as one capable of bringing faith to life. No doubt, such confidence grew out of the belief he shared with many Jews, namely, that all wisdom originates in God and, if taken to heart, steers the exponent in right pathways, enabling them to enjoy the blessings of God.

'Jesus, the sage' – here is a persona relatively unexplored by the church, which has tended to be preoccupied with 'Jesus, the saviour', 'Jesus, the Son of God' and other titles belonging to the rarefied dialects of theological discourse where their significance resides.[19] Perhaps it is time for a *sapiential renaissance* to give a fresh perspective and renewed momentum to the practice and communication of faith – for a rediscovery of the value of wisdom for life.[20] The benefits of such an initiative are not difficult to identify. In the first place, it would provide *a common currency for communicating certain aspects of Jesus' faith* without recourse to unfamiliar theological categories or interpretations. This may well help to increase Jesus' accessibility and to demonstrate his enduring significance. It would also provide us with *a vehicle for mediating God's reconciling purposes* in the sense that wisdom transcends boundaries of time, culture and creed, affirming our common humanity, uniting us in a common pursuit and, hopefully, drawing us into worship of the only wise God.

Attending to wisdom would also concentrate our attention on this life as a invitation to join Jesus in discerning the contours of God's abundant vitality and creativity within the web of interactions and relationships constituting existence as we know it. That is, to live wholeheartedly and unreservedly in God's world. This would demand of us a greater sensitivity and perceptiveness to where God's wisdom can be found, together with a readiness to be surprised and reformed by what we discover – wisdom is no respecter of persons and we would need humility to acknowledge all her children (cf. Luke 7.35)! How such a faith would cohabit with the certitudes of Christian belief is a moot point and one deserving sagacious consideration. It is also unclear what impact it would have upon our understanding of Christian definition and authority or, for that matter, upon our structures and patterns of ministry. There is a likelihood, however, that we would *be drawn increasingly into the world to share in the responsibility for valuing wisdom, for becoming proficient in living wisely and for celebrating wisdom's heritage, opportunities and origins.*

## Living Generously

From what we can gather, access to Jesus' table was the gift of all God's people. In contrast to other Jewish groups, he appears to have practised an 'open table', although participation was not without responsibility. Meals were eaten 'face to face' with whoever happened to be present, facilitating encounter and requiring a measure of openness and reconciliation. The blessing of God was invoked over the company and the provisions, reinforcing the substantial, organic and interrelated nature of divine generosity and communicating an expectation, even an obligation, to enjoy. To eat with Jesus, then, was to partake of divine hospitality and to celebrate a share in God's abundant life – capable of satisfying human need, realizing the integrity of God's people and resourcing joyous living. We also know that Jesus celebrated different types of meals, from massive picnics to more intimate encounters, and did not attempt to categorize them in terms of theological significance. It seems that wherever food and drink were shared in God's presence, Jesus expected blessings to flow.

We do know, however, that Jesus used one meal or set of meals towards the end of his life to interpret his eucharistic ministry. On this occasion, he draws attention to the *costliness of blessing*. There is, of course, an implicit sacrificial economy in operation at all meals – life, whether animal or vegetable, is taken so that life may be given; food is purchased, prepared and offered; conversation draws us into mutual vulnerability and places us at the mercy of others. In addition to such considerations, Jesus makes explicit the personal cost of extending divine hospitality through sacrificial service which, for him, would soon culminate in the offering of life. A life offered for God's sake and for the sake of all God's people. But Jesus did not stop there: he went on to entrust this costly ministry of divine hospitality to his apprentices, colleagues and friends.

The importance of Jesus' ministry of hospitality was not lost on his followers and, through the centuries, has generated a rich tradition of performance and understanding which supports contemporary expressions. It would be impossible here to review eucharistic practice or to account for today's manifestations.[21] Instead, and perhaps somewhat naively, we shall simply offer a number of observations arising from a comparison between Jesus' exposition and certain present-day characteristics. The first relates *to what we think Jesus entrusted to us*. Great emphasis is now placed upon the costliness of Jesus' sacrificial ministry and he rightfully occupies a central place within celebrations.[22] And yet once we elevate him into the category of unique and unrepeatable there is a danger of losing sight of the *corporateness* of his vocation and his expectation that we should continue where he left off. When this happens, the continuity in divine blessing mediated through fresh embodiments of Jesus' faith risks being compromised, if not severed. We see this, for example, when eucharists are reduced to meals held in Jesus' memory and do not venture into expositions of joyous living where Jesus is remembered by practising the ministry he entrusted to us.

The second observation concerns *who should be invited to the*

*Lord's Table.* One ramification of seeing the eucharist as essentially about Jesus and his ultimate sacrifice is that, in certain respects, the stakes are raised. Participants are expected to possess at least a rudimentary understanding of why the eucharist is Jesus' meal and in what sense he is present. This has the effect of restricting access and subtly shifting the emphasis from a celebration of God's boundless hospitality into a membership meal for the initiated. Jesus seemed willing to eat with anyone, with all that implied about forgiveness, reconciliation and purity; his church, apparently, is not! To a measure, this is an oversimplification for, as we noted earlier, we do not know whether Jesus welcomed Gentiles; his ministry was, however, open to all God's people – embracing, at least, the Jewish nation. This, in turn, requires us to clarify the constitution of God's people today and to define how, if it is not a birthright, one is incorporated.[23]

A further corollary arising from accessibility to the eucharist relates to *approach*. In extending eucharistic hospitality, Jesus sought to bring the best out in God's people by blessing them in God's name, inviting them to share in the fruits of God's goodness and encouraging them to take themselves seriously as responsible children of the promise. There was a centripetal dynamism here that drew people out of exile – sin, illness or however experienced – into God's abundance. It was both existentially demanding and personally liberating in that it communicated grace and precipitated transformation. In contrast, many contemporary celebrations of the eucharist interrupt this flow of divine generosity by stressing the unworthiness of participants and reminding them of their transgressions.[24] In effect, of confirming the distance between exile and restoration by defining people in terms of their past failings rather than their inheritance of faith. This seems at variance to Jesus' practice and, in its extremist forms, reduces the eucharist to little more than an antidote for sin.

Our third reflection relates to *where God is to be found in the eucharist*. Jesus' table-fellowship was one way in which he sought to amplify God's presence and to demonstrate the capacity for the ordinary stuff of life to yield blessing. Yet ambiguity surrounds in what sense eating together with Jesus made God real. Even at the Last Supper, it is unclear how Jesus mediates divine presence. Is it the bread and wine? Is it the taking and blessing? Is it the giving, receiving and sharing? Is it the consuming? Is it the life of service and sacrifice? Is it the commitment to remember and repeat? In truth, it is not defined with any precision, but is communicated through faith-filled attention to the practice of hospitality in a spirit of generosity, openness and love. And this, in turn, should caution us from seeking to tie God down in the eucharist to a particular action, substance or moment. Instead, it should *spawn a broad spectrum of eucharistic improvisation through which different distillations of divine presence may emerge.* Further, our eucharists should *locate us firmly within this world and supply us with a means of redeeming time in God's name and of allowing God's passions and predilections to stir us in the pursuit of God's causes.*

Our final observation is about *performance.* The challenge of translating Jesus' eucharistic hospitality across cultures with varying access to food, eating habits and expectations of meals is not inconsiderable. Jesus used customary foodstuffs for his time and place. His eucharists were mealtimes and, as such, an established part of daily routine, integrating naturally with the rest of his life and ministry. He belonged to a faith tradition ever mindful of God's blessings or the lack of them. Many of these circumstances no longer characterize the contexts in which the church seeks to celebrate the eucharist. In addition, other factors have led to the ritualizing and regulating of performance, the disassociation of eucharistic practice from regular mealtimes, and the use of special foods administered by authorized personnel. What was once an organic component of daily living has become specialized and fashioned according to particular theological perceptions and preferences. We must constantly ask ourselves, 'What has all this to do with Jesus?' And if we need a touchstone, surely it must be *whether our celebrations of the eucharist still possess the capacity to transform or whether they have become dislocated not only from their source, but also from faith-filled living.*[25]

Throughout this section, we have concentrated on the eucharist as the paradigmatic exposition of joyous living, but what Jesus celebrated at table has far-reaching implications.[26] For instance, how can the blessings of God be celebrated when people are hungry, homeless and oppressed, denied the dignity of gainful employment, the opportunity of financial stability and the ability to read and write? It seems Jesus' eucharistic hospitality contains the seeds for human flourishings on a global scale.[27]

## Nurturing Love

Jesus was remembered as one who knew himself to be valuable in

God's eyes and who, secure in his Father's love, possessed a remarkable capacity for communicating value and love to others. Although we cannot know for certain how Jesus came to embody this quality of love, it is not difficult to identify a number of contributory factors.[28] He appears to have belonged to a family and community where he was cherished, cared for and sustained. He inherited the Jewish faith-tradition, which introduced him to the blessings of life, taught him to pray, and inducted him in the privileges and responsibilities of being a member of God's people. Through exposure to the Scriptures and worship he will have been shaped by the promises of God, become familiar with the story of salvation and, in particular, with God's commissioning of certain Jews to fulfil God's salvific purposes. In all probability, his own sense of vocation was formed through absorbing these influences within a climate of God's perceived absence; and with vocation, the conviction of being chosen by God. Jesus also appears to have felt the sufferings of fellow-Jews acutely, so much so, that he was prepared to spend his life alleviating need and communicating joy. But, above all this, Jesus exhibits an intuitive connectedness with God supported by an extraordinary perceptiveness, a visionary imagination and a wilful pursuit of divine things.

If we are to learn anything about love from Jesus, then, the starting point must be *motivation*. Jesus' capacity for love was formed within him through belonging to communities committed to one another by blood or faith. Communities where love evolved shape and definition in patterns of behaviour, mutual obligation and shared destiny. And within this nexus of sustaining relationships, Jesus came to know himself to be loved of God and found the confidence and the means to live out of that love. This is surely a vocation the church must never tire from pursuing, namely, to be a place of belonging and new identity, where love gains meaning and bestows creative potential. To be effective, however, this pursuit extends beyond celebrating Jesus' exposition of love and encouraging emulation; communities of faith must *share in the responsibility for the formation of loving persons* with all this entails in terms of understanding the dynamics of love and evolving structures capable of encouraging and sustaining loving relationships within church and community.[29]

A key quality shining through Jesus' ministry in this sphere is *integrity*. First, integrity in the formation of love. Love for Jesus is quintessentially relational – a way of being human in which one's identity and worth are communicated through formative and sustaining relationships. In this sense, Jesus does not possess love, it is rather his pedigree, revealing as much about his origins as about his character. And the church can afford to be no less honest about love. To encourage the impression that God can transform us overnight or that there are 'quick-fix' spiritual answers to circumvent the growing pains of love may be appealing, but is likely to prove unsustainable. If Jesus' exposition of love was born of thirty years formation, it is unlikely to take us any less! Although the church of today is often called to minister within consumer-driven societies where persons are encouraged to define themselves as individuals, the formative ways of love remain non-negotiable, offering access to an authentic humanity, but at a cost. We need to embrace this as a strength.[30]

Equally, there is a need for integrity in how we define love. Here the church faces significant hermeneutical problems in that the word carries many meanings, not all of which are compatible with Jesus' faith.[31] The issue is not simply one of secular versus religious understandings, but a distinct shift towards the affectional dynamics of love at the expense of the volitional. This gives rise to a brand of 'feelings-driven' love which keeps close company with liking, sentimentalism and infatuation. The concern is not with whether love should be fulfilling, but with what happens when it becomes equated with particular pleasurable feelings, which then arbitrate on love's proximity and become a singular pursuit, apparently, in love's name.[32]

Worship, especially certain styles and components, can readily foster this outlook; and there is a growing expectation in some quarters for services to deliver these experiences. But how entertaining is the church called to be? The corrective to all this must surely be the central place Jesus affords to the love *commandment*, which takes us beyond affection to the qualities capable of forming communities of reconciliation and worth.[33] Participation in such communities will draw us out of ourselves and require us to embrace demanding disciplines such as compassion and forbearance, hospitality and service, courtesy and consideration, commitment and dedication. According to Jesus, this is the true *ecstasis* of love – a willingness to serve others in love's name, and to be served. This quality of love may not be as pleasurable as other strains, but it is the church's foundation and inheritance – an essential ingredient in Jesus' habitus of faith.

Finally, Jesus exhibits a profound integrity in the practice of love. In one sense, his approach defies generalization in that he is remembered as relating to people in many different ways and with surprisingly different outcomes. And yet the fact that such variety of encounter has been preserved bears witness to a quality of engagement characteristic of him. We must be careful at this juncture not to slip into misleading platitudes, such as, 'Jesus accepted everybody' or 'Jesus loved the sinner, but hated the sin'. Instead, we should draw attention to *his personal investment in relationships and, in particular, his eschewing of falsehood and dedication to restoring each person's dignity*. What this entailed was particular to each person, but it almost always afforded opportunity for growth or change. And he appears no less honest and wholehearted in his relationship with God, equally capable of delighting in God's presence (e.g. Matt. 11.25–7/Luke 10.21–2) and despairing of God's absence (e.g. Matt. 27.46/Mark 15.34). Clearly, it is impossible to legislate in favour of practising this quality of love, but churches must surely strive to be places where it is encountered, celebrated and nurtured.

## Keeping Faith

One of the severest challenges facing any ideology revolving around a founder figure is how to keep the movement alive once he or she has died. The tendency is for the initial momentum to dissipate, clarity of vision to be lost and group cohesion to diminish.[34] A number of strategies for preservation are possible, stretching from attempts to replicate the original in some way to thoroughgoing mutation, where the initial manifestation soon becomes lost within a wave of 'new strains'. It does not seem inappropriate to draw on the vocabulary and insights of evolution here for, in certain respects, ideology is governed by comparable priorities and constraints to those of organic life. Further, it is insightful to reflect on Jesus' legacy in these terms.[35]

Earlier in the book, we described how first-century Palestine witnessed many different embodiments of Jewish faith (e.g. Essene, Pharisee, Sadducee), each in its own way seeking to keep the vision of Israel alive – to preserve the heart of Jewish identity while responding to the changing circumstances in which it must survive. Jesus and John the Baptist also belong within this milieu. What is interesting is how the 'essence' is variously conceived; significantly, there is great variation, including the Temple and its sacrificial cult, Torah and its observance, the land and political freedom, the maintenance of purity and the pursuit of holiness. Perhaps even more pertinent to our investigations is Jesus' own conception: forgiveness, prayer, wisdom, joyous living, love and vocation. The habitus of faith as we have described it. Of course, Jesus practised it within the context of his Jewish heritage; but, as the flourishings of his faith among non-Jews soon demonstrated, it was not inextricably linked to his Jewishness. And here lies the genius – *to locate the essence of faith within a generative core of insights, practices and disciplines readily transferable and capable of giving rise to seemingly limitless improvisation*. Whether Jesus was fully aware of the potential of his habitus is a matter of speculation, but this in no way diminishes his remarkable achievement – one that cost him his life, but has brought millions to life.

And, surely, this is the church's true vocation – to maintain access to the faith of Jesus. So easily stated, yet so difficult to accomplish. History would suggest, however, his faith is a particularly robust strain possessing intrinsic vitality which has consistently borne fruit over six hundred or so generations, sometimes in the most arid of conditions, and within almost every culture and nation of the world. But this can only be grounds for confidence, not complacency. Perhaps the key issue arising from these reflections is whether Jesus' faith has become too intimately associated with certain aspects of previous flourishings which are in danger of losing their power to communicate. For instance, Jesus' significance has become enshrined within doctrines and creeds formulated among world views, controversies and cultures which now seem alien, irrelevant or impenetrable. Again, the liturgical celebration of Jesus' faith for many denominations is constrained by so-called 'classical' formulations of the fourth, fifth and, in some cases, sixteenth centuries. Further, the church's episcopacy, with all the institution implies in terms of authority and patterns of ministry, was established to maintain the continuity, catholicity and orthodoxy of faith. We trust that when these different initiatives were taken it was to give access to Jesus and his faith.[36] But are they still able to perform this function? And, if so, how can their 'conductivity' be increased?

In this chapter, we have attempted to outline some of the ways in which the findings of our historical investigations feed into a contemporary agenda for what it means to be the church. To explore these in a more detailed and rigorous manner is the task of further study, but hopefully sufficient has been said to indicate the fruitfulness and perhaps even the urgency of such an undertaking. If there is one contention underpinning these pages it is that *the birth of faith should be sought in the person and ministry of Jesus and not in what transpired after the crucifixion.* In fact, belief in Jesus' resurrection and the experiences of Pentecost are best understood within the context of the community of faith Jesus called into being when alive – a group of disciples Jesus resourced to continue in his vocation after his death. If this contention is along the right lines then it may be time to explore the implications of resetting the compass within the church's theological map from Jerusalem to Galilee to see whether rediscovering the legacy of Jesus can supply us with those vital co-ordinates of faith capable of maintaining his accessibility in this and future generations.

# NOTES

1 Useful background information can be found in Dunn (1991); and Küng (1995), esp. pp. 21–162.

2 We find diversity not only in how Jesus came to be appreciated, but also in the kind of lifestyles and communities that grew out of his faith. See Bauer (1972); Crossan (1998); Riley (1997); and Witherington (1998).

3 On the matters raised in this paragraph, see Bradshaw (1992); Fox (1988); Horsley and Silberman (1997); Küng (1995); Lüdemann (1996); Meeks (1993); and Stark (1996).

4 See, especially, the exposition of Gregory Jones (1995) [from which the title of this section comes]; also Dallen (1986); Ford (1999), pp. 107–36; R. Williams (1982a); and the collection of essays in *Concilium* 184 (1986). I am grateful to Stephen Burns for help with bibliography in this and the following sections of Chapter 6.

5 Especially, Borobio (1986), pp. 95–112. For assessments and explorations of the church's penitential ministry, see Dudley and Rowell (1990); Fink (1987); and Kennedy (1987).

6 See the insightful study of Andreas Köstenberger (1998), especially the final chapter.

7 There are many resonances here with Dietrich Bonhoeffer's 'religionless Christianity'; see Bonhoeffer (1971), pp. 278–82; and the contributions of David Ford (1999), pp. 241–65, and (1997). John Macquarrie (1982 and 1990) offers one of the most convincing expositions of human being and corresponding Christology.

8 Wallis (1995b), pp. 225–50. For a concerted attempt to restore the humanity of Jesus Christ, the Son of God, see J. B. Torrance (1981), pp. 127–47; and the essays collected together in Hart and Thimell (1989).

9 See, for example, the presentations of Mackey (1979); Macquarrie (1990), esp. Part 3; and Peacocke (1993), esp. Part 3.

10 Jacques Pohier (1985), esp. pp. 200–57, offers an important prolegomenon.

11 Clearly, this is a multi-disciplinary task; see the contributions of Burns (1996); and C. Elliott (1995). The Holocaust has become a 'test-case' for what is demanded of forgiveness at personal and corporate levels; for example, Rubenstein and Roth (1987); and Wollaston (1996). Brian Frost (1991) offers a broader perspective.

12 This line of exploration is taken further by Cracknell (1986), pp. 69–109; and Ward (1991).

13 The standard historical survey is that of Josef Jungmann (1965); also T. F. Torrance (1975), pp. 139-214.

14 For example, recent relational interpretations of the Trinity, see Taylor (1987), pp. 104–21.

15 Cf. James Mackey's (1983) interpretation of the Trinity as a doctrine about Jesus.

16 This, of course, is well traversed territory; see Grillmeier (1975); and Hanson (1988).

17 For example, many of the songs, prayers and liturgies of the Iona Community reflect this ambience (e.g. *Iona Community Worship Book, The Pattern of our Days, A Wee Worship Book, Wild Goose Songbooks, Volumes 1–3*).

18 Major reviews of theological hermeneutics can be found in Thiselton (1980 and 1992). George Lindbeck (1984) has generated an important debate about the relationship between doctrinal statements and the practice of faith; see McGrath (1990); and *Modern Theology* 4 (1988).

19 But see, for example, Schüssler Fiorenza (1995). The wisdom of Jesus is stressed in certain cultures; see Porter, Hayes and Tombs (1997); and Wessels (1990).

20 There are hopeful signs here; for instance, Alves (1990); Barton (1999); Brown and Loades (1996); Davidson (1990); Etchells (1998); McClendon (1990); Page (1991); and Taylor (1981).

21 Helpful overviews are supplied by Bouyer (1968); H. Davies (1993); Heron (1983); Jones, Wainwright, and Yarnold (1978), Part 3; and Wakefield (1998).

22 On the whole question of what has become known as 'eucharistic sacrifice', see Buchanan (1984); Hanson (1979); Stevenson (1989 and 1986); and R. Williams (1982b).

23 This keys into a number of current debates, including, whether sacramental initiation is complete in baptism, and whether children should be full participants at the eucharist. See, for example, Buchanan (1990); Holeton (1991); Meyers (1995); Dennis (1995); and Turk (1988).

24 Most eucharistic rites include a penitential section in the ante-communion and many include a version of Thomas Cranmer's Prayer of Humble Access: 'We do not presume to come to this thy table (o mercifull lord) trusting in our owne righteousnes, but in thy manifold and great mercies: we be not woorthie so much as to gather up the cromes

under thy table: but thou art the same lorde whose propertie is always to haue mercie: Graunt us therefore (gracious lorde) so to eate the fleshe of thy dere sonne Jesus Christ, and to drynke his bloud in these holy Misteries, that we may contunuallye dwell in hym, and he in us, that our synfull bodyes may bee made cleane by his body, and our soules washed through hys most precious bloud. Amen.'

25 See David Ford's insightful exposition of the 'eucharistic self' (1999, pp. 137–65).

26 It is important to remember that 'joyous living' for Jesus does not describe a set of feelings, but a way of being, characterized by a genuine openness to God within ourselves and in our relationship to all God's people and God's world. The opposite of joy is not sadness, but living as if there was no God. The implications of joy for the life of faith are explored by Hardy and Ford (1984); and Ramon (1988).

27 On this, Balasuriya (1979); and Wainwright (1978), pp. 123–54.

28 Thought-provoking assessments are offered by Dominian (1998); and Margaret Magdalen (1994).

29 The work of James Fowler on faith development makes a substantial contribution here; see, among his many writings, Fowler (1981 and 1987). Also from a burgeoning literature, Astley (1991); Astley and Francis (1992); and Fowler, Nipkow and Schweitzer (1992). Also Conn (1986); and McFadyen (1990).

30 A helpful contemporary exposition of love from a relational perspective is offered by Vincent Brümmer (1993), especially Part 4; also Ford (1999), pp. 216–40.

31 See the classic study of Anders Nygren (1932–39); also Brümmer (1993).

32 A helpful discussion of the matters raised in this paragraph is provided by James Averill and Elma Nunley (1992).

33 See Bonhoeffer (1954); Jones (1995), esp. pp. 163–204; Vanier (1989); and a number of the essays collected in Anderson and Morrill (1998).

34 Useful introductions to the social dynamics of various forms of religious movements are supplied by I. M. Lewis (1986); Reed (1978); and Wilson (1982).

35 See the remarkable exposition of Gerd Theissen (1984), especially Parts 3 and 4, who explores the notion of Jesus as a 'mutant', in evolutionary terms, giving rise to a new Spirit-inspired expression of humanity. John Bowker (1995) offers a broader discussion of communities of faith from this perspective.

36 Many of Hans Küng's writings help to bring these issues into focus; see, for example, his massive Küng (1995).

# Summary and Conclusion

We have covered a good deal of ground in the previous pages and, we hope, in a responsible manner, amounting to a journey with continuity and direction. We set out to answer the question, What happened to Jesus' followers after his death? Grief at the loss of their beloved leader and friend was identified as their overarching response; a grief which we found resonated with contemporary studies into the anatomy of loss and which, to a measure, was shaped by and expressed through their Jewish heritage. Our search for a satisfactory account of the disciples' pattern of life after the crucifixion drew us into an investigation of Jesus' personal practice of faith, where we identified six fundamental characteristics: experiencing forgiveness, relating to God as Father, becoming wise, celebrating God's generosity, embracing the discipline of love and pursuing God's Kingdom. We observed how this habitus of faith was not only embodied by Jesus himself, but constituted the substance of the apprenticeship he offered to his closest followers and which, in due course, he entrusted to them. One of the remarkable capacities of Jesus' faith we uncovered was its transferability, not simply in the sense that others were able to practise it, but because it gave access to a quality of human being in relation to God exemplified by Jesus himself.

Our attention turned next to how Jesus' habitus of faith, together with insights drawn from the Hebrew Scriptures and intertestamental literature, brought form to the disciples' grief, enabling them to continue in his legacy, to honour his memory and so to maintain his accessibility and relevance. This brought into focus Jesus' major contribution to faith which, in turn, helped to explain why he became intimately associated with a particular experience of human being in relation to God and was venerated for enabling others to discover this for themselves. We also explored how Jesus' faith, constituting a generative core and fundamental grammar, soon spawned fresh embodiments and performances as one or more components

160

brought faith to life in Jew and non-Jew alike – a phenomenon which helps to explain both the diversity of earliest Christianity and its universal appeal. Finally, we attempted to open up a conversation between Jesus' practice of faith and contemporary Christian expressions to see in what ways the former can bring fresh impetus, direction and vitality to the latter.

If these comments in some sense gather up the cairns along the way and represent the destination (surely another cairn!) reached, then perhaps we may conclude by offering one strong impression formed en route. It concerns Jesus' relation to faith. Although we sought to identify the defining characteristics of Jesus' faith and to demonstrate how they were communicated to and embraced by others, the remarkable thing is that they never cease to be his. That is to say, faith is not abstracted from Jesus nor Jesus extracted from faith; it remains inextricably linked to his person as the one who not only brings it to life, but possesses the capacity to enliven it in others. While the need to account for this remarkable phenomenon inevitably demands the attention of his followers and admirers, generating rich seams of christological reflection, we should be cautious about allowing this pursuit to become a singular preoccupation. For if this study has established anything, it is surely that the enduring appeal of Jesus resides not so much in solving the mystery of his identity, but of discovering how he enables us to engage with the mystery of ours.

# Appendix 1:
# Mourning Jesus:
# A Liturgy for Holy Saturday

The following order of service attempts to give liturgical expression to the thesis of this book by inviting participants to explore the grief of Jesus' first followers and to appreciate how faith, informed by Jesus' habitus, began to shape a response within them. In recent years, this liturgy has been introduced to the observance of the *Triduum* at the Parish Church of St Michael and All Angels, Houghton-le-Spring.

On Good Friday, a large cross is constructed on the dais where the nave altar table would normally stand; the paschal candle is placed adjacent and lit. A life-size body of Jesus, constructed out of wire meshing and swathed in a loin cloth, is secured to the cross. At the conclusion of the Three Hours, the paschal candle is extinguished and, as part of the discipline of love, the corpse is removed from the cross, wrapped in linen bandages, and placed on the high altar, which was stripped of all adornments at the conclusion of the Maundy Thursday eucharist. The high altar and sanctuary serve as Jesus' tomb. On the evening of Holy Saturday, the community of faith gathers in the chancel, remaining seated in the choir stalls throughout the service.

## ORDER OF SERVICE

*Though the fig tree does not blossom, and no fruit is on the vines;*
*though the produce of the olive fails and the fields yield no food;*
*though the flock is cut off from the fold and there is no herd in the stalls,*
*yet I will rejoice in the Lord; I will exult in the God of my salvation.*
*(Habakkuk 3. 17–18)*

### Setting the Scene – The Burial of Jesus

After these things, Joseph of Arimathea, who was a disciple of Jesus, though a secret one because of his fear of the Jews, asked Pilate to let him take away the body of Jesus. Pilate gave him permission; so he came and removed his body. Nicodemus, who had at first come to Jesus by night, also came, bringing a mixture of myrrh and aloes, weighing about a hundred pounds. They took the body of Jesus and wrapped it with the spices in linen cloths, according to the burial custom of the Jews. Now there was a garden in the place where he was crucified, and in the garden there was a new tomb in which no one had ever been laid. And so, because it was the Jewish day of Preparation, and the tomb was nearby, they laid Jesus there. (John 19.38–42)

### A Jewish Prayer of Mourning

If ever my grief were measured
or my sorrow put on a scale,
it would outweigh the sands of the ocean.
For God has hidden my way
and put hedges across my path.

I sit and gnaw on my grief;
my groans pour out like water.
My worst fears have happened;
my nightmares have come to life.
Silence and peace have abandoned me.

(*The Book of Job*, translated by Stephen Mitchell,
Berkeley: North Point, 1987)

## Songs of Sorrow and Lament

PSALM 137

*The lament is sung repeatedly as a Bowl of Ash, a symbol of mourn-
ing, is passed round. Worshippers are invited to mark themselves or
one another with ash in an appropriate way.*

(Anonymous, reproduced from *Songs of God's People*,
Oxford: Oxford University, 1988)

PSALM 88 (*said, antiphonally*)

1   O Lord, my God, my Saviour,
    by day and night I cry to you.
2   Let my prayer enter into your presence;
    incline your ear to my lamentation.
3   For I am full of trouble:
    my life is at the brink of the grave.

4　I am counted among those who go down to the Pit;
　　I have become like one who has no strength;

5　Lost among the dead,
　　like the slain who lie in the grave,

6　Whom you remember no more,
　　for they are cut off from your hand.

7　You have laid me in the depths of the Pit,
　　in dark places and in the abyss.

8　Your anger weighs upon me heavily,
　　and all your great waves overwhelm me.

9　You have put my friends far from me;
　　　you have made me to be abhorred by them;
　　I am in prison and cannot get free.

10　My sight has failed me because of trouble;
　　Lord, I have called upon you daily;
　　　I have stretched out my hands to you.

11　Do you work wonders for the dead?
　　will those who have died stand up and give you thanks?

12　Will your loving-kindness be declared in the grave?
　　your faithfulness in the land of destruction?

13　Will your wonders be known in the dark?
　　or your righteousness in the country where all is
　　　forgotten?

14　But as for me, O Lord, I cry to you for help;
　　in the morning my prayer comes before you.

15　Lord, why have you rejected me?
　　why have you hidden your face from me?

16　Ever since my youth,
　　　I have been wretched and at the point of death;
　　I have borne your terrors with a troubled mind.

17　Your blazing anger has swept over me;
　　your terrors have destroyed me;

18　They surround me all day long like a flood;
　　they encompass me on every side.

19　My friend and my neighbour you have put away from
　　　me,
　　and darkness is my only companion.

(Translation from *Celebrating Common Prayer*,
London: Mowbray, 1992)

## Attending to the Scriptures – Isaiah 53

*Isaiah helps to redeem Jesus' crucifixion from meaninglessness and waste by revealing God's hand in righteous suffering and sacrificial death.*

## Act of Devotion

SONG OF SONGS 8.7–8 *(said, in unison)*

> **Set me as a seal upon your heart,**
> **as a seal upon your arm;**
>
> **For love is strong as death**
> **passion fierce as the grave;**
> **its flashes are flashes of fire,**
> **a raging flame.**
>
> **Many waters cannot quench love,**
> **neither can the floods drown it.**
>
> **If all the wealth of our house**
> **were offered for love,**
> **it would be utterly scorned.**

(Setting from Celebrating Common Prayer)

*A candle is kindled and placed at the foot of the high altar where Jesus is laid.*

> We kindle a flame for Jesus, our master and friend.
> **for the gift of faith,**
> **for the offering of love,**
> **for the birth of hope,**
> **may God's name be praised,**
> **now and for ever. Amen.**

## Words of Comfort

*During the recitation of the psalms, worshippers are invited to light a candle and to place it at the entrance of the tomb.*

PSALM 23 (*said, antiphonally*)

1    The Lord is my shepherd;
      I shall not be in want.

2    He makes me lie down in green pastures
      and leads me beside still waters.

3    He revives my soul
      and guides me along right pathways for his name's sake.

4    Though I walk through the valley of the shadow of
           death
       I shall fear no evil;
    for you are with me;
       your rod and your staff, they comfort me.

5    You spread a table before me
       in the presence of those who trouble me;
    you have anointed my head with oil,
       and my cup is running over.

6    Surely your goodness and mercy shall follow me
       all the days of my life,
    and I shall dwell in the house of the Lord for ever.

PSALM 139 (*said, antiphonally*)

1    Lord, you have searched me out and known me;
      you know my sitting down and my rising up;
       you discern my thoughts from afar.

2    You trace my journeys and my resting-places
      and are acquainted with all my ways.

3    Indeed, there is not a word on my lips,
      but you, O Lord, know it altogether.

4    You press upon me behind and before
      and lay your hand upon me.

5    Such knowledge is too wonderful for me;
      it is so high that I cannot attain to it.

6    Where can I go then from your Spirit?
      where can I flee from your presence?

7    If I climb up to heaven, you are there;
      if I make the grave my bed, you are there also.

8    If I take the wings of the morning
      and dwell in the uttermost parts of the sea,

9    Even there your hand will lead me

and your right hand hold me fast.

10  If I say, 'Surely the darkness will cover me,
and the light around me turn to night',

11  Darkness is not dark to you;
the night is as bright as the day;
darkness and light to you are both alike.

12  For you yourself created my inmost parts;
you knit me together in my mother's womb.

13  I will thank you because I am marvellously made;
your works are wonderful and I know it well.

14  My body was not hidden from you,
while I was being made in secret
and woven in the depths of the earth.

15  Your eyes beheld my limbs, yet unfinished in the womb
all of them were written in your book,
they were fashioned day by day,
when as yet there was none of them.

16  How deep I find your thoughts, O God!
how great is the sum of them!

17  If I were to count them,
they would be more in number than the sand;
to count them all,
my life span would need to be like yours.

18  O that you would slay the wicked, O God!
You that thirst for blood, depart from me.

19  They speak despitefully against you;
your enemies take your name in vain.

20  Do I not hate those, O Lord, who hate you?
and do I not loathe those who rise up against you?

21  I hate them with a perfect hatred;
they have become my own enemies.

22  Search me out, O God, and know my heart;
try me and know my restless thoughts.

23  Look well whether there be any wickedness in me
and lead me in the way that is everlasting.

> (Translation from *Celebrating Common Prayer*,
> London: Mowbray, 1992)

## Attending to Scripture – Ruth 1.1–17

*Ruth embodies the way of love in the face of death.*

**Re-membering Jesus . . .**

*The following biddings are led by different members of the gathering in an extemporary manner.*

I remember when he came to us by the lakeside . . .
our hearts raced within us when he called us by name.
**We will remember and give thanks.**

I remember his stories and sayings . . .
and, how through them, God's kingdom came close.
**We will remember and give thanks.**

I remember his love of the Scriptures . . .
and how they came to life in his hands.
**We will remember and give thanks.**

I remember the boat trips across the waters . . .
and his talent for sleeping through the fiercest storms.
**We will remember and give thanks.**

I remember when he restored the dignity of the forgotten
    ones . . .
and looked upon them with eyes of compassion.
**We will remember and give thanks.**

I remember when he touched lepers with hands of
    kindness . . .
and cleansed them from their scourge.
**We will remember and give thanks.**

I remember being overwhelmed by God's forgiveness . . .
as he lifted up my head and revived my soul.
**We will remember and give thanks.**

I remember his miracles of healing . . .
embracing human need with transforming hands of love.
**We will remember and give thanks.**

I remember when he taught us to pray . . .
we learned to call God Father and to share the Father's heart.
**We will remember and give thanks.**

I remember his delight in children . . .
and his willingness to learn from their ways.
**We will remember and give thanks.**

I remember his meal-times and open-tables . . .
when all feasted on the food of friendship and the wine of
    gladness.
**We will remember and give thanks.**

I remember when he confounded the pretentious . . .
with words of wisdom that disclosed their conceit.
**We will remember and give thanks.**

I remember his fascination with nature . . .
how it spoke to him of the glory of God.
**We will remember and give thanks.**

I remember his friendship and openness . . .
his genuine concern for the well-being of all.
**We will remember and give thanks.**

I remember his passion for truth and justice . . .
how he challenged the mighty ones in God's name.
**We will remember and give thanks.**

I remember his tenderness towards women . . .
and his readiness to share the kingdom with them.
**We will remember and give thanks.**

I remember seeing in him the person I longed to be . . .
and daring to believe that person could live.
**We will remember and give thanks.**

I remember when he told us of his forthcoming death . . .
and we silenced him, hoping it would never come to pass.
**We will remember and give thanks.**

I remember when he gathered us together at Passover time . . .
and entrusted to us what God had entrusted to him.
**We will remember and give thanks.**

I remember when they came to arrest him . . .
terror filled our hearts and we were overwhelmed with fear.
**We will remember and give thanks.**

I remember when they strung him up on a cross to die . . .
and seeing God's tears welling within his mother's eyes.
**We will remember and give thanks, now and always.**
**Amen.**

**Praying with Jesus**

We pray as Jesus taught us.

**Our Father, in heaven,**
**let your name be made holy,**
**let your kingdom come,**
**let your will be done,**
**as in heaven so also on earth.**
**Give us this day the bread of Life.**
**And forgive us our debts,**
**as we also have forgiven our debtors.**
**And let our faith not be tested beyond endurance,**
**but deliver us from Evil,**
**for the kingdom and the power**
**and the glory are yours,**
**now and for ever. Amen.**

**Embracing the Legacy of Jesus**

**We will honour you, Jesus . . .**
  **through the telling of the stories,**
  **through the study of the Scriptures,**
  **through the following of the Way,**
  **through the breaking of the bread,**
  **through the practice of forgiveness,**
  **through the loving of the people,**
  **through the prayers of the kingdom,**
  **through the sharing of the faith.**
**We will honour you, in God's holy name. Amen.**

### Blessing God's Holy Name – The Mourner's Kaddish Prayer

Magnified and sanctified be the great name of God in the
world which he created according to his will. May he establish
his Kingdom in your life and in your days, and in the lifetime
of all his people: quickly and speedily may it come; and let us
say, Amen!

**Amen. Blessed be God for ever!**

Blessed, praised and glorified, exalted, extolled and honoured,
magnified and lauded be the name of the Holy One; blessed be
God! Though he be high above all the blessings and hymns,
praises and consolations, which are uttered in the world; and
let us say, Amen!

**Amen. Blessed be God for ever!**

May there be abundant peace from heaven and life for us and
for all people; let us say, Amen!

**Amen. Blessed be God for ever!**

(Translation from *Celebrating Common Prayer*,
London: Mowbray, 1992)

# Appendix 2:
# 'Holy Saturday' in the Early Church

Throughout this study, we have offered a radically different approach to Holy Saturday in comparison to those treatments concerned with Jesus' whereabouts in the period between his crucifixion and resurrection, the so-called 'harrowing of hell'. The following pages review this alternative trajectory within the early church and attempt to account for it.[1] The biblical point of departure tends to be 1 Peter 3.18b–20 and 4.6:

> He was put to death in the flesh, but made alive in the spirit, in which also he went and made a proclamation to the spirits in prison, who in former times did not obey, when God waited patiently in the days of Noah, during the building of the ark, in which a few, that is, eight persons, were saved through water . . . For this is the reason the gospel was proclaimed even to the dead, so that, though they had been judged in the flesh as everyone is judged, they might live in the spirit as God does.

Although Augustine[2] questioned whether these verses refer to the dis-incarnate Son's activities in hell, most scholars before and many afterwards came to accept this interpretation.[3] What then was the purpose of this happening? One line of explanation considers the *descensus* to be the ultimate expression of the Son's identification with humanity through the incarnation, that is, the completion of the process of condescension necessary to secure our salvation. Athanasius expresses it thus:

> For man dies, not by his own power, but by necessity of nature and against his will, but the Lord, being Himself immortal, but having a mortal flesh, had power, as God, to become separate from the body and to take it again, when He would. Concerning this too speaks David in the Psalm, 'Thou shalt not leave My soul in hades, neither shalt Thou suffer Thy Holy One to see corruption.' For it beseemed that the flesh, corruptible as it was, should

no longer after its own nature remain mortal, but because of the Word who had put it on, should abide incorruptible. For as He, having come in our body, was conformed to our condition, so we, receiving Him, partake of the immortality that is from Him.[4]

Another approach emphasizes how the dis-incarnate Son continues his incarnate ministry of proclaiming the good news of salvation and releasing imprisoned souls from the punishment for sin and the grip of death. As the *Gospel of Peter* describes it, the soldiers guarding the tomb witness Jesus being led out by two angels and hear a voice from heaven saying, '"Have you preached to those who sleep?", and from the cross there was heard the answer, "Yes"' (10.41–2). Interestingly, there is significant variation over the scale and compass of this operation. At one extreme, hell is emptied of all who, from the time of Adam, have been ensnared by sin:

> And Hades took Satan and said to him, 'O Beelzebub, heir of fire and torment, enemy of the saints, through what necessity did you contrive that the King of Glory should be crucified, so that he should come here and strip us naked? Turn and see that not one dead man is left in me, but all that you gained through the tree of knowledge you have lost through the tree of the cross . . . While Hades was thus speaking with Satan, the King of Glory stretched out his right hand, and took hold of our forefather Adam and raised him up. Then he turned to the rest and said, 'Come with me, all you who have died through the tree which this man touched. For behold, I raise you all up again through the tree of the cross.'[5]

At the other, it is only the righteous who are released and who ascend with their Lord:

> Death was struck with dismay on beholding a new visitant descend into Hades, not bound by the chains of the place . . . All the just were ransomed, whom death had swallowed; for it behoved the King whom they had proclaimed, to become the redeemer of His noble heralds . . . Of this our Saviour the Prophet Jonas formed the type, when he prayed out of the belly of the whale, and said, 'I cried in my affliction,' and so on; 'out of the belly of hell,' and yet he was in the whale; but though in the whale, he says that he is in Hades; for he was a type of Christ, who was to descend into Hades.[6]

If these interpretations underline the dis-incarnate Son's power to break the bonds of death, more nuanced treatments stress the fresh opportunity for response to God afforded by preaching the gospel. Some maintain the offer of salvation is extended to all:

> The soul when it was deified descended into Hades, in order that, just as the Sun of Righteousness rose for those upon the earth, so likewise He might bring light to those who sit under the earth in darkness and shadow of death: in order that just as He brought the message of peace to those upon the earth, and of release to the prisoners, and of sight to the blind, and became to those who believed the Author of everlasting salvation and to those who did not believe a reproach of their unbelief, so He might become the same to those in Hades: That every knee should bow to Him, of things in heaven, and things in earth and things under earth. And thus after He had freed those who had been bound for ages, straightway He rose again from the dead, shewing us the way of resurrection.[7]

While others limit it to those who have not previously had a chance to respond to the good news:

> Wherefore the Lord preached the Gospel to those in Hades ... And it were the exercise of no ordinary arbitrariness, for those who had departed before the advent of the Lord (not having the Gospel preached to them and having afforded no ground from themselves in consequence of believing or not) to obtain either salvation or punishment. For it is not right that these should be condemned without trial, and that those alone who lived after the advent should have the advantage of the divine righteousness.[8]

The question of how the Son was able to gain access to hell and continue his ministry there exercised many. Much use is made of Psalm 24.7–8, as the Son is depicted as the King of Glory demanding entry into Hades and being met by closed gates, which are subsequently shattered to demonstrate his authority over evil and death:

> Again the voice sounded, 'Lift up the gates.' When Hades heard the voice the second time, he answered as if he did not know it and said, 'Who is this King of Glory?' The angels of the Lord said, 'The Lord strong and mighty, the Lord mighty in battle.' And

immediately at this answer the gates of brass were broken in pieces and the bars of iron were crushed and all the dead who were bound were loosed from their chains, and we with them. And the King of Glory entered as a man, and all the dark places of Hades were illuminated.[9]

Another theme receiving considerable attention is how the incarnate Son's sinless body acts as the bait which deceives Satan into thinking that he is simply receiving the soul of an ordinary human; but when he discovers the Son's true identity, it is too late:

For the motive behind the mystery of the incarnation, which I previously explained, was just this: the divine power of the Son of God, like a hook wrapped in a covering of human flesh and, as the Apostle Paul said, 'in habit found as a man', was to lure on the Prince of the World to a conflict, and while Christ offered him His human flesh as a bait, the Deity concealed within was to hold him fast with a hook, as a result of the shedding of His immaculate blood. Only He who Himself knows no stain of sin could abolish the sins of all men, at any rate of those who had marked the doorposts of their faith with His blood.[10]

Sacrificial imagery is employed again in Melito of Sardis' powerful homily *On the Passover*, which explores how God is able to release us from sin and death by means of the Son's identification with humanity through the incarnation and, more specifically, through his death, depicted as a Passover:

The Lord, when he had clothed himself with man
    and suffered because of him that was suffering
    and been bound because of him that was held fast
    and been judged because of him that was condemned
    and been buried because of him that was buried,
arose from the dead and uttered this cry:
'Who takes issue with me? – let him stand against me.
    I released the condemned;
    I brought the dead to life;
    I raise up the buried.
I am the one,' says the Christ,
'I am the one that destroyed death
    and triumphed over the enemy
    and trod down Hades
    and bound the strong one

and carried off man to the heights of heaven;
I am the one,' says the Christ.[11]

Clearly, most if not all of this kind of speculation concerning Holy Saturday assumes a Christology in which Jesus is interpreted theologically as one who is intimately, if not essentially, related to God.[12] From this perspective, it is interesting how the dis-incarnate Son is rarely raised from the dead.[13] Rather, as God, he has authority over Satan and death; and as one who is without sin, he is never incapacitated by the powers of Hades, but enters a free agent capable of raising himself.[14]

The question of what 'part' of Jesus entered Hades remains unclear. Origen, for example, suggests that it was the human soul of Christ which descended and which, after being raised by God, became immortal:

Anyone who is interested may realize that it is not the dead man that is immortal, but he who rose from the dead. Not only was the dead man not immortal, but even Jesus, who was a composite being, was not immortal before his death since he was going to die. No one who is going to die at some future date is immortal, but he becomes immortal when he will no longer die.[15]

Tertullian similarly thought it was the human Jesus who died and was buried,[16] although he maintained that whatever descended must be a soul possessing corporeality, albeit different from bodily substance, for 'whatever is incorporeal is incapable of being kept and guarded in any way; it is also exempt from either punishment or refreshment' (*De Anima* VII). These attempts to rationalize the business of Holy Saturday take seriously the biblical witness to the conviction that Jesus 'died' and 'was buried' (e.g. 1 Cor. 15.3–4), and reflect an understanding of Christ in which human and divine subjects coexist and are yet open to different fates.[17]

Athanasius, the champion of Nicene orthodoxy and defender of the full divinity of the incarnate Son, represents a later stage in christological debate and one which attempts to remove all hints of dualism of this kind. However, the price paid appears to be that the human subject within Jesus no longer coexists with, but is replaced by, the divine Word, reducing the incarnation to a form of embodiment:[18]

But in the Body which was circumcised, and carried and ate and drank, and was weary, and was nailed on the tree and suffered, there was the impassible and incorporeal Word of God. This Body it was that was laid in a grave, when the Word had left it, yet was not parted from it, to preach, as Peter says, also to the spirits in prison. And this above all shews the foolishness of those who say that the Word was changed into bones and flesh. For if this had been so, there were no need of a tomb. For the Body would have gone by itself to preach to the spirits in Hades. But as it was, He Himself went to preach, while the Body Joseph wrapped in a linen cloth, and laid it away at Golgotha. And so it is shewn to all that the Body was not the Word, but Body of the Word . . . And verily it is strange that He it was Who suffered and yet suffered not. Suffered, because His own Body suffered, and He was in it, which thus suffered; suffered not, because the Word, being by Nature God, is impassible.[19]

A more sophisticated treatment of how the human and divine characteristics of Jesus can be accommodated is provided by John of Damascus, who adopts a similar approach to the Cappadocian Fathers in conceiving of the relationship between the divine and the human in dynamic, perichoretic terms. Here it is not possible to speak of Jesus' human and divine components separately in that, through the incarnation, a thoroughgoing interpenetration took place which fused body and soul with the divine Word:

Wherefore, although He died as man and His Holy Spirit severed from His immaculate body, yet His divinity remained inseparable from both, I mean, from His soul and His body, and so even thus His one hypostasis was not divided into two hypostases. For body and soul received simultaneously in the beginning their being in the subsistence of the Word, and although they were severed from one another by death yet they continued, each of them, having the one subsistence of the Word. So that the one subsistence of the Word is alike the subsistence of the Word, and of soul and body. For at no time had either soul or body a separate subsistence of their own, different from that of the Word, and the subsistence of the Word is for ever one, and at no time two. So that the subsistence of Christ is always one. For although the soul was separated from the body topically, yet hypostatically they were united through the Word.[20]

This brief survey hopefully communicates something of the richness of speculation which developed around Holy Saturday. In certain respects, this literature reflects the tendency of the early church to construct mythological stories, informed by theological conviction, to account for those periods in Jesus' life where our sources are silent.[21] The danger, however, is that by overemphasizing one conviction about Jesus, another is undermined. Certainly, it is not difficult to understand how the discussions of Holy Saturday presented above diminish the humanity of Jesus and are tantamount to denying that he died at all.[22] For while the depiction of the afterlife as a place where the souls of the living continue in some form is consistent with Jewish and Graeco-Roman conceptions, the portrayal of Jesus in Hades as a free agent with authority over his own destiny, as well as those of others, is manifestly incompatible with any meaningful concept of death.[23] Further, it confirms beyond doubt that such interpretations bear little if any relationship to the response of Jesus' bereaved disciples following his death; rather, they are the product of later strands of christological reflection.

## NOTES

1 Excellent reviews can be found in Bauckham (1992a), pp. 145–59; and MacCulloch (1930). The patristic period generated most interest in Holy Saturday, although see Aquinas, *Summa Theologiae*, 3.52.1–8. In the current century, Hans Urs von Balthasar is the scholar who has done most to reappropriate Holy Saturday within theological reflection (especially 1990, pp. 148–88); cf. Saward (1990), pp. 105–33; see also Lash (1990), pp. 109–19; and A. E. Lewis (1987), pp. 335–62.

2 'Consider, however, I pray you, whether all that the Apostle Peter says concerning spirits shut up in prison, who were unbelieving in the days of Noah, may not after all have been written without any reference to hell, but rather to those times the typical character of which he has transferred to the present time. For that transaction had been typical of future events, so that those who do not believe the gospel in our age, when the Church is being built up in all nations, may be understood to be like those who did not believe in that age while the ark was a preparing; also, that those who have believed and are saved by baptism may be compared to those who at that time, being in the ark, were saved by water; wherefore he says, "So baptism by a like figure saves you"'(Augustine, *Epistolae* CLXIV (Ad Evodium),V. 15).

3 See the thorough discussion of Dalton (1989). Other New Testament references suggesting Christ's descent to hell include: Matt. 12.40; 27.52–3; Acts 2.24–32; Eph. 4.9–10; Rev. 1.18.

4 Athanasius, *Contra Arianos* III.57; also Ambrose, *De Fide* II.103; Cyril of Jerusalem, *Catecheses* IV.15, and Gregory of Nyssa, *Epistulae* XVII.

5 *Acts of Pilate* (Christ's Descent into Hell) 23–4 (7–8); cf. Eusebius, *Demonstratio Evangelica* IV.12; VIII.1; X. 8.

6 Cyril of Jerusalem, *Catecheses* IV. 19–20; also Irenaeus, *Adversus Haereses* IV.27.2; Epiphanius of Salamis, *Panarion* 3.4.4; *Martyrdom of Isaiah* 9.13–18.

7 John of Damascus, *De Fide Orthodoxa* III.29; Origen, *Contra Celsum* II.43; *De Principiis* II.5.3; *Sibylline Oracles* VIII.310–13.

8 Clement of Alexandria, *Stromata* VI.6.

9 *Acts of Pilate* (Christ's Descent into Hell) 21.3 (5.3).

10 Rufinus, *Commentarius in Symbolum Apostolorum* 16 (tr. J. N. D. Kelly, 1955); also: Cyril of Jerusalem, *Catecheses* IV.15; Eusebius, *Demonstratio Evangelica* VIII.1; X.8.

11 Melito of Sardis, *Peri Pascha* 100–2 (tr. S. G. Hall, 1979).

12 On the christological implications of the *descensus*, Grillmeier (1949), pp. 1–53, 184–203.

13 But see Origen, *Contra Celsum* II.16.

14 E.g. Ambrose, *De Fide* III.27, 111; Eusebius, *Demonstratio Evangelica* IV.12; VIII.1; X.8; Rufinus, *Commentarius in Symbolum Apostolorum* 17; 29; 30.

15 Origen, *Contra Celsum* II.16 (tr. H. Chadwick, 1953); similarly, Irenaeus, *Adversus Haereses* V.31.2; *Fragment* XXVI.

16 'Now although Christ is God, yet, being also man, "He died according to the Scriptures," and "according to the same Scriptures was buried." With the same law of His being He fully complied, by remaining in Hades in the form and condition of a dead man; nor did He ascend into the heights of heaven before descending into the lower parts of the earth, that He might there make the patriarchs and prophets partakers of Himself' (*De Anima* LV).

17 Grillmeier (1975), pp. 106–49.

18 The question of whether Athanasius' understanding of the incarnation belongs within the Alexandrian *logos-sarx* interpretation, resulting in what Richard Hanson describes as a 'Space-suit Christology' (p. 448), or whether his soteriologically motivated approach is closer to Antiochene *logos-anthropos* solutions is still hotly debated; see: Dragas (1985), pp. 289–399; Grillmeier (1975), pp. 308–28; Hanson (1988), pp. 446–58; and T. F. Torrance (1988), pp. 146–90.

19 Athanasius, *Epistolae* LIX (Ad Epictetum), 5–6; also, *Contra Arianos* III.57.

20 John of Damascus, *De Fide Orthodoxa* III.27.

21 The infancy gospels are another example of where, in this case, Jesus' early years are rewritten from the perspective of his divinity.

22 Balthasar (1990), pp. 152–60, who stresses that one of the key theological insights of Holy Saturday is God's solidarity, through the Son, with humanity in death.

23 The situation is further compounded by the conviction that when the divine soul of the incarnate Son was in Hades, it remained

omnipresent! 'When He descended to Hades, He was never absent from Paradise (just as He was always in Heaven when He was preaching on earth as the Son of Man), but promised His martyr a home there, and held out to him the transports of perfect happiness. Bodily fear cannot touch Him Who reaches indeed down as far as Hades but by the power of His nature is present in all things everywhere' (Hilary of Poitiers, *De Trinitate* X.34; cf. also Gregory of Nyssa *Epistulae* XVII). A similar line is taken by Aquinas: 'Hence: (1) The body which was then in the tomb is not a part of the uncreated person but of Christ's assumed nature. So even if the body of Christ was not in hell, this does not mean that the whole Christ was not there. It does, however, show that not everything pertaining to his human nature was there. (2) A complete human nature results from the union of soul and body; but not so the totality of the divine person. Hence, once the union of soul and body was dissolved by death, the whole Christ remained, although human nature did not remain in its totality. (3) While the person of the whole Christ is in every place, it is not wholly so, because it is not circumscribed by any place. All places taken together could not contain his immensity. Rather, his immensity contains all things. Only of such things which are in place corporally and are circumscribed by place can it be said that, if they are wholly in place, no part of them is outside it. But this does not apply to God' (*Summa Theologiae* 3a.52.3; tr. Eyre and Spottiswoode edition, 1974).

# Bibliography

## Primary Sources

Unless otherwise indicated, the following editions have been used:

### THE BIBLE AND OLD TESTAMENT APOCRYPHA

*The New Revised Standard Version of the Bible, Anglicized Edition.* Division of Christian Education of the National Council of the Churches of Christ in the United States of America, 1989, 1995.

### JEWISH SOURCES

*The Dead Sea Scrolls in English*, ed. G. Vermes. London: Penguin, 1995, 4th edn.

*Old Testament Pseudepigrapha*, ed. J. H. Charlesworth. London: Darton, Longman & Todd, 1983 and 1985, 2 vols.

*Mekilta de Rabbi Ishmael*, ed. J. Z. Lauterbach. Philadelphia: Jewish Publication Society of America, 1933, 3 vols.

*Midrash Rabbah*, ed. H. Freedman and M. Simon. London: Soncino, 1939, 10 vols.

*The Mishnah: Translated from the Hebrew with Introduction and Brief Explanatory Notes*, ed. H. Danby. Oxford: Oxford University, 1933.

### EARLY CHRISTIAN SOURCES

*The Ante-Nicene Christian Library: Translations of the Writings of the Fathers Down to AD 325*, ed. A. Roberts and J. Donaldson. Edinburgh: T. & T. Clark, 1884–8, 24 vols.

*The Apocryphal New Testament: A Collection of Apocryphal Christian Literature in an English Translation based on M. R. James*, ed. J. K. Elliott. Oxford: Clarendon, 1993.

*The Apostolic Fathers: A New Translation and Commentary*, ed. R. M. Grant. London: Thomas Nelson, 1965–68, 6 vols.

*A Select Library of the Nicene and Post-Nicene Fathers of the Christian Church*, ed. P. Schaff and H. Wace. Grand Rapids, Michigan: Eerdmans, 1956, 2 series, many vols.

## Secondary Literature

Achtemeier, P. J. (1970), 'Toward the Isolation of Pre-Markan Miracle Catenae', *Journal of Biblical Literature* 89, pp. 265–91.

—— (1972), 'The Origin and Function of the Pre-Marcan Miracle Catenae', *Journal of Biblical Literature* 91, pp. 198–221.

—— (1976), 'Jesus and the Disciples as Miracle Workers in the Apocryphal New Testament', in E. S. Fiorenza (ed.), *Aspects of Religious Propaganda in Judaism and Early Christianity*. Notre Dame: Notre Dame University, pp. 149–86.

Ainsworth-Smith, I. and Speck, P. (1982), *Letting Go: Caring for the Dying and Bereaved*. London: SPCK.

Allison, D. C. (1993), *The New Moses: A Matthean Typology*. Edinburgh: T. & T. Clark.

Alves, R. A. (1990), *The Poet, The Warrior, The Prophet*. London: SCM.

Anderson, E. B. and Morrill, B. T. (eds) (1998), *Liturgy and the Moral Self: Humanity at Full Stretch Before God*. Collegeville, MI: Pueblo.

Anderson, G. A. (1991), *A Time to Mourn, A Time to Dance: The Expressions of Grief and Joy in Israelite Religion*. Pennsylvania: Pennsylvania University.

Arnold, C. E. (1992), 'Joy', in Freedman, *Dictionary*, Vol. 3, pp. 1022–3.

Ashton, J. (1991), *Understanding the Fourth Gospel*. Oxford: Clarendon.

Astley, J. (ed.) (1991), *How Faith Grows: Faith Development and Christian Education*. London: Church House Publishing.

Astley, J. and Francis, L. (eds) (1992), *Christian Perspectives on Faith Development*. Grand Rapids, MI: Eerdmans.

Aune, D. (1987), *The New Testament in its Literary Environment*. Philadelphia: Westminster.

—— (1991), 'Oral Traditions and the Aphorisms of Jesus', in Wansbrough, *Jesus*, pp. 211–65.

—— (1996), 'Following the Lamb: Discipleship in the Apocalypse', in Longenecker, *Patterns*, pp. 269–84.

Averill, J. R. and Nunley, E. P. (1992), *Voyages of the Heart: Living an Emotionally Creative Life*. New York: Macmillan.

Avis, P. (ed.) (1993), *The Resurrection of Jesus Christ*. London: Darton, Longman & Todd.

Bahr, G. J. (1965), 'The Use of the Lord's Prayer in the Primitive Church', *Journal of Biblical Literature* 84, pp. 153–9.

Bailey, K. E. (1976), *Poet and Peasant*. Grand Rapids, MI: Eerdmans.

Bailey, L. R. (1979), *Biblical Perspectives on Death*. Philadelphia: Fortress.

Baird, J. A. (1969), *Audience Criticism and the Historical Jesus*. Philadelphia: Westminster.

Balasuriya, T. (1979), *The Eucharist and Human Liberation*. London: SCM.

Balthasar, Hans Urs von (1990), *Mysterium Paschale*, tr. and intro. A. Nichols. Edinburgh: T. & T. Clark.

Bammel, E. and Moule, C. F. D. (eds) (1984), *Jesus and the Politics of his Day*. Cambridge: Cambridge University.

Banks, R. (1975), *Jesus and the Law in the Synoptic Tradition*. Cambridge: Cambridge University.

Barr, J. (1988), 'Abba isn't Daddy', *Journal of Theological Studies* (n.s) 39, pp. 28–47.

Barrett, C. K. (1966), *The Holy Spirit and the Gospel Tradition*. London: SPCK, new edn.

—— (1978), *The Gospel According to St John: An Introduction with Commentary and Notes on the Greek Text*. London: SPCK, 2nd edn.

Barton, S. C. (ed.) (1999), *Where Shall Wisdom Be Found? Wisdom in the Bible, the Church and the Contemporary World*. Edinburgh: T. & T. Clark.

Barton, S. C. and Stanton G. (eds) (1994), *Resurrection: Essays in Honour of Leslie Houlden*. London: SPCK.

Bauckham, R. (1992a), 'Descent to the Underworld', in Freedman, *Dictionary*, Vol. 2, pp. 145–59.

—— (1992b), 'The Worship of Jesus', in Freedman, *Dictionary*, Vol. 3, pp. 812–19.

—— (1996), 'Life, Death, and the Afterlife in Second Temple Judaism' in Longenecker, *Life*, pp. 80–95.

—— (ed.) (1998), *The Gospels for All Christians: Rethinking the Gospel Audiences*. Edinburgh: T. & T. Clark.

Bauer, W. (1972), *Orthodoxy and Heresy in Earliest Christianity*, tr. R. A. Kraft and G. Krodel. London: SCM.

Beasley-Murray, G. R. (1972), *Baptism in the New Testament*. Exeter: Paternoster.

—— (1986), *Jesus and the Kingdom of God*. Grand Rapids, MI: Eerdmans.

Behm, J. (1965), 'κλάω', in Kittel and Friedrich, *Dictionary*, Vol. 3, pp. 726–43.

Belleville, L. L. (1996), ' "Imitate Me, Just as I Imitate Christ": Discipleship in the Corinthian Correspondence', in Longenecker, *Patterns*, pp. 120–42.

Bender, A. P. (1894–5), 'Beliefs, Rites, and Customs of the Jews, connected with Death, Burial, and Mourning', *Jewish Quarterly Review* 6, pp. 317–47, 664–71; 7, pp. 101–18, 259–69.

Berger, K. (1973–4), 'Die königlichen Messiastraditionen des Neuen Testaments', *New Testament Studies* 20, pp. 1–44.

Best, E. (1981), *Following Jesus: Discipleship in the Gospel of Mark*. Sheffield: JSOT.

—— (1983), *Mark: The Gospel as Story*. Edinburgh: T. & T. Clark.

Betz, J. (1996), 'The Eucharist in the Didache' in Draper, *Didache*, pp. 244–75.

Blue, B. (1994), 'Acts and the House Church' in D. W. J. Gill and C. Gempf (eds), *The Book of Acts in Its First Century Setting*. Grand Rapids, MI: Eerdmans, Vol. 2, pp. 119–222.

Boff, L. (1980), *Jesus Christ Liberator: A Critical Christology for Our Time*, tr. P. Hughes. London: SPCK.

Bokser, B. M. (1985), 'Wonder-Working and the Rabbinic Tradition: The Case of Hanina ben Dosa', *Journal for the Study of Judaism* 16, pp. 42–91.

Bonhoeffer, D. (1954), *Life Together*, tr. J. W. Doberstein. London: SCM.

—— (1971), *Letters and Papers from Prison*, tr. J. Bowden, F. Clarke, and R. Fuller. London: SCM, enlarged edn.

Borg, M. J. (1992), 'The Teaching of Jesus Christ', in Freedman, *Dictionary*, Vol. 3, pp. 804–12.

—— (1993), *Jesus, A New Vision: Spirit, Culture and the Life of Discipleship*. London: SPCK.

—— (1998), *Conflict, Holiness and Politics in the Teaching of Jesus*. Harrisburg, PA: Trinity [this edn].

Bornkamm, G. (1997), 'Towards the Interpretation of John's Gospel', tr. by the editor in J. Ashton (ed.), *The Interpretation of John*. Edinburgh: T. & T. Clark, 2nd edn, pp. 97–119.

Bornkamm, G., Barth, G. and Held, H. J. (eds) (1963), *Tradition and Interpretation in Matthew*, tr. P. Scott. Philadelphia: Westminster.

Borobio, D. (1986), 'Sacramental Forgiveness of Sins', in *Concilium* 184, pp. 95–112.

Bourdieu, P. (1977), *Outline of a Theory of Practice*, tr. R. Nice. Cambridge: Cambridge University.

Bouyer, L. (1968), *Eucharist: Theology and Spirituality of the Eucharistic Prayer*, tr. C. U. Quinn. Notre Dame: Notre Dame University.

Bowker, J. W. (1966), 'Intercession in the Quran and the Jewish Tradition', *Journal for the Study of Judaism* 11, pp. 69–82.

—— (1969), *The Targums and Rabbinic Literature: An Introduction to Jewish Interpretation of Scripture*. Cambridge: Cambridge University.

—— (1995), *Is God a Virus? Genes, Culture and Religion*. London: SPCK.

Bowlby, J. (1979), *The Making and Breaking of Affectional Bonds*. London: Routledge.

—— (1981), *Attachment and Loss, Volume 3 – Loss: Sadness and Depression*. London: Penguin. [this edn].

Bradshaw, P. (1992), *The Search for the Origins of Christian Worship*. London: SPCK.

Branick, V. (1989), *The House Church in the Writings of Paul*. Wilmington, DE: Michael Glazier.

Brooke, G. J. (1980), 'The Lord's Prayer Interpreted through John and Paul', *Downside Review* 98, pp. 298–311.

Brown, D. and Loades, A. (eds) (1996), *Christ: The Sacramental Word – Incarnation, Sacrament and Poetry*. London: SPCK.

Brown, R. E. (1981), *The Gospel According to John I–XII: A New Translation with Introduction and Commentary*. New York: Doubleday, 2nd edn.

—— (1994), *The Death of the Messiah: From Gethsemane to the Grave*. New

York: Doubleday, 2 vols.

Brueggemann, W. (1972), *In Man We Trust: The Neglected Side of Biblical Faith*. Atlanta, GA: John Knox.

—— (1986), *Hopeful Imagination: Prophetic Voices in Exile*. Philadelphia: Fortress.

—— (1987), *Hope within History*. Atlanta: John Knox.

—— (1995a), 'From Hurt to Joy, from Death to Life', in Miller, *Psalms*, pp. 67–83.

—— (1995b), 'The Formfulness of Grief', in Miller, *Psalms*, pp. 84–97.

Brümmer, V. (1993), *The Model of Love: A Study in Philosophical Theology*. Cambridge: Cambridge University.

Buber, M. (1951), *Two Types of Faith*, tr. N. P. Goldhawk. London: Routledge & Kegan Paul.

Buchanan, C. (ed.) (1984), *Essays on Eucharistic Sacrifice in the Early Church*. Nottingham: Grove Books.

—— (1990), *Children in Communion*. Nottingham: Grove Books.

Büchler, A. (1922), *Types of Jewish-Palestinian Piety from 70 BCE to 70 CE* London: Jews' College.

Bultmann, R. (1952), *Theology of the New Testament, Volume 1*, tr. K. Grobel. London: SCM.

—— (1958), *Jesus and the Word*, tr. L. P. Smith and E. H. Lantero. New York: Charles Scribner.

—— (1971), *The Gospel of John: A Commentary*, tr. G. R. Beasley-Murray. Oxford: Basil Blackwell.

Burchard, C. (1987), 'The Importance of Joseph and Aseneth for the Study of the New Testament: A General Survey and a Fresh Look at the Lord's Supper', *New Testament Studies* 33, pp. 102–34.

Burge, G. M. (1987), *The Anointed Community: The Holy Spirit in the Johannine Tradition*. Grand Rapids, MI: Eerdmans.

Burns, S. (1996), 'Abuse and Forgiveness – Theological and Psychological Aspects'. Unpublished M. Litt. thesis, Cambridge University.

Burridge, R. A. (1992), *What Are the Gospels? A Comparison with Graeco-Roman Biography*. Cambridge: Cambridge University.

—— (1998), 'About People, by People, for People: Gospel Genre and Audiences', in Bauckham, *Gospels*, pp. 113–45.

Buxton, R. F. (1986), 'Holy Saturday', in J. G. Davies (ed.), *A New Dictionary of Liturgy and Worship*. London: SCM, pp. 258–9.

Cameron, R. (1992), 'Gospel of Thomas', in Freedman, *Dictionary*, Vol. 6, pp. 535–40.

Carnley, P. (1987), *The Structure of Resurrection Belief*. Oxford: Clarendon.

Casey, M. (1990), 'The Original Aramaic Form of Jesus' Interpretation of the Cup', *Journal of Theological Studies (n.s.)* 41, pp. 1–12.

—— (1991), *From Jewish Prophet to Gentile God: The Origins and Development of New Testament Christology*. Cambridge: J. Clarke.

Catchpole, D. R. (1993), *The Quest for Q*. Edinburgh: T. & T. Clark.

Cavallin, H. C. C. (1974), *Life After Death: Paul's Argument for the Resurrection of the Dead in 1 Corinthians 15, Part 1*. Lund: C. W. K. Gleerup.

Charlesworth, J. H. (1986), 'Jewish Hymns, Odes, and Prayers (*c.* 167 BCE –135 CE)', in R. A. Kraft and G. W. E. Nickelsburg (eds), *Early Judaism and Its Modern Interpreters*. Atlanta, GA: Scholars, pp. 411–36.

—— (1988), *Jesus within Judaism: New Light from Exciting Archaeological Discoveries*. New York: Doubleday.

—— (1992a), 'Jewish Prayers in the Time of Jesus', *Princeton Seminary Bulletin*, Supplementary Issue 2, pp. 36–55.

—— (ed.) (1992b), *The Messiah: Developments in Earliest Judaism and Christianity*. Minneapolis: Fortress.

—— (ed.) (1994), *The Lord's Prayer and Other Prayer Texts from the Greco-Roman Era*. Valley Forge, PA: Trinity.

Chenderlin, F. (1982), *'Do This as My Memorial.' The Semantic and Conceptual Backgound and Value of Ανάμνησις in 1 Corinthians 11.24–25*. Rome: Biblical Institute.

Childs, B. S. (1962), *Memory and Tradition in Israel*. London: SCM.

Chilton, B. D. (1979), *God in Strength: Jesus' Announcement of the Kingdom*. Freistadt: F. Plöchl.

—— (1983), *The Glory of Israel: The Theology and Provenience of the Isaiah Targum*. Sheffield: JSOT.

—— (1984), *A Galilean Rabbi and His Bible: Jesus' Use of the Interpreted Scripture of His Time*. Wilmington, DE: Michael Glazier.

—— (1988), 'Jesus and the Repentance of E. P. Sanders', *Tyndale Bulletin* 39, pp. 1–18.

—— (1992), 'The Purity of the Kingdom as Conveyed in Jesus' Meals', in E. H. Lovering (ed.), *Society of Biblical Literature 1992 Seminar Papers*. Atlanta, GA: Scholars, pp. 473–88.

—— (1994), *A Feast of Meanings: Eucharistic Theologies from Jesus through Johannine Circles*. Leiden: E. J. Brill.

—— (1996), *Pure Kingdom: Jesus' Vision of God*. Grand Rapids MI: Eerdmans.

—— (1997), *Jesus' Prayer and Jesus' Eucharist: His Personal Practice of Spirituality*. Valley Forge, PA: Trinity.

—— (1998), *Jesus' Baptism and Jesus' Healing: His Personal Practice of Spirituality*. Harrisburg, PA: Trinity.

Chilton, B. D. and MacDonald, J. I. H. (1987), *Jesus and the Ethics of the Kingdom*. London: SPCK.

Clements, R. E. (1980), 'זכר et. al.', in G. J. Botterweck and H. Ringgren (eds), *Theological Dictionary of the Old Testament*, tr. D. E. Green. Grand Rapids, MI: Eerdmans, Vol. 4, pp. 64–87.

Collins, J. J. (1974), 'Apocalyptic Eschatology as the Transcendence of Death', *Catholic Biblical Quarterly* 36, pp. 21–43.

—— (1992), 'Dead Sea Scrolls', in Freedman, *Dictionary*, Vol. 2, pp. 85–101.

Conn, W. (1986), *Christian Conversion: A Developmental Interpretation of Autonomy and Surrender*. New York: Paulist.

Conzelmann, H. (1961), *The Theology of St Luke*, tr. G. Buswell. New York: Harper & Row.

Cousar, C. B. (1992), 'Jerusalem, Council of', in Freedman, *Dictionary*, Vol. 3, pp. 766–8.

Cracknell, K. (1986), *Towards a New Relationship: Christians and People of Other Faith*. London: Epworth.

Crenshaw, J. L. (1998), *Education in Ancient Israel: Across the Deadening Silence*. New York: Doubleday.

Crossan, J. D. (1973), *In Parables: The Challenge of the Historical Jesus*. New York: Harper & Row.

—— (1983), *In Fragments: The Aphorisms of Jesus*. New York: Harper & Row.

—— (1988), *The Cross that Spoke: The Origins of the Passion Narrative*. San Francisco: Harper & Row.

—— (1991), *The Historical Jesus: The Life of a Mediterranean Jewish Peasant*. Edinburgh: T. & T. Clark.

—— (1995), *Who Killed Jesus? Exposing the Roots of Anti-Semitism in the Gospel Story of the Death of Jesus*. New York: HarperSanFrancisco.

—— (1998), *The Birth of Christianity: Discovering What Happened in the Years Immediately after the Execution of Jesus*. San Francisco: HarperSan-Francisco.

Cullmann, O., *The Christology of the New Testament*, tr. S. C. Guthrie and C. A. M. Hall. London: SCM, 2nd edn.

Cupitt, D. (1979), *Explorations in Theology – Volume 6*. London: SCM.

Dahl, N. A. (1976), *Jesus in the Memory of the Church*. Minneapolis: Augsburg.

Dallen, J. (1986), *The Reconciling Community: The Rite of Penance*. New York: Pueblo.

Dalton, W. J. (1989), *Christ's Proclamation to the Spirits: A Study of 1 Peter 3:18—4:6*. Rome: Pontifical Biblical Institute, 2nd edn.

Daly, R. J. (1978), *The Origins of the Christian Doctrine of Sacrifice*. London: Darton, Longman & Todd.

Davidson, R. (1990), *Wisdom and Worship*. London: SCM.

Davies, D. J. (1997), *Death, Ritual and Belief: The Rhetoric of Funerary Rites*. London: Cassell.

Davies, E. W. (1981), 'Inheritance Rights and the Hebrew Levirate Marriage', *Vetus Testamentum* 31, pp. 138–44, 257–88.

Davies, H. (1993), *Bread of Life and Cup of Joy: Newer Ecumenical Perspectives on the Eucharist*. Grand Rapids, MI: Eerdmans.

Davies, W. D. (1966), *The Setting of the Sermon on the Mount*. Cambridge: Cambridge University.

Davis, S. T., Kendall, D., and O'Collins, G. (eds) (1997), *The Resurrection:*

*An Interdisciplinary Symposium on the Resurrection of Jesus.* Oxford: Oxford University.

De Boer, M. C. (1988), *The Defeat of Death: Apocalyptic Eschatology in 1 Corinthians 15 and Romans 5.* Sheffield: JSOT.

De Boer, W. P. (1962), *The Imitation of Paul: An Exegetical Study.* Kampen: Kok.

Dennis, J. (chairperson) (1995), *On the Way: Towards an Integrated Approach to Christian Initiation.* London: Church House Publishing.

Derrett, J. D. M. (1973), *Jesus's Audience: The Social and Psychological Environment in which He Worked.* London: Darton, Longman & Todd.

De Vaux, R. (1961), *Ancient Israel: Its Life and Institutions,* tr. J. McHugh. London: Darton, Longman & Todd.

Dix, D. G. (1945), *The Shape of the Liturgy.* London: A. & C. Black, 2nd edn.

Dodd, C. H. (1936), *The Apostolic Preaching and its Developments.* London: Hodder & Stoughton.

—— (1953), *The Interpretation of the Fourth Gospel.* Cambridge: Cambridge University.

Dominian, J. (1998), *One Like Us: A Psychological Interpretation of Jesus.* London: Darton, Longman & Todd.

Downing, F. G. (1988), *Christ and the Cynics: Jesus and Other Radicals in First Century Traditions.* Sheffield: JSOT.

—— (1992), *Cynics and Christian Origins.* Edinburgh: T. & T. Clark.

Dragas, G. D. (1985), *St Athanasius Contra Apollinarem.* Athens: no publisher.

Draper, J. A. (ed.) (1996), *The Didache in Modern Research.* Leiden: E. J. Brill.

Droge, A. J. and Tabor, J. D. (1992), *A Noble Death: Suicide and Martyrdom among Christians and Jews in Antiquity.* San Fransisco: Harper.

Dudley, M. and Rowell, G. (eds) (1990), *Confession and Absolution.* London: SPCK.

Duling, D. C. (1975), 'Solomon, Exorcism, and the Son of David', *Harvard Theological Review* 68, pp. 235–52.

—— (1977–78), 'The Therapeutic Son of David: An Element in Matthew's Christological Apologetic', *New Testament Studies* 24, pp. 392–410.

Dungan, D. L. (1971), *The Sayings of Jesus in the Churches of Paul.* Oxford: Blackwell.

Dunn, J. D. G. (1970), *Baptism in the New Testament: A Re-examination of the New Testament Teaching on the Gift of the Spirit in Relation to Pentecostalism Today.* London: SCM.

—— (1975), *Jesus and the Spirit: A Study of the Religious and Charismatic Experience of Jesus and the First Christians as Reflected in the New Testament.* London: SCM.

—— (1977), *Unity and Diversity in the New Testament: An Inquiry into the Character of Earliest Christianity.* London: SCM.

—— (1980), *Christology in the Making: An Inquiry into the Origins of the Doctrine of the Incarnation*. London: SCM.

—— (1990), *Jesus, Paul and the Law: Studies in Mark and Galatians*. London: SPCK.

—— (1991), *The Partings of the Ways Between Christianity and Judaism and their Significance for the Character of Christianity*. London: SCM.

—— (1998), *The Theology of Paul the Apostle*. Edinburgh: T. & T. Clark.

Dupont, J. (1970), 'The Conversion of Paul, and its Influence on his Understanding of Salvation by Faith', tr. R. P. Martin in W. W. Gasque and R. P. Martin (eds), *Apostolic History and the Gospel*, Exeter: Paternoster, pp. 176–94.

Durkheim, E. (1952), *The Elementary Forms of the Religious Life*, tr. J. W. Swain. London: Routledge & Kegan Paul.

Ebeling, G. (1963), *Word and Faith*, tr. J. W. Leitch. London: SCM.

Elliott, C. (1995), *Memory and Salvation*. London: Darton, Longman & Todd.

Elliott, J. H. (1985), 'Backward and Forward "In His Steps": Following Jesus from Rome to Raymond and Beyond. The Tradition, Redaction, and Reception of 1 Peter 2:18–25', in Segovia, *Discipleship*, pp. 184–208.

Etchells. R. (1998), *A Reading of the Parables of Jesus*. London: Darton, Longman & Todd.

Evans, C. A. (1995), *Jesus and His Contemporaries: Comparative Studies*. Leiden: E. J. Brill.

Evans, C. F. (1970), *Resurrection in the New Testament*. London: SCM.

Fee, G. D. (1994), *God's Empowering Presence: The Holy Spirit in the Letters of Paul*. Peabody, MA: Hendrickson.

Feeley-Harnik, G. (1994), *The Lord's Table: The Meaning of Food in Early Judaism and Christianity*. Washington: Smithsonian Institution.

Fenton, J. (1993), 'The Four Gospels: Four Perspectives on the Resurrection', in Avis, *Resurrection*, pp. 39–49.

Fink, P. E. (ed.) (1987), *Alternative Futures for Worship – Volume 4: Reconciliation*. Collegeville, MN: Liturgical.

Flusser, D. (1981), *Die rabbinischen Gleichnisse und der Gleichniserzähler Jesus: Teil 1 – Das Wesen der Gleichnisse*. Bern: Peter Lang.

Ford, D. F. (1995), 'What Happens in the Eucharist?', *Scottish Journal of Theology* 48, pp. 359–81.

—— (1997), *The Shape of Living*. London: HarperCollinsReligious.

—— (1999), *Self and Salvation: Being Transformed*. Cambridge: Cambridge University.

Fortna, R. T. (1992), 'Signs/Semeia Source', in Freedman, *Dictionary*, Vol. 6, pp. 18–22.

Fowler, J. W. (1981), *Stages in Faith: The Psychology of Human Development and the Quest for Meaning*. San Francisco: Harper & Row.

—— (1987), *Faith Development and Pastoral Care*. Philadelphia: Fortress.

Fowler, J. W., Nipkow, K. E. and Schweitzer, F. (eds) (1992), *Stages of Faith and Religious Development*. London: SCM.

Fox, R.L. (1988), *Pagans and Christians in the Mediterranean World from the Second Century AD to the conversion of Constantine*. London: Penguin.

Freedman, D. N. (ed.) (1992), *The Anchor Bible Dictionary*. New York: Doubleday, 6 vols.

Freyne, S. (1998), *Galilee: From Alexander the Great to Hadrian, 323 BCE to 135 CE – A Study in Second Temple Judaism*. Edinburgh: T. & T. Clark.

Froehlich, K. (1992), 'The Lord's Prayer in Patristic Literature', *Princeton Seminary Bulletin*, Supplementary Issue 2, pp. 71–87.

Frost, B. (1991), *The Politics of Peace*. London: Darton, Longman & Todd.

Frost, E. (1954), *Christian Healing: A Consideration of the Place of Spiritual Healing in the Church of Today in the Light of the Doctrine and Practice of the Ante-Nicene Church*. London: A. R. Mowbray & Co, 3rd edn.

Fuchs, E. (1964), *Studies in the Historical Jesus*, tr. A. Scobie. London: SCM.

Fuller, R. H. (1963), 'The Double Origin of the Eucharist', *Biblical Research* 8, pp. 60–72.

Furnish, V. P. (1973), *The Love Command in the New Testament*. London: SCM.

Gaventa, B. R. (1986), *From Darkness to Light: Aspects of Conversion in the New Testament*. Philadelphia: Fortress.

Gelpi, D. L. (1977), *Charism and Sacrament: A Theology of Christian Conversion*. London: SPCK.

George, A. R. (1953), *Communion with God in the New Testament*. London: Epworth.

Gerhardsson, B. (1961), *Memory and Manuscript: Oral Tradition and Written Transmission in Rabbinic Judaism and Early Christianity*. Lund: C. W. K. Gleerup.

Gibbard, S. M. (1966), 'The Eucharist in the Ignatian Epistles', *Studia Patristica*, Vol. 8 (Texte und Untersuchungen 93); Berlin: Akademie-Verlag, pp. 214–18.

Gill, P. (1994), 'Death in the Christian Community: Theology, Funeral Ritual and Pastoral Care From the Perspective of Victor Turner's Ritual Process Model', *Modern Believing* 35, pp. 17–24.

Goppelt, L. (1981), *Theology of the New Testament – Volume 1: The Ministry of Jesus and its Theological Significance*, tr. J. E. Alsup. Grand Rapids, MI: Eerdmans.

Gowan, D. E. (1998), *Theology of the Prophetic Books. The Death and Restoration of Israel*. Louisville KN: Westminster/John Knox.

Grayston, K. (1990), *Dying, We Live: A New Enquiry into the Death of Christ in the New Testament*. London: Darton, Longman & Todd.

Green, E. M. B. (1965), *The Meaning of Salvation*. London: Hodder & Stoughton.

Green, W. S. (1982), 'Palestinian Holy Men: Charismatic Leadership and Rabbinic Tradition', in W. Haase (ed.), *Aufstieg und Niedergang der*

*Römischen Welt.* Berlin: Walter de Gruyter, Vol. 2.19.2, pp. 619–47.

Greenwood, R. (1994), *Transforming Priesthood.* London: SPCK.

Grillmeier, A. (1949), 'Der Gottessohn im Totenreich: Soteriologische und christologische Motivierung der Descensuslehre in der älteren christlichen Überlieferung', *Zeitschrift für Theologie und Kirche* 71, pp. 1–53, 184–203.

—— (1975), *Christ in Christian Tradition, Volume 1: From the Apostolic Age to Chalcedon (AD 451),* tr. J. Bowden. London: Mowbrays, rev. edn.

Gundry, R. H. (1976), *SOMA in Biblical Theology with Emphasis on Pauline Anthropology.* Cambridge, Cambridge University.

Hahn, F. (1969), *The Titles of Jesus in Christology: Their History in Early Christianity,* tr. H. Knight and G. Ogg. London: Lutterworth.

Hahn, F. and Klein, H. (eds.) (1982), *Glaube im Neuen Testament: Studien zu Ehren von Herman Binder anlässlich seines 70 Geburtstags.* Neukirchen-Vluyn: Neukirchener.

Hanson, R. P. C. (1979), *Eucharistic Offering in the Early Church.* Nottingham: Grove Books.

—— (1988), *The Search for the Christian Doctrine of God: The Arian Controversy 318–381.* Edinburgh: T. & T. Clark.

Hardy, D. W. and Ford, D. F. (1984), *Jubilate: Theology in Praise.* London: Darton, Longman & Todd.

Harris, H. A. (1998), 'Should we say that Personhood is Relational?', *Scottish Journal of Theology* 51, pp. 214–34.

Harris, M. J. (1983), *Raised Immortal: Resurrection and Immortality in the New Testament.* London: Marshall, Morgan & Scott.

Hart, T. and Thimell, D. (eds) (1989), *Christ in our Place: The Humanity of God in Christ for the Reconciliation of the World.* Exeter: Paternoster.

Harvey, A. E. (1982), *Jesus and the Constraints of History.* London: Duckworth.

—— (1990), *Strenuous Commands: The Ethics of Jesus.* London: SCM.

Harvey, N. P. (1985), *Death's Gift: Chapters on Resurrection and Bereavement.* London: Epworth.

Hawthorne, G. F. (1996), 'The Imitation of Christ: Discipleship in Philippians', in Longenecker, *Patterns,* pp. 163–79.

Hays, R. B. (1996), *The Moral Vision of the New Testament: Community, Cross, New Creation – A Contemporary Introduction to New Testament Ethics.* San Francisco: Harper.

Hengel, M. (1979), *Acts and the History of Earliest Christianity,* tr. J. Bowden. London: SCM.

—— (1981a), *The Atonement: The Origins of the Doctrine in the New Testament,* tr. J. Bowden. London: SCM.

—— (1981b), *The Charismatic Leader and his Followers,* tr. J. C. G. Greig. Edinburgh: T. & T. Clark.

Hengel, M. with Deines, R. (1991), *The Pre-Christian Paul,* tr. J. Bowden. London: SCM.

Hermisson, H.-J. and Lohse, E. (1981), *Faith*, tr. D. W. Stott. Nashville, TN: Abingdon.

Heron, A. (1983), *Table and Tradition: Towards an Ecumenical Understanding of the Eucharist*. Edinburgh: Handsel.

Higgins, A. J. B. (1952), *The Lord's Supper in the New Testament*. London: SCM.

Hofius, O. (1967), *Jesu Tischgemeinschaft mit den Sündern*. Stuttgart: Calwer.

—— (1993), 'The Lord's Supper and the Lord's Supper Tradition: Reflections on 1 Corinthians 11:23b–25', tr. B. D. Smith, in Meyer, *Loaf*, pp. 75–115.

Holeton, D. R. (1991), *Christian Initiation in the Anglican Communion*. Nottingham: Grove Books.

Hollenbach, P. W. (1982), 'The Conversion of Jesus: From Jesus the Baptizer to Jesus the Healer', in W. Haase (ed.), *Aufstieg und Niedergang der Römischen Welt*. Berlin: Walter de Gruyter, Vol. 2.25.1, pp. 196–219.

Holm, J. with Bowker, J. (eds) (1994), *Rites of Passage*. London: Pinter.

Horn, F. W. (1992), 'Holy Spirit', tr. D. M. Elliott in Freedman, *Dictionary*, Vol. 3, pp. 260–80.

Horsley, R. A. (1987), *Jesus and the Spiral of Violence: Popular Jewish Resistance in Roman Palestine*. San Francisco: Harper & Row.

—— (1989), *Sociology and the Jesus Movement*. New York: Crossroad.

—— (1995), *Galilee: History, Politics, People*. Philadelphia: Trinity.

—— (1996), *Archaeology, History, and Society in Galilee: The Social Context of Jesus and the Rabbis*. Valley Forge, PA: Trinity.

Horsley, R. A. and Hanson, J. S. (1985), *Bandits, Prophets and Messiahs: Popular Movements at the Time of Jesus*. Minneapolis: Winston.

Horsley, R. A. and Silberman, N. A. (1997), *The Message and the Kingdom: How Jesus and Paul Ignited a Revolution and Transformed the Ancient World*. New York: Grosset/Putnam.

Houlden, J. L. (1992), 'Lord's Prayer', in Freedman, *Dictionary*, Vol. 4, pp. 346–62.

Hurtado, L. W. (1988), *One God, One Lord: Early Christian Devotion and Ancient Jewish Monotheism*. London: SCM.

—— (1998), 'First-Century Jewish Monotheism', *Journal for the Study of the New Testament* 71, pp. 3–26.

Jackson, E. N. (1985), *Understanding Grief: Its Roots, Dynamics, and Treatment* London: SCM [this edn].

Jasper, R. C. D. and Cuming, G. J. (1987), *Prayers of the Eucharist: Early and Reformed*. New York: Pueblo, 3rd edn.

Jenks, A. W. (1992), 'Eating and Drinking in the Old Testament', in Freedman, *Dictionary*, Vol. 2, pp. 250–4.

Jeremias, J. (1964), *The Eucharistic Words of Jesus*, tr. N. Perrin. London: SCM.

—— (1967), *The Prayers of Jesus*, tr. J. Bowden, C. Burchard and J. Reumann. London: SCM.

—— (1971), *New Testament Theology, Volume 1: The Proclamation of Jesus*, tr. J. Bowden. London: SCM.

—— (1972), *The Parables of Jesus*, tr. S. H. Hooke. London: SCM, rev. edn.

Jewett, R. (1979), *Dating Paul's Life*. London: SCM.

—— (1993), 'Tenement Churches and Communal Meals in the Early Church: The Implications of a Form-Critical Analysis of 2 Thessalonians 3:10', *Biblical Research* 38, pp. 23–43.

—— (1994), 'Tenement Churches and Pauline Love Feasts', *Quarterly Review* 14, pp. 43–58.

Johnson, A. R. (1964), *The Vitality of the Individual in the Thought of Ancient Israel*. Cardiff: University of Wales.

Johnson, L. T. (1981), *Sharing Possessions: Mandate and Symbol of Faith*. London: SCM.

—— (1986), *The Writings of the New Testament: An Interpretation*. London: SCM.

—— (1998), *Religious Experience in Earliest Christianity: A Missing Dimension in New Testament Studies*. Minneapolis: Fortress.

Jones, C., Wainwright, G. and Yarnold, E. (eds) (1978), *The Study of Liturgy*. London: SPCK.

Jones, L. G. (1995), *Embodying Forgiveness: A Theological Analysis*. Grand Rapids, MI: Eerdmans.

Joyce, P. (1993), 'Lamentations and the Grief Process: A Psychological Reading', *Biblical Interpretation* 1, pp. 304–20.

Jungmann, J. A. (1965), *The Place of Christ in Liturgical Prayer*, tr. A. Peele. London: Geoffrey Chapman.

Kaiser, O. and Lohse, E. (1981), *Death and Life*, tr. J. F. Steely. Nashville, TN: Abingdon.

Kanda, S. H. (1973), 'The Form and Function of the Petrine and Pauline Miracle Stories in the Acts of the Apostles'. Unpublished doctoral thesis, Claremont Graduate School.

Käsemann, E. (1969), *New Testament Questions of Today*, tr. W. J. Montague and W. F. Bunge. London: SCM.

Kee, H. C. (1986), *Medicine, Miracle and Magic in New Testament Times*. Cambridge: Cambridge University.

Kelber, W. H. (1983), *The Oral and Written Gospel: The Hermeneutics of Speaking and Writing in the Synoptic Tradition, Mark, Paul, and Q*. Philadelphia: Fortress.

Kennedy, R. J. (ed.) (1987), *Reconciliation: The Continuing Agenda*. Collegeville, MN: Liturgical.

Kim S. (1981), *The Origin of Paul's Gospel*. Tübingen: J. C. B. Mohr (Paul Siebeck).

Kingsbury, J. D. (1983), *The Christology of Mark's Gospel*. Philadelphia: Fortress.

Kittel, G. and Friedrich, G. (eds) (1964–76), *Theological Dictionary of the*

*New Testament*, tr. G. W. Bromiley. Grand Rapids, MI: Eerdmans, 10 vols.

Klassen, W. (1992a), 'Judas Iscariot', in Freedman, *Dictionary*, Vol. 3, pp. 1091–6.

—— (1992b), 'Love (New Testament and Jewish Literature)', in Freedman, *Dictionary*, Vol. 4, pp. 381–96.

—— (1996), *Judas: Betrayer or Friend of Jesus*. London: SCM.

Klauck, H.-J. (1986), *Herrenmahl und hellenistischer Kult: Eine religionsgeschichte Untersuchung zum ersten Korintherbrief*. Münster: Aschendorff, 2nd edn.

—— (1993), 'Presence in the Lord's Supper: 1 Corinthians 11:23–26 in the Context of Hellenistic Religious History', tr. B. D. Smith in Meyer, *Loaf*, pp. 57–74.

Kloppenborg, J. S. (1987), *The Formation of Q: Trajectories in Ancient Wisdom Collections*. Philadelphia: Fortress.

—— (1990), '"Easter Faith" and the Sayings Gospel of Q', *Semeia* 49, pp. 71–99.

Knoch, O. (1993), '"Do This in Memory of Me!" (Luke 22:20; 1 Cor 11:24–25) – The Celebration of the Eucharist in the Primitive Christian Communities', tr. S. Keesmaat in Meyer, *Loaf*, pp. 1–10.

Knox, J. (1963), *The Church and the Reality of Christ*. London: Collins.

Koenig, J. (1985), *New Testament Hospitality: Partnership with Strangers as Promise and Mission*. Philadelphia: Fortress.

—— (1992), 'Hospitality' in Freedman, *Dictionary*, Vol. 3, pp. 299–301.

Koester, H. (1971), 'GNOMAI DIAPHOROI: The Origin and Nature of Diversification in the History of Early Christianity', in J. M. Robinson and H. Koester, *Trajectories in Early Christianity*. Philadelphia: Fortress, pp. 114–57.

Köstenberger, A.J. (1998), *The Missions of Jesus and the Disciples according to the Fourth Gospel with Implications for the Fourth Gospel's Purpose and the Mission of the Contemporary Church*. Grand Rapids, MI: Eerdmans.

Kübler-Ross, E. (1970), *On Death and Dying*. London: Tavistock.

Kung, H. (1995), *Christianity: Its Essence and History*, tr. J. Bowden. London: SCM.

Kurz, W. S. (1985), 'Kenotic Imitation of Paul and of Christ in Philippians 2 and 3', in Segovia, *Discipleship*, pp. 103–26.

Kuschel, K.-J. (1992), *Born before All Time? The Dispute over Christ's Origin*. tr. J. Bowden. London: SCM.

Lampe, G. W. H. (1965), 'Miracles and Early Christian Apologetic' in Moule, *Miracles*, pp. 205–18.

—— (1976), *The Seal of the Spirit: A Study in the Doctrine of Baptism and Confirmation in the New Testament and Fathers*. London: SPCK, 2nd edn.

Lane, W. L. (1996), 'Standing before the Moral Claim of God: Discipleship in Hebrews', in Longenecker, *Patterns*, pp. 203–24.

Lash, N. (1990), 'Friday, Saturday, Sunday', *New Blackfriars* 71, pp. 109–19.

LaVerdiere, E. (1996), *The Eucharist in the New Testament and the Early Church.* New York: Pueblo.

Lewis, A.E. (1987), 'The Burial of God: Rupture and Resumption as the Story of Salvation', *Scottish Journal of Theology* 40, pp. 335–62.

Lewis. I. M. (1986), *Religion in Context: Cults and Charisma.* Cambridge: Cambridge University.

Lewis, T. J. (1992), 'Abode of the Dead', in Freedman, *Dictionary,* Vol. 2, pp. 101–5.

Lietzmann, H. (1969), *An Die Korinther I–II.* Tübingen: J. C. B. Mohr (Paul Siebeck), 5th edn with supplement by W. G. Kümmel.

—— (1979), *Mass and the Lord's Supper: A Study in the History of Liturgy,* tr. D. H. G. Reeve. Leiden: E. J. Brill.

Lindars, B. (1961), *New Testament Apologetic.* London: SCM.

—— (1987), ' "Joseph and Asenath" and the Eucharist', in B. P. Thompson (ed.), *Scripture: Meaning and Method. Essays presented to Anthony Tyrrell Hanson for his Seventieth Birthday.* Hull: Hull University, pp. 181–99.

—— (1993), 'The Resurrection and the Empty Tomb', in Avis, *Resurrection,* pp. 116–35.

Lindbeck, G. A. (1984), *The Nature of Doctrine: Religion and Theology in a Postliberal Age.* London: SPCK.

Littlewood, J. (1992), *Aspects of Grief: Bereavement in Adult Life.* London: Routledge.

Loewe, R, (1990), 'Jewish Exegesis', in R. J. Coggins and J. L. Houlden (eds), *A Dictionary of Biblical Interpretation.* London: SCM, pp. 346–54.

Lohmeyer, E. (1965), *The Lord's Prayer,* tr. J. Bowden. London: Collins.

Longenecker, R. N. (ed.) (1996), *Patterns of Discipleship in the New Testament.* Grand Rapids, MI: Eerdmans.

—— (ed.) (1998), *Life in the Face of Death: The Resurrection Message of the New Testament.* Grand Rapids, MI: Eerdmans.

Loos, H. van der (1968), *The Miracles of Jesus.* Leiden: E. J. Brill.

Lorenzen. T. (1995), *Resurrection and Discipleship: Interpretative Models, Biblical Reflections, Theological Consequences.* New York: Orbis.

Lüdemann, G. (1984), *Paul: Apostle to the Gentiles – Studies in Chronology,* tr. F. S. Jones. London: SCM.

—— (1989), *Early Christianity according to the Traditions of Acts,* tr. J. Bowden. London: SCM.

—— (1994), *Resurrection of Jesus: History, Experience, Theology,* tr. J. Bowden. London: SCM.

—— (1996), *Heretics: The Other Side of Early Christianity,* tr. J. Bowden. London: SCM.

Lüdemann, G., with Özen, A. (1995), *What Really Happened to Jesus?,* tr. J. Bowden. London: SCM.

Lunny, W. J. (1989), *Sociology of the Resurrection.* London: SCM.

MacCulloch, J. A. (1930), *The Harrowing of Hell: A Comparative Study of an Early Christian Doctrine.* Edinburgh: T. & T. Clark.

Mack, B. L. (1988), *A Myth of Innocence: Mark and Christian Origins*. Philadelphia: Fortress.

—— (1993), *The Lost Gospel: The Book of Q and Christian Origins*. San Francisco: Harper.

Mackey, J. P. (1979), *Jesus the Man and the Myth: A Contemporary Christology*. London: SCM.

—— (1983), *The Christian Experience of God as Trinity*. London: SCM.

Macquarrie, J. (1982), *In Search of Humanity: A Theological and Philosophical Approach*. London: SCM.

—— (1990), *Jesus Christ in Modern Thought*. London: SCM.

Malina, B. J. (1981), *The New Testament World: Insights from Cultural Anthropology*. London: SCM.

Malina, B. J. and Rohrbaugh, R.L. (1992), *Social-Science Commentary on the Synoptic Gospels*. Minneapolis: Fortress.

Margaret Magdalen, Sister (1994), *The Hidden Face of Jesus: Reflections on the Emotional Life of Christ*. London: Darton, Longman & Todd.

Marmorstein, A. (1968), *The Doctrine of Merits in Old Rabbinical Literature*. New York: KTAV [this edn].

Marshall, C. D. (1989), *Faith as a Theme in Mark's Narrative*. Cambridge: Cambridge University.

Marshall, I. H. (1980), *Last Supper and Lord's Supper*. Exeter: Paternoster.

Martin, F. (1988), *Narrative Parallels to the New Testament*. Atlanta, GA: Scholars.

Martin-Achard, R. and Nickelsburg, G. W. E. (1992), 'Resurrection', in Freedman, *Dictionary*, Vol. 5, pp. 684–91.

Martyn, J. L. (1979), *History and Theology in the Fourth Gospel*. Nashville, TN: Abingdon, 2nd edn.

Marxsen, W. (1969), *Mark the Evangelist: Studies in the Redaction History of the Gospel*, tr. J. Boyce, D. Juel, W. Poehlmann and R. A. Harrisville. Nashville, TN: Abingdon.

—— (1970), *The Resurrection of Jesus of Nazareth*, tr. M. Kohl. London: SCM.

—— (1979), *The Beginnings of Christology together with The Lord's Supper as a Christological Problem*, tr. P. J. Achtemeier and L. Nieting. Philadelphia: Fortress.

—— (1992), *Jesus and the Church: The Beginnings of Christianity*, tr. P. E. Devenish. Philadelphia: Trinity.

Mazza, E. (1996), 'Didache 9–10: Elements of a Eucharistic Interpretation', in Draper, *Didache*, pp. 76–99.

McArthur, H. K. (1970–1), 'On the Third Day', *New Testament Studies* 18, pp. 81–6.

McArthur, H. K. and Johnston, R. M. (1990), *They Also Taught in Parables: Rabbinic Parables from the First Centuries of the Christian Era*. Grand Rapids, MI: Zondervan.

McClendon, J. W. (1990), *Biography as Theology: How Life Stories Can Remake Today's Theology*. Philadelphia: Trinity, new edn.

McDonald, J. I. H. (1980), *Kerygma and Didache: The Articulation and Structure of the Earliest Christian Message*. Cambridge: Cambridge University.

McFadyen, A. I. (1990), *The Call to Personhood: A Christian Theory of the Individual in Social Relationships*. Cambridge: Cambridge University.

McGrath, A. E. (1986), *Iustitia Dei: A History of the Christian Doctrine of Justification – Volume 1*. Cambridge: Cambridge University.

—— (1990), *The Genesis of Doctrine: A Study in the Foundation of Doctrinal Criticism*. Oxford: Blackwell.

Mealand, D. L. (1977), 'Community of Good and Utopian Allusions in Acts II–IV', *Journal of Theological Studies (n.s.)* 28, pp. 96–9.

Meeks, W. A. (1993), *The Origins of Christian Morality: The First Two Centuries*. New Haven, CT: Yale University.

Meier, J. P. (1991 and 1994), *A Marginal Jew: Rethinking the Historical Jesus*. New York: Doubleday, 2 vols.

Meyer, B. F. (1979), *The Aims of Jesus*. London: SCM.

—— (ed.) (1993), *One Loaf, One Cup: Ecumenical Studies of 1 Cor 11 and Other Eucharistic Texts*. Macon, GA: Mercer University.

Meyers, R. (ed.) (1995), *Children at the Table: A Collection of Essays on Children and the Eucharist*. New York: Church Hymnal Corporation.

Michaels, J. R. (1996), 'Going to Heaven with Jesus: From 1 Peter to Pilgrim's Progress', in Longenecker, *Patterns*, pp. 248–68.

Miller, M. H. (1971), Character of the Miracles in Luke-Acts'. Unpublished doctoral thesis, Berkeley, California: Graduate Theological Union.

Miller, P. D. (1994), *They Cried to the Lord: The Form and Theology of Biblical Prayer*. Minneapolis: Fortress.

—— (ed.) (1995), *The Psalms and the Life of Faith*. Minneapolis: Fortress.

Moloney, F. J. (1997), *A Body Broken for a Broken Body: Eucharist in the New Testament*. Blackburn, Victoria: HarperCollins, rev. edn.

Moltmann-Wendel, W. (1993), *The Women Around Jesus*. tr. J. Bowden. New York: Crossroad.

Morrice, W. G. (1984), *Joy in the New Testament*. Exeter: Paternoster.

Moule, C. F. D. (ed.) (1965), *Miracles: Cambridge Studies in their Philosophy and History*. London: Mowbray.

—— (1978), 'As we forgive . . . : A Note on the Distinction between Deserts and Capacity in the Understanding of Forgiveness', in E. Bammel, C. K. Barrett and W. D. Davies (eds), *Donum Gentilicium: New Testament Studies in Honour of David Daube*. Oxford: Clarendon, pp. 68–77.

Muilenburg, J. (1986), 'The Intercession of the Covenant Mediator (Exodus 33:1a, 12–17)', in P. R. Ackroyd and B. Lindars (eds). *Words and Meanings: Essays Presented to David Winton Thomas*. Cambridge: Cambridge University, pp. 159–81.

Murphy-O'Connor, J. (1992), 'Teacher of Righteousness', in Freedman, Dictionary, Vol. 6, pp. 340–1.

Neale, D. A. (1991), *None but the Sinners: Religious Categories in the Gospel of Luke*. Sheffield: JSOT.

Neirynck, F. (1979), 'The Miracle Stories in the Acts of the Apostles', in J. Kremer (ed.), *Les Acts des Apôtres: Traditions, rédaction, théologie*. Gembloux: Leuven University, pp. 169–213.

Neusner, J. (1971), *The Rabbinic Traditions about the Pharisees before 70, Part 3 – Conclusions*. Leiden: E. J. Brill.

—— (1973), *The Idea of Purity in Ancient Judaism: The Haskell Lectures, 1972–1973*. Leiden: E. J. Brill.

Neusner, J. and Chilton, B. D. (1996), *The Body of Faith: Israel and the Church*. Valley Forge, PA: Trinity.

Neusner, J., Green, W. S., and Frerichs, E. S. (eds) (1987), *Judaisms and their Messiahs at the Turn of the Christian Era*. Cambridge: Cambridge University.

Newsom, C. A. (1992), 'Angels (Old Testament)', in Freedman, *Dictionary*, Vol. 1, pp. 248–53.

Nickelsburg, G. W. E. (1972), *Resurrection, Immortality, and Eternal Life in Intertestamental Judaism*. Cambridge, MA: Harvard University.

—— (1992a), 'Resurrection', in Freedman, *Dictionary*, Vol. 5, pp. 680–91.

—— (1992b), 'Son of Man', in Freedman, *Dictionary*, Vol. 6, pp. 137–50.

Nolan, A. (1977), *Jesus Before Christianity: The Gospel of Liberation*. London: Darton, Longman & Todd.

Nygren, A. (1932–39), *Agape and Eros: A Study of the Christian Idea of Love and A History of the Christian Idea of Love*, tr. A. G. Hebert and P. S. Watson. London: SPCK, 3 vols.

O'Rahilly, A. (1941a), 'Jewish Burial', *Irish Ecclesiastical Record* 58, pp. 123–35.

—— (1941b), 'The Burial of Christ', *Irish Ecclesiastical Record* 58, pp. 302–16, 493–503; 59, pp. 150–71.

Osborn, E. (1981), 'The Love Commandment in Second Century Christian Writings', *Second Century* 1, pp. 223–43.

Oulton, J. E. L. and Chadwick, H. (1954), *Alexandrian Christianity: Selected Translations of Clement and Origen with Introductions and Notes*. London: SCM.

Page, R. (1991), *The Incarnation of Freedom and Love*. London: SCM.

Palmer, D. W. (1993), 'Acts and the Ancient Historical Monograph', in B. W. Winter and A. D. Clarke (eds), *The Book of Acts in Its First Century Setting: Volume 1 – Ancient Literary Setting*. Grand Rapids, MI: Eerdmans, pp. 1–29.

Parkes, C. M. (1986), *Bereavement: Studies of Grief in Adult Life*. London: Penguin, 2nd edn.

Parkes, C. M. and Weiss, R. S. (1983), *Recovery from Bereavement*. New York: Basic Books.

Patte, D. (1975), *Early Jewish Hermeneutic in Palestine*. Missoula, MI: Scholars.

Peacocke, A. (1993), *Theology for a Scientific Age: Being and Becoming – Natural, Divine and Human*. London: SCM, enlarged edn.

Perkins, P. (1984), *Resurrection: New Testament Witness and Contemporary Reflection*. London: Geoffrey Chapman.

Perrin, N. (1967), *Rediscovering the Teaching of Jesus*. London: SCM.

—— (1976), *Jesus and the Language of the Kingdom: Symbol and Metaphor in New Testament Interpretation*. London: SCM.

Petuchowski, J. J. (1978), 'The Liturgy of the Synagogue', in Petuchowski and Brocke, *Lord's Prayer*, pp. 45–57.

Petuchowski, J. J. and Brocke, M. (1978), *The Lord's Prayer and Jewish Liturgy*, tr. E. R. Petuchowski. London: Burns & Oates.

Piper, J. (1980), *'Love Your Enemies': Jesus' Love Command in the Synoptic Gospels and the Early Christian Paraenesis*. Cambridge: Cambridge University.

Pohier, J. (1985), *God – In Fragments*, tr. J. Bowden. London: SCM.

Porter, S. E., Hayes, M. A. and Tombs, D. (eds) (1997), *Images of Christ: Ancient and Modern*. Sheffield: Sheffield Academic.

Priest, J. (1992), 'A Note on the Messianic Banquet', in Charlesworth, *Messiah*, pp. 222–38.

Ramon, Brother (1988), *Fulness of Joy: The Presence of God in Human Life*. Basingstoke: Marshall Pickering.

Raphael, B. (1984), *The Anatomy of Bereavement: A Handbook for Caring Professions*. London: Hutchinson.

Reed, B. (1978), *The Dynamics of Religion: Process and Movements in Christian Churches*. London: Darton, Longman & Todd.

Rhodes, A. B. (1977), 'Israel's Prophets as Intercessors', in A. L. Merrill and T. W. Overholt (eds), *Scripture in History and Theology: Essays in Honour of J. Coert Rylaarsdam*. Pittsburgh, PA: Pickwick, pp. 107–28.

Richardson, A. (1941), *The Miracle-Stories of the Gospels*. London: SCM.

Riches, J. (1980), *Jesus and the Transformation of Judaism*. London: Darton, Longman & Todd.

Riesner, R. (1984), *Jesus als Lehrer: Eine Untersuchung zum Ursprung der Evangelien-Überlieferung*. Tübingen: J. C. B. Mohr (Paul Siebeck), 2nd edn.

—— (1991), 'Jesus as Preacher and Teacher' in Wansbrough, *Jesus*, pp. 185–210.

Riggs, J. W. (1984), 'From Gracious Table to Sacramental Elements: The Tradition-History of Didache 9 and 10', *Second Century* 4, pp. 83–101.

—— (1995), 'The Sacred Food of Didache 9–10 and Second Century Ecclesiologies', in C. N. Jefford (ed.), *The Didache in Context: Essays on Its Text, History and Transmission*. Leiden: E. J. Brill, pp. 256–83.

Riley, G. J. (1997), *One Jesus, Many Christs: How Jesus Inspired not One True Christianity, but Many*. San Francisco: HarperSanFrancisco.

Robinson, H. W. (1964), *Corporate Personality in Ancient Israel*. Minneapolis: Fortress [this edn].

Robinson, J. A. T. (1956), 'The "Parable" of the Sheep and the Goats', *New Testament Studies* 2, pp. 225–37.

Robinson, J. M. (1971), 'LOGOI SOPHON: On the Gattung of Q' in J. M. Robinson and H. Koester, *Trajectories in Early Christianity*. Philadelphia: Fortress, pp. 71–113.

Rosenblatt, P. C., Walsh, R. P. and Jackson, D. A. (1976), *Grief and Mourning in Cross-Cultural Perspective*. Human Relations Area Files.

Rothkoff, A. (1972), 'Mourning', in C. Roth (ed.), *Encyclopaedia Judaica*. Jerusalem: Encyclopaedia Judaica, Vol. 12, pp. 486–92.

Rowland, C. (1985), *Christian Origins: An Account of the Setting and Character of the most Important Messianic Sect of Judaism*. London: SPCK.

—— (1992), 'Parousia', in Freedman, *Dictionary*, Vol. 5, pp. 166–70.

Rowley, H.H. (1956), *The Faith of Israel: Aspects of Old Testament Thought*. London: SCM.

Rubenstein, R. L. and Roth. J. K. (1987), *Approaches to Auschwitz: The Legacy of the Holocaust*. London: SCM.

Sanders, E. P (1977), *Paul and Palestinian Judaism: A Comparison of Patterns of Religion*. London: SCM.

—— (1983), 'Jesus and the Sinners', *Journal for the Study of the New Testament* 19, pp. 5–36.

—— (1985), *Jesus and Judaism*. London: SCM.

—— (1992), *Judaism: Practice and Belief 63 BCE – 66 CE*. London: SCM.

—— (1993), *The Historical Figure of Jesus*. London: Penguin.

Sanders, E. P. and Davies, M. (1989), *Studying the Synoptic Gospels*. London: SCM.

Sanders, J. A. (1992), 'Canon (Hebrew Bible)', in Freedman, *Dictionary*, Vol. 1, pp. 837–52.

Saward, J. (1990), *The Mysteries of March: Hans Urs von Balthasar on Incarnation and Easter*. London: Collins.

Sawicki, M. (1994), *Seeing the Lord: Resurrection and Early Christian Practices*. Minneapolis: Fortress.

Schatzmann, S. (1989), *A Pauline Theology of Charismata*. Peabody, MA: Hendrickson.

Schiffman, L. H. (1979), 'Communal Meals at Qumran', *Revue de Qumran* 10, pp. 45–56.

Schillebeeckx, E. (1979), *Jesus: An Experiment in Christology*, tr. H. Hoskins. London: Collins.

Schoedel W. R. (1985), *Ignatius of Antioch: A Commentary on the Letters of Ianatius of Antioch*. Philadelphia: Fortress.

Schrage, W. (1988), *The Ethics of the New Testament*, tr. D. E. Green. Edinburgh: T. & T. Clark.

Schramm, G. (1992), 'Meal Customs (Jewish)', in Freedman, *Dictionary*, Vol. 4, pp. 648–50.

Schürmann, H. (1962), 'Die vorösterlichen Anfänge der Logientradition', in H. Ristow and K. Matthiae (eds.), *Der historische Jesus und der keryg-*

*matische Christus: Beiträge zum Christusverständnis in Forschung und Verkündigung.* Berlin: Evangelische, pp. 342–70.

Schüssler Fiorenza, E. (1983), *In Memory of Her: A Feminist Theological Reconstruction of Christian Origins.* London: SCM.

—— (1995), *Jesus: Miriam's Child. Sophia's Prophet – Critical Issues in Feminist Christology.* London: SCM.

Schweitzer, A. (1954), *The Quest of the Historcal Jesus: A Critical Study of Its Progress from Reimarus to Wrede*, tr. W. Montgomery. London: A. & C. Black, 3rd edn.

Schweizer, E. (1968), 'πνεῦμα κτλ', in Kittel and Friedrich, *Dictionary*, Vol. 6, pp. 396–455.

—— (1971a), 'σάρξ κτλ', in Kittel and Friedrich, *Dictionary*, Vol. 7, pp. 98–151.

—— (1971b), 'σῶμα κτλ', in Kittel and Friedrich, *Dictionary*, Vol. 7, pp. 1024–94.

—— (1992), 'Body' in Freedman, *Dictionary*, Vol. 1, pp. 767–72.

Schwöbel C. and Gunton, C. E. (eds) (1991), *Persons, Divine and Human.* Edinburgh: T. & T. Clark.

Scott, B. B. (1989), *Hear Then the Parable: A Commentary on the Parables of Jesus.* Minneapolis: Fortress.

Segovia, F. F. (ed.) (1985), *Discipleship in the New Testament.* Philadelphia: Fortress.

Selvidge, M. J. (1980), 'Woman, Cult, and Miracle Recital: Mark 5:24–34'. Unpublished PhD thesis, St Louis University.

—— (1984), 'Mark 5.25–34 and Leviticus 15.19–20', *Journal of Biblical Literature* 103, pp. 619–23.

Seybold, K. and Mueller, U. B. (1981), *Sickness and Healing*, tr. D. W. Scott. Nashville: Abingdon.

Smith, D. E. (1992), Greco-Roman Sacred Meals', in Freedman, *Dictionary*, Vol. 4, pp. 653–5.

Sobrino, J. (1978), *Christology at the Crossroads: A Latin American Approach*, tr. J. Drury. London: SCM.

—— (1994), *Jesus the Liberator: A Historical-Theological Reading of Jesus of Nazareth*, tr. P. Burns and F. McDonagh. Tunbridge Wells: Burns & Oates.

Spiegel, Y. (1978), *The Grief Process*, tr. E. Duke. London: SCM.

Spong, J. S. (1994), *Resurrection: Myth or Reality?* San Francisco: Harper.

Stacey, D. (1994), 'The Lord's Supper as Prophetic Drama', *Epworth Review* 21, pp. 65–74.

Stanley, D. M. (1958), 'Become Imitators of Me: The Pauline Conception of Apostolic Tradition', *Biblica* 40, pp. 859–77.

Stanton, G. N. (1974), *Jesus of Nazareth in New Testament Preaching.* Cambridge: Cambridge University.

Stark, R. (1996), *The Rise of Christianity: How the Obscure, Marginal Jesus Movement Became the Dominant Religious Force in the Western World in a Few Centuries.* Princeton, NJ: Princeton University.

Stauffer, E. (1964), 'ἀγαπάω', in Kittel and Friedrich, *Dictionary*,Vol. 1, pp. 35–55.

Stevenson, K. W. (1986), *Eucharist and Offering*. New York: Pueblo.

—— (1989), *Accept this Offering: The Eucharist as Sacrifice Today*. London: SPCK.

Stewart, R. A. (1961), *Rabbinic Theology: An Introductory Study*. Edinburgh: Oliver & Boyd.

Strawson, W. (1959), *Jesus and the Future Life*. London: Epworth.

Stroker, W. D. (1989), *Extracanonical Sayings of Jesus*. Atlanta, GA: Scholars.

Suhl, A. (1968), *Die Wunder Jesu: Ereignis und Überlieferung*. Gütersloh: Gerd Mohn.

Tannehill, R. C. (1977), 'The Disciples in Mark: The Function of the Narrative Role', *Journal of Religion* 57, pp. 386–405.

Taylor, J. V. (chairperson), (1981), *Believing in the Church: The Corporate Nature of Faith: A Report by The Doctrine Commission of the General Synod of the Church of England*. London: SPCK.

—— (chairperson) (1987), *We Believe in God: A Report by The Doctrine Commission of the General Synod of the Church of England*. London: Church House Publishing.

Thatcher, A. (1993), *Liberating Sex: A Christian Sexual Theology*. London: SPCK.

Theissen, G. (1978), *The First Followers of Jesus: A Sociological Analysis of the earliest Christianity*, tr. J. Bowden. London: SCM.

—— (1982), *The Social Setting of Pauline Christianity: Essays on Corinth*, tr. J. H. Schütz. Philadelphia: Fortress.

—— (1983), *The Miracle Stories of the Early Christian Tradition*, tr. F. McDonagh. Edinburgh: T. & T. Clark.

—— (1984), *Biblical Faith: An Evolutionary Approach*, tr. J. Bowden. London: SCM.

—— (1992), *The Gospels in Context: Social and Political History in the Synoptic Tradition*, tr. L. M. Maloney. Edinburgh: T. & T. Clark.

Thiselton, A. C. (1980), *The Two Horizons: New Testament Hermeneutics and Philosophical Description with special reference to Heidegger, Bultmann, Gadamer and Wittgenstein*. Exeter: Paternoster.

—— (1992), *New Horizons in Hermeneutics: The Theory and Practice of Transforming Biblical Reading*. Grand Rapids, MI: Zondervan.

Thomas, L.-V. (1987), 'Funeral Rites', tr. K. Anderson in M. Eliade (ed.), *The Encyclopedia of Religion*. New York: Macmillan, Vol. 5, pp. 450–8.

Thompson, M. (1991), *Clothed with Christ: The Example and Teaching of Jesus in Romans 12.1—15.13*. Sheffield: JSOT.

Torrance, J. B. (1981), 'The Vicarious Humanity of Christ', in T. F. Torrance (ed.), *The Incarnation: Ecumenical Studies in the Nicene-Constantinopolitan Creed, AD 381*. Edinburgh: Handsel, pp. 127–47.

Torrance. T. F. (1975), *Theology in Reconciliation: Essays towards Evangelical and Catholic Unity in East and West*. London: Geoffrey Chapman.

—— (1988), *The Trinitarian Faith: The Evangelical Theology of the Ancient Catholic Church*. Edinburgh: T. & T. Clark.

Townsend, J. T. (1992), 'Education (Greco-Roman Period)', in Freedman, *Dictionary*, Vol. 2, pp. 312–17.

Tuckett, C.M. (1996) 'Synoptic Tradition in the Didache', in Draper (ed.), *Didache*, pp. 92–128.

—— (1997), 'Q and the "Church": The Role of the Christian Community within Judaism according to Q', in M. Bockmuehl and M. B. Thompson (eds), *A Vision for the Church: Studies in Early Christian Ecclesiology*. Edinburgh: T. & T. Clark, pp. 65–77.

Turk, M. (chairperson) (1988), *Children in the Way: New Directions for the Church's Children* (A Report for the General Synod Board of Education). London: Church House Publishing.

Turner, V. (1995), *The Ritual Process: Structure and Anti-Structure*. New York: de Gruyter [this edn].

Twelftree, G. H. (1993), *Jesus the Exorcist: A Contribution to the Study of the Historical Jesus*. Tübingen: J. C. B. Mohr (Paul Siebeck).

Urbach, E. E. (1987), *The Sages: Their Concepts and Beliefs*, tr. I. Abrahams, Cambridge, MA: Harvard University.

Van Henten, J. W. (ed.) (1989), *Die Entstehung der Jüdischen Martyrologie*. Leiden: E. J. Brill.

—— (1993), 'The Tradition-Historical Background of Rom. 3.25: A Search for Pagan and Jewish Parallels', in M. C. De Boer (ed.), *From Jesus to John: Essays on Jesus and New Testament Christology in Honour of Marinus de Jonge*. Sheffield: JSOT, pp. 101–28.

—— (1997), *The Maccabean Martyrs as Saviours of the Jewish People: A Study of 2 and 4 Maccabees*. Leiden: E. J. Brill.

Vanier, J. (1989), *Community and Growth*, tr. A. Shearer. London: Darton, Longman & Todd, revised and expanded edn.

Verhey, A. (1992), 'Remember, Remembrance', in Freedman, *Dictionary*, Vol. 5, pp. 667–9.

Vermes, G. (1972), 'Hanina ben Dosa', *Journal of Jewish Studies* 23, pp. 28–50.

—— (1976), *Jesus the Jew*. London: Fontana [this edn].

—— (1983), *Jesus and the World of Judaism*. London: SCM.

—— (1993), *The Religion of Jesus the Jew*. London: SCM.

Vokes, F. E. (1970), 'The Lord's Prayer in the First Three Centuries', *Studia Patristica* Vol. 10 (Texte und Untersuchungen 107); Berlin: Akademie-Verlag, pp. 253–60.

Wainwright, G. (1978), *Eucharist and Eschatology*. London: Epworth, 2nd edn.

Wallis, I.G. (1992), 'Christ's Continuing Ministry of Healing', *Expository Times* 104, pp. 42–5.

—— (1995a), *The Faith of Jesus Christ in Early Christian Traditions*. Cambridge: Cambridge University.

—— (1995b), 'Jesus, Human Being and the Praxis of Intercession: Towards a Biblical Perspective', *Scottish Journal of Theology* 48, pp. 225–50.

—— (1995c), 'Jesus the Believer', *Modern Believing* 36, pp. 10–17.

Walters, G. (1997), *Why Do Christians Find it Hard to Grieve?* Carlisle: Paternoster.

Wakefield, G. S. (1998), *An Outline of Christian Worship.* Edinburgh: T. & T. Clark.

Wansbrough, H. (ed.) (1991), *Jesus and the Oral Gospel Tradition.* Sheffield: JSOT.

Ward, K. (1991), *A Vision to Pursue: Beyond the Crisis in Chrstianity.* London: SCM.

Weber, H.-R. (1979), *The Cross: Tradition and Interpretation,* tr. E. Jesset. London: SPCK.

Weder, H. (1992), 'Disciple, Discipleship', in Freedman, *Dictionary,* Vol. 2, pp. 207–10.

Wenham, D. (1995), *Paul: Follower of Jesus or Founder of Christianity.* Grand Rapids, MI: Eerdmans.

Wessels. A. (1990), *Images of Jesus: How Jesus is Perceived and Portrayed in Non-European Cultures,* tr J. Vriend. London: SCM.

Westerholm, S. (1978), *Jesus and Scribal Authority.* Lund: C. W. K. Gleerup.

Westermann, D. C. (1972), 'Salvation and Healing in the Community: The Old Testament Understanding', tr. R. Wilkinson in *International Review of Mission* 61, pp. 9–19.

Whitaker, E. C. (1970), *Documents of the Baptismal Liturgy.* London: SPCK. 2nd edn..

White, V. (1996), *Paying Attention to People: An Essay on Individualism and Christian Belief.* London: SPCK.

Wild, R. A. (1985), ' "Be Imitators of God": Discipleship in the Letter to the Ephesians', in Segovia, *Discipleship,* pp. 127–43.

Wiles, M. F. (1965), 'Miracles in the Early Church', in Moule, *Miracles,* pp. 221–34.

Wilkins, M. J. (1992), 'Imitate, Imitators', in Freedman, *Dictionary,* Vol. 3, p. 392.

Williams R. (1982a), *Resurrection: Interpreting the Easter Gospel.* London: Darton, Longman & Todd.

—— (1982b), *Eucharistic Sacrifice: The Roots of a Metaphor.* Nottingham: Grove Books.

Williams, S. K. (1975), *Jesus' Death as Saving Event: The Background and Origin of a Concept.* Missoula, MT: Scholars.

Wilson, B. (1982), *Religion in Sociological Perspective.* Oxford: Oxford University.

Witherington, B. (1984), *Women in the Ministry of Jesus: A Study of Jesus' Attitudes to Women and their Roles as Reflected in His Earthly Life.* Cambridge: Cambridge University.

—— (1994), *Jesus the Sage: The Pilgrimage of Wisdom.* Minneapolis: Fortress.

—— (1995), *The Jesus Quest: The Third Search for the Jew of Nazareth*. Downers Grove: Inter-Varsity.

—— (1998), *The Many Faces of the Christ: The Christologies of the New Testament and Beyond*. New York: Crossroad.

Wolff, H. W. (1974), *Anthropology of the Old Testament*, tr. M. Kohl; London: SCM.

Wollaston, I. (1996), *A War Against Memory? The Future of Holocaust Remembrance*. London: SPCK.

Worden, J. W. (1991), *Grief Counselling and Grief Therapy: A Handbook for the Mental Health Practitioner*. London: Routledge, 2nd edn.

Wrede, W. (1971), *The Messianic Secret*, tr. J. C. G. Greig. Cambridge: J. Clarke.

Wright, D. P. and Jones, R. N. (1992), 'Leprosy', in Freedman, *Dictionary*, Vol. 4, pp. 277–82.

Wright, N. T. (1992), *The New Testament and the People of God*. Minneapolis: Fortress.

—— (1996), *Jesus and the Victory of God*. Minneapolis: Fortress.

Young, B. H. (1989), *Jesus and his Jewish Parables: Discovering the Roots of Jesus' Teaching*. New York: Paulist.

—— (1995), *Jesus the Jewish Theologian*. Peabody, MA: Hendrickson.

Zizioulas, J. D. (1985), *Being as Communion: Studies in Personhood and the Church*. London: Darton, Longman & Todd.

# Index of Subjects and Names

# Index of Biblical and Other Primary Sources